Case Studies in Merchandising Apparel and Soft Goods

Case Studies

in Merchandising
Apparel
and Soft Goods

Michele M. Granger
Stephens College

Fairchild Publications
New York

Contents

Chapter One
The Nature of the Organization *39*

Chapter Four
The External Environment *121*

Chapter Five
Product Identification *151*

Chapter Eight
Product Placement—Marketing Channels of Distribution *207*

Chapter Nine
Promotion *227*

Preface

The purpose of this book is to place the student in the work setting of the apparel and soft goods industry, from the secondary level of apparel manufacturing to the tertiary level of retail sales. An interdisciplinary approach, which combines clothing/textiles and business administration as it applies to the apparel and soft goods industry, is analyzed from a marketing perspective. The five "Ps" of the marketing model (i.e., product, people, place, promotion, and price) form the foundation for the structure of this text. The traditional definition of the fashion industry has been broadened to encompass apparel, accessories, shoes, home furnishings, and fabrics in the chapter examples and the subsequent case studies.

The case study analysis method has been selected as the route through which the student has the opportunity to function as a business consultant. Despite the hours allocated to carefully prepare lectures and the skills needed to encourage active discussion, the instructor may not always be able to assist and assess the student's ability to apply knowledge until application of textbook theory is the performance objective. The case study method requires such application; it is student-centered and problem-based with the ultimate educational goal of critical thinking. The vast majority of the case studies in this book represent actual situations, real-life examples that have actually occurred. In some cases, the names have been changed to protect the anonymity of the people and businesses that were involved in the situations. In other cases, the players in the case studies have granted permission for their names and stories to be included.

Following the table of contents, there is a brief introduction about the case study teaching method to the instructor. (Additional information about the case study approach has also been included in the *Instrutor's Guide* with supplementary assignment suggestions and listings of alternative solutions for each case study.) After that, you will find a section entitled, "To the Student." This material is included to provide the reader with a definition and purpose of the case study, tips for class preparation, suggestions for the written case study analysis, and ideas for discussion of the case study in class as either a member or the leader of a group. A case study analysis form and an instructor's evaluation form are also provided. Additionally, in this section, a sample case study and its solution are included as a visual example of the case study process from start to finish. Finally, after the preface and acknowledgments, a chart of Case Summaries has been constructed to enable the instuctor and student to identify the primary topics within each case study. This chart is particularly useful in assisting the student with determining the central issues of the case studies.

Chapter 1 covers the nature of the organization from organization classifications to business ownership. Types of products sold, the level of nonstore selling, and the types of services offered are introduced through a brief narrative then clarified in a series of case studies. Special emphasis has been placed on the extent of departmentalization within the organization to include the operations function, the merchandising function, the human resource function, the control function, and the public relations function. Finally, Chapter 1 examines the structure of the organization and its communication channels.

Chapter 2 discusses the customers of apparel and soft goods organizations. The consumer's buying motives are examined in relation to the customer decision process to purchase. Consumer demographics are considered as they relate to market segmentation attempts. Additional factors that identify consumer groups are examined, including lifestyles, social classes, reference groups, and culture.

Chapter 3 investigates the company mission and the development of the organization's mission statement. Objectives and goals are examined from a variety of perspectives—those of the student intern, the employee, and the manager. Finally, market positioning is explored in terms of the organization's competitive environment. A closer look at the organization's macroenvironment is detailed in Chapter 4. In this section, the external environment of the organization is analyzed from its economic, social/demographic, political/legal, natural, and technological surroundings.

Chapter 5 encompasses product identification in terms of product levels, product classifications, branding, packaging, and labeling. In Chapter 6, the product receives further examination in terms of how it is offered to the customer. Types, levels, and forms of service are explored. Finally, decisions relating to the product line and mix are presented through a series of case studies. Chapter 7 presents decisions relating to price and the product, from wholesale and retail pricing decisions to pricing strategies. Placement of the product is the focus of Chapter 8 as it investigates the physical distribution of the product. From conventional to multichannel marketing channels, the channel design alternatives and management of distributors are analyzed.

Chapter 9 examines promotion of both the product and the organization. Decisions relating to identifying the target market, choosing a message, selecting the media type, setting the promotion budget, and determining the promotion mix are presented through the case studies in this section. Personal and nonpersonal communication channels are explored. Visual merchandising is analyzed as a form of promotion. Finally, the evaluation decisions relating to collecting feedback on promotional efforts are examined.

Chapter 10 explores the impact of human relations in the workplace. This section primarily deals with the attitude, initiative, assertiveness, and professional conduct of entry-level employees. It examines human relations from the perspectives of the management trainee to the business owner.

Additionally, we have included a glossary of merchandising and retailing terminology at the end of the book, as a quick reference.

When appropriate, we have also cross-referenced these glossary terms to a case study for ease-of-learning. Within the glossary listing itself, we have cross-referenced other terms that we felt would help the student's understanding of the listing. For the teacher and learner interested in further reading about the apparel and soft goods industry, there is a reference reading list that incorporates specific texts with which this book is compatible for the case study application of concepts and theories. Finally, for ease-of-learning, an index of all the cases has also been included.

To illustrate the concepts being examined in the cases, we have incorporated many merchandising and retailing forms and charts. While these forms and charts may not relate directly to the cases being studied, they do illustrate clearly a concept that is being explored within the case. For clarity, we have included brief descriptions under these forms and charts.

Each chapter begins with a brief introductory narrative and concludes with a series of case studies. Throughout the chapters, moral and ethical concerns appear in several case studies. These sub-problems are among the most difficult to resolve as they are affected by personal values and cultural influences. Current and future industry trends and issues have been incorporated into the content of many of the case studies. While some of the problems are new, others present common dilemmas that have faced employers and employees alike for years. Although a few of the problems may seem simple, they are often the ones that the student must first confront and resolve to build the confidence necessary to climb the success ladder.

From a teacher's perspective, it is my optimistic hope that the students using this book will recognize the value of effective problem-solving, the power of critical thinking, and the benefit of life-long learning.

Acknowledgments

I wish to thank my students and colleagues—past, present, and future—for sharing a love of learning and for always teaching this teacher. Much appreciation is extended to my students Amy Allin, Ann Edwards, Rachel Kennedy, Jaina Sheets, and Dapheney Lemon for their original material upon which some of the case studies were based.

Closer to home, I want to thank my daughter Annie for her life support; one that results from her personality that is filled with resilient good cheer, persistence, affection, thoughtfulness, and wisdom beyond her years. My want is that I will give her as much as she has given me. I also want to thank my parents, Sally and John Granger, and my brother and sister, Joseph and Patty, for constantly reminding me that I am "the best one of us all." Whether they believe it or not is difficult to tell, but it certainly does encourage me. Additionally, I am thankful for my sister-in-law, Wendy, a model of patience, which is a necessity to live with my brother. I owe gratitude to my grandmother, Leona Tucker, a woman of courage and independence, for her examples of kindness and strength. To my nieces and nephews, Shane, Megan, Michael, Katelynn, Sarah, and Thomas, I thank you for being a legacy of family love to Annie and me. To my friends, Emmi, Sarah, and Dave, I thank you for your love and support.

The editor and I would like to thank the following reviewers for their insightful, constructive, and thoughtful reviews: Laura Bliss,

Stephens College; Tselane Brown, Houston Community College; Gail Dalpian, Johnson and Wales University; Mary Ann Eastlick, University of Arizona; Deborah McDowell, Southwest Missouri State; Carolyn Olsen, Southeast Community College; Glenda Lowry, PhD, Marshall University; Helen Xenakis, Fashion Institute of Technology; and Adrienne Zinn, Los Angeles Trade-Technical College. We are grateful for the guidance that you showed us when this book was being conceived, written, and edited.

Finally, thank you to Pamela Kirshen Fishman and Ilana Scheiner of Fairchild Books and Visuals for supporting this project and starting the ball rolling. A huge amount of appreciation is also extended to Susan Jeffers Casel, editor of this book, for her thoughtful and detailed critiques as well as her encouraging "midwifery" as she guided this project from conception to production. She truly pushed me to my maximum abilities and created a much stronger product than the one I had originally submitted.

Case Studies in Merchandising Apparel and Soft Goods

Case Summaries

To the Instructor

The Value of the Case Study Method

Since the case method of study was developed at the Harvard Business School in the 1920s, case analysis has enabled instructors to introduce realism, involvement, and application into their classrooms. A case allows the student to gain hands-on experience without leaving the classroom—a sort of "Magic Bus" field trip in which the instructor is the tour guide.

There are several advantages to the case study method of teaching and learning. First, this type of study encourages critical thinking as the student applies previously learned theories of the principles of apparel and soft goods marketing to actual industry situations. Second, in addition to knowledge about a specific discipline, the student gains valuable life skills as s/he participates in the process of orderly thinking. As the student becomes involved in the analysis required for logical decision-making, s/he develops the abilities to break down problems and evaluate them rationally and objectively. Finally, the student gains interpersonal skills as s/he learns to express thoughts, ideas, and feelings within a group—as opposed to "being a sponge" and just memorizing the facts. As a member of a group, the student gains the diversity of perspectives from other students and from the instructor. For the instructor who has student goals of critical thinking abilities, problem-solving applications, and communication skills, the case study method of analysis offers tremendous opportunities. It is important to recognize that instruction through the case study method requires a different approach for an instructor than the traditional methods of teaching used in the traditional lecture classroom.

From a pedagogical viewpoint, the four types of teaching/learning systems commonly found in the college classroom are :

1 The subject-based/teacher-centered system

2 The subject-based/student-centered system

3 The problem-based/teacher-centered system

4 The problem-based/student-centered system

The conventional lecture/discussion course is usually subject-based and teacher-centered. The student learning style—surface learning—features a literal reproduction of material that requires extensive memorization. For example, in a subject-based/teacher-centered course, a student may ask, "Do I have to learn about resident buying offices for the upcoming midterm examination?"

In contrast, the case study method of teaching is problem-based/student-centered. It requires active learning. The goal for the student is a learning style that integrates new knowledge with old, fosters an attempt to understand meanings, and looks for explanations rather than facts. As opposed to surface learning, facts and concepts from foundation courses are integrated and applied in the context of real-life situations. Problem-based/student-centered learning results in a deeper type of knowledge, not simply memorizing and repeating material. The student learns to both speak and write more fluently and concisely. For example, in the problem-based/student-centered course, a student may ask, "How does a buyer determine whether or not to use the resident buying office catalog?"

Both of these teaching/learning methods (subject-based/teacher-centered or problem-based/student-centered) supplement and complement each other. Both methods require different roles for the instructor and the student; however, if the teacher and the learner view themselves as partners in the educational process, this role variance can be challenging and fulfilling.

The Student's Role in Case Study Analysis

Ideally, the student's role should change from that of a passive subordinate to that of an active future colleague. The problem-based/student-centered system can simultaneously incorporate reasoning skills, support of the group process, and assist in self-directed learning. When students actively participate in their education, they become self-directed learners. As teachers, it is inherent in our profession that we constantly evaluate for the ultimate goal of education. When we believe that the ultimate goal of education is to transfer the work of pursuing knowledge to the individual, we help our students to prepare for lifelong learning. Students truly become educated when they realize that college is preparing them for lifelong learning by offering them the skills to learn intelligently.

The Instructor's Role in Case Study Analysis

Through the case method of study, the instructor moves into the roles of facilitator and guide. The instructor supports the learning process through modeling, coaching, and fading away as the student becomes engaged in the stages of problem-solving.

In what ways can you, the instructor, help the student make the transition from teacher-centered to student-centered learning? Overall, student-centered learning validates student metacognition by encouraging the student to "think about thinking." The instructor may also aid the student by keeping the analysis process on track as the student pursues the case objectives. Additionally, the teacher can help the student develop problem-solving skills by probing the student's knowledge through such questions as:

- Do you agree with your peer's explanation?
- How do you know that?
- Are you sure about that?
- What made you think that?
- Have you thought of all of the possibilities?

Finally, the instructor can modulate the pace of classroom case analysis for the students. If the cases are too easy or the number of cases analyzed is too few, the students will become bored. If the cases are too complex or the number of cases analyzed is too large, the students will become overwhelmed, frustrated, and burned-out.

Teaching through case study analysis provides the professor with opportunities to vary instructional techniques while maximizing individual teaching skills. The instructor may want to consider the following six case study analysis methods:

1 Committee

2 Collaborative

3 Role playing

4 Individual

5 Tutorial

6 Mentoring

Some instructors elect to use all six methods within a semester in an effort to provide stimulation and diversity within the course. Others prefer to utilize one or two of the methods with which they are most comfortable and familiar. Note to Instructor: for analysis of these methods, see the *Instructor's Guide*.

The initial transition from theory learning to problem-solving application can be simultaneously thrilling, frustrating, and overwhelming for both the student and instructor. The student may ask, "What is a case and what do you want me to do with it?" Common complaints from students include a lack of sufficient information and the impossible quest for the perfect answer. In the following section, the case study is defined, analyzed, and anticipated obstacles are previewed for the student.

To the Student

The Case Study and the Student

You are about to embark on an amazing adventure, an adventure that will transport you into the merchandising world without leaving the classroom. You will have the opportunity to work as a "business consultant" for a variety of apparel and soft goods companies—from small specialty stores to major department store giants. You will be provided with the opportunity to view business problems from a manager's position before you have been hired into an entry-level position. You will gain the perspective of a variety of executive positions in the fashion retailing world, including entrepreneurship, human resources, management, promotion and advertising, public relations, and merchandising.

The vehicle responsible for this remarkable transition is the case study. The primary objective of the case method of teaching is to provide the highest level of realism and involvement into the instruction of merchandising management and marketing decision-making. The use of case studies as a learning device emphasizes the application of theories and principles to actual industry problems. The emphasis is not on narration of abstract theories or principles. Case studies enable you to be a part of the realities of the merchandising management and marketing business as you participate in the decision-making process required by actual industry situations. You may have worked with case study analysis in the past, but for others, it is an entirely new and intimidating learning experience.

Beginners frequently ask:

- What is a case study?
- What am I supposed to do with it?
- How do I know if I have found the right answer?

Within the next few pages, these questions will be answered and the mystery of case study analysis will be revealed.

The Definition and Purpose of the Case Study

A case study is a written description of a business problem. The purpose of the case study is to provide a business situation in which you, the student, can evaluate a difficulty(s) and propose a recommended solution(s). Case analysis is simply studying an organization's or employee's situation and deciding what—if anything—can be done to resolve the issue. Sometimes it appears that the problem is readily identifiable, but frequently this is not the situation. Usually, you will be required to play the role of a business consultant by sifting through the information and determining the information that is important and that which should be disregarded. Sometimes the data will appear conflicting or incomplete. It is your assignment to arrive at the real problem, to develop viable alternatives, and then to create workable solutions. You may become frustrated when you perceive there is a lack of sufficient information; however, situations in which incomplete information is available are all-too-common in the business world. Making reasonable assumptions and decisions under uncertainty and with imperfect information is part of the reality of business.

Finally, be prepared to not discover the correct, definitive answer. In case analysis, you and your peers will develop a wide variety of alternatives with reasonable arguments in favor of each of them. You may find it frustrating that you are unable to nail down precisely what the company or employee should do—such frustration is part of "the real world." There are few pat answers in real life. One of the most critical (and initially, the most troubling) lessons a student learns through case analysis is that the world is not black and white—quite often, you will be dealing with shades of gray.

Preparation for Class

Courses based on case study analysis require a more involved and unique preparation than the preparation needed for the typical lecture/discussion class. Whether your assignment is to lead the class (or a committee) in discussion or to contribute to the review as a member of the class (or a committee), you must literally master the case before going to class. You must be prepared to answer the following questions:

- What do you think?

- What would you do?

- Do you agree with another student's analysis?

- If so, why?

- If not, what do you suggest?

The process of case discussion can be both intimidating and frustrating for students who are not prepared or who have not thought critically about the case. To effectively discuss and analyze a case study, you must first examine the structure of the industry situation given in the case. All of the cases are constructed in a similar format. The case study is broken down into:

- The section and the title, which provide the topic for the narrative.

- Introductory paragraphs, which describe the organization and primary characters within the case situation.

- Several paragraphs that detail the business situation and incorporate the problem, the central issue, and any secondary issues. Additionally, statements that identify the actual problem will appear in various places within the case study.

- A concluding paragraph, which summarizes the scenario. (Please note: the 1-3 page case study offers sufficient—but not necessarily complete—information reflecting the topic(s) and issue(s) involved.)

- The case study questions listed at the end of the case study. From these (there are at least two for almost every case study), you should choose that character's perspective (if there is more than one character involved) that you will take in your response and your preferred course of action. Sometimes the questions are quite specific and require specific answers; other times, you are given the right to choose to go your own way. In any case, if you have a preferred solution that does not fit with any of the questions asked, ask your instructor whether you should pursue your own course of action.

The following are step-by-step pointers and tips that will assist you. To help maximize your case analysis process, you should:

1 Read the case study several times prior to beginning the analysis. Skim the case first. During a second, more thorough, reading, make notes on what appear to be key facts. A third review will help to clarify any questions you may have and should enable you to develop alternatives due to your familiarity with the material.

2 Determine the problem statement, central issue, and a secondary problem and/or central issue, if you believe they exist. The problem statement is a brief description of the dilemma requiring resolution. The central issue is the underlying theory or principle on which the problem is based. For example, in Department Store X, employee turnover is high. In this case, turnover is the problem, while the central issue may be inadequate compensation, poor training, difficult working hours, difficulties with management, unclear job expectations, or a combination of these. As there may be more than one central issue, there may be secondary problem statements also. Identifying the problem and its underlying central issue(s) is one of the most critical parts of conflict resolution in the business world. If you are not solving the actual problem, you can literally create new ones in actual industry situations. Initially, you may have some difficulty differentiating between the problem statement and the central issue. With practice and attention to all the details, you will be able to differentiate between the two with ease. After determining the problem statement and the central issue, you should choose which of the questions listed at the end of the case study that you intend to answer.

3 State your assumptions, if necessary. As some cases do not provide all of the information needed to make a decision, some assumptions may be required. It is your responsibility to make sure your assumptions are reasonable. Also, be prepared to defend them.

4 Identify all of the viable alternatives. Be open, reasonable, and realistic. Remember, money will not solve every problem, especially when there is no additional funding available. You cannot assume that there is an unlimited budget. Instead, look for workable, creative solutions.

5 Evaluate the alternatives. Avoid searching for "the right answer" until you have weighed the strengths and weaknesses of each alternative. Make a recommendation based on this evaluation—choosing not "the right answer," but the best answer as based on your examination of the advantages and disadvantages of each alternative solution.

6 Select and justify a preferred alternative solution based on the results of your evaluation. Remember, there is no right or wrong answer; however, there is an obvious, logical choice. Briefly justify why you have chosen that specific alternative.

7 Determine an implementation strategy—an action plan to put your solution into effect. Break your plan of action into specific steps, preferably within a time frame. You should also note the personnel to whom each task is delegated, and discuss a budget, if applicable. Sometimes, you will work all of the way through the implementation section only to realize that your preferred alternative is difficult or even impossible to put into action. When this occurs, re-evaluate the alternatives and reconsider your decision. This implementation section can also serve as a doublecheck for what not to do.

Remember, if your preferred solution and alternatives do not match any of the questions listed at the end of a particular case study, go to your instructor to find out whether you should pursue your chosen course of action. It may be that your solution is one that no one else has thought of and is just right for the problem!

The next section is a brief list of case study analysis tips developed by students who have participated in a case analysis course. These suggestions will help to assist and guide you as you begin your case study analysis.

Case Study Analysis Tips

- If you choose to make an assumption(s) about a particular case study, briefly clarify and justify it before determining the problem statement. Remember, all assumptions must be realistic.

- Suggesting the need for more research as a selected alternative is usually prohibitive in the real world in terms of cost and time. As it may simply postpone the problem-solving process, it is not a recommended solution.

- Do not be vague in your recommendations, especially in your implementation strategy.

- Dwelling on past mistakes by management or other personnel or restating the facts of the case cannot substitute for constructing alternative solutions.

- Do not judge the complexity of a case by its length. Some of the shortest case studies may require the greatest analysis time.

- Remember to develop realistic alternatives. Keep in mind that, most of the time, funding is limited.

- Be concise throughout the case study analysis. Be explicit in when constructing alternatives.

- Be prepared to defend your solution and alternatives when discussing your case study analysis in class.

- Use titles reflecting employment positions when referring to characters in the cases, rather than their personal names.

Class Participation

The following information will help you to be fully prepared to actively participate in your case study analysis course but you should keep in mind that your level of participation will vary with your role or assignment for each class session. For example, as a discussion leader, you will have a very high level of participation and involvement as you direct the class analyses of cases. As a member of the class when another student is in the leadership position, your active involvement may be somewhat minimized. Remember, you will be required to contribute to every class session in some way—large or small. Ten suggestions that will maximize your class participation potential are:

1 Be prepared. Read the case study repeatedly; write your analysis thoroughly; think it over carefully. You will be amazed how easy it is to participate when you are truly prepared.

2 Be assertive. If you do not speak up, you will miss out on the opportunity to share your preparation. Although this is difficult for some people, it is a necessary attribute for business success. Learning to be effectively assertive now, in college, will put you one step ahead as a young career executive.

3 Be courteous. Avoid interrupting others. Recognize the importance and impact of business etiquette as it pertains to group discussions. When you disagree, remember to challenge the point or perspective, not the person.

4 Have something valuable to contribute. One of the most frustrating aspects of group discussion for you, your peers, and faculty is to have someone making "off-the-cuff" remarks or talking for the sake of being heard or dominating the discussion. Carefully listen to the flow of the discussion and contribute when you have something appropriate and valuable to say.

5 Recognize the limitations of your analysis. One of the advantages of group discussion is that you will benefit from the collective viewpoint. Two heads are better than one (and 25—or whatever number of students are enrolled in your class—are even better). Realize that often you will not identify every available alternative for a case study and that you and/or some of your colleagues will develop viable alternatives the instructor and author have not discovered!

6 Be flexible. Do not be rigid about defending your solution if you truly believe, after participating in the class discussion, that another alternative is more appropriate. Be open to other points of view and to objectively evaluating your perspective.

7 Expect to be challenged. Do not Take It Personally (don't TIP). You are not being challenged as an individual—your analysis is being questioned. Do not feel sorry for yourself or become upset. If your analysis and logic are sound, your solution will stand up under the most careful scrutiny. If it is not, you will learn something and have the opportunity to improve on the next go-around.

8 Justify your position. After the discussion, if you still believe that your preferred solution is superior, defend your position. Use facts, preparation, and effective communication skills to support your perspective.

9 Recognize the value of good communication skills. Learn how to listen, speak, and write effectively. Organize your thoughts and present them in an orderly, logical fashion.

10 Relax and listen carefully to all the different opinions given in the class discussion.

The next section is a list of communication skills for directors of group discussion. These skills can help you to maximize your effectiveness as a communicator, leader, and executive of tomorrow. Review the list now to identify your strengths as well as areas for improvement. When it is your turn to take the position of the discussion leader, review this list on the evening before your class session. An awareness of effective communication abilities will give you an edge as you prepare to direct the group discussion.

Group Leadership Communication Skills to Enhance Case Study Discussion
Because these skills are essential not only for the purpose of case study analysis but also for succeeding in the real-life world of merchandising and retailing, we have listed them here for you. They are not in order of importance as they are all equally vital for success:

- Active listening: the ability to hear and understand direct and subtle messages, including both verbal cues and body language.

- Paraphrasing: the ability to restate correctly what another person says without sounding mechanical or applying one's own perspective.

- Reflecting: the ability to summarize the feeling or opinion expressed by the speaker or group members.

- Clarifying: the ability to focus on the underlying issues to assist others to gain a clearer picture of their thoughts and/or feelings.

- Initiating: the ability to effectively open group discussions through "icebreakers," a brief summary of the process to follow, an anecdote, and so forth.

- Interpreting: the ability to reflect upon and to present another's thoughts in a different way without affecting the meaning of the message.

- Questioning: the ability to ask—without sounding like an interrogator—open-ended questions that will stimulate discussion.

- Linking: the ability to relate what one person is doing or saying to the concerns of the other members.

- Confronting: the ability to directly challenge the viewpoint or perspective of a person in a way that does not cause the person to become defensive.

- Blocking: the ability to intervene or to stop counterproductive behaviors (such as gossiping, storytelling, or losing sight of the subject matter) without attacking or controlling.

- Facilitating: the ability to help others to openly express themselves and work through barriers of communication.

- Empathizing: the ability to sense the subjective feelings of others in a group and to understand much of what the others are experiencing.

- Supporting: the ability to align with group members when it is productive (and not counterproductive) to do so.

- Summarizing: the ability to identify key elements of a discussion session through a concise and informative conclusion statement.

- Humoring: the ability to laugh with others and to laugh at one's self.

Case Study Analysis Form

On page 24, you will find a case study analysis form, which may be modified or utilized as is at the discretion of your instructor. Although the case study form accommodates four alternative solutions with their respective advantages and disadvantages, you may develop more or less than four alternatives depending upon the particular case study and your level of effort and expertise. Remember that the format is a guide to assist you in analyzing a wide variety of case studies.

Case Study Evaluation Form

Following the case study analysis form, you will also find a suggested case study evaluation form that may be adjusted, used as presented, or deleted by your instructor. It is included to provide you with an overview of areas of evaluation some teachers have designated as significant in case study analysis. Your individual instructor will determine how your written and oral case study contributions and will be evaluated and will share these expectations and evaluation criterion with you and the other the students in your class.

Sample Case Study

On page 30, you will find a sample case study and its corresponding analysis by a student, which is not intended to illustrate a perfect analysis. Instead, the purpose is to provide an example of an acceptably written case analysis for which you may find additional alternatives, a better solution, or other points of discussion.

Name_____

Date_____ **Case Study Number**_____

Case Study Title_____

Immediate Problem_____

_____

_____

_____

Central Issue_____

_____

Alternative Solution 1_____

_____

_____

_____

Advantages

a_____

_____

b_____

_____

c_____

_____

Disadvantages

a_____

_____

b_____

_____

c_____

_____

Alternative Solution 2_____

_____

_____

Advantages

a_____

_____

b_____

_____

c_____

_____

Disadvantages

a_____

_____

b_____

_____

c_____

Alternative Solution 3_____

_____

_____

_____

Advantages

a_____

_____

b_____

_____

c_____

_____

Disadvantages

a_____

_____

b_____

_____

c_____

_____

Alternative Solution 4_____

_____

_____

_____

_____

Advantages

a_____

_____

b_____

_____

c_____

_____

Disadvantages

a_____

_____

b_____

_____

c_____

_____

Selected Alternative and Justification_____

_____

_____

_____

Implementation_____

_____

_____

_____

_____

_____

Case Study Evaluation Form for Instructor Use

Name_____

Date_____ **Case Study Number**_____

Points
Earned

Points
Available

Immediate Problem

○ Should be more concise

○ Needs to be more specific

○ Incorrect assessment of problem

○ Other_____

Central Issue

○ Restated immediate problem

○ There are additional central issues

○ Incorrect assessment of central issue

○ Other_____

Alternative Solutions

○ Incomplete; there are other alternatives

○ Unrealistic solutions

○ Duplicates (Alternatives ____ and ____)

○ Alt.____does not solve immediate problem

○ Other_____

Solution/Defense

○ Incomplete response

○ Should be more concise

○ Other_____

Points Earned   Points Available

◯   ◯   **Implementation**

◯ Justifies, does not provide how-to steps

◯ Needs to be more specific

◯ Other_____

◯   ◯   **Miscellaneous** (Those that apply are circled)

Illegible   Incorrect Format   Incorrect Number of Pages   Submitted Late

◯ Other_____

Discussion of Case Study Analysis Strengths_____

_____

_____

_____

_____

_____

_____

_____

_____

_____

_____

◯   ◯   **Total Points**

The New Kid on the Block

Patty McCoy determined that she wanted to become a fashion buyer while she was enrolled in a clothing and textiles course in high school. She attended a private liberal arts college, majoring in fashion merchandising and graduating with a Bachelor of Science degree. During summer breaks throughout her college years, she worked in various retail positions at local specialty stores. Additionally, she completed a retailing internship with a major department store during her junior year. The excellent evaluation provided by her internship employer was significant in her ability to procure an entry-level management position upon graduation. Patty was elated that her education and work experiences were significant factors in securing her first post-graduation job as an assistant department manager within a major department store.

Patty anticipated her first day on the job with both excitement and nervousness. She reported to the department manager of children's wear, Wendy Cox, for a review of her job responsibilities. Ms. Cox appeared overwhelmed and anxious as she reeled off a list of the day's tasks that included (but was not limited to) rearranging the sales floor fixtures, putting away a rack of new stock receipts, setting up a holiday display, clearing out the fitting rooms, and preparing a new weekly work schedule for the departmental sales associates. Ms. Cox explained to Patty that she would receive very little assistance from the sales associates as they were older, experienced salespersons who were commissioned employees. She then guided Patty to the sales floor where she introduced her to the full-time sales staff of four women. They welcomed Patty and then quickly returned to their sales books, the telephone, and the customers shopping in the department.

As the first day finally came to an end, Patty was exhausted and a bit frustrated. Even with Ms. Cox's assistance, she was unable to complete the day's tasks. The holiday display was unfinished; the fitting rooms remained cluttered with merchandise; and the employee schedule was incomplete. The rest of the week was a repetition of her first day on the job. Ms. Cox would deliver a list of job responsibilities in the morning, followed by Patty's valiant attempts to complete the work. Although the sales associates never offered assistance, Patty politely asked them individually for help with putting away merchandise and installing the new display. One associate replied that she was busy helping a customer; another assisted for a few minutes and then suddenly vanished to another part of the department.

At the conclusion of her first week of employment, Patty asked Ms. Cox for advice regarding the lack of assistance from the sales associates. Ms. Cox seemed receptive to Patty's observations and verified that the sales personnel in other departments did help with stockwork and displays. Ms. Cox stated that her own job responsibilities were so great that she did not have the time to adequately train and supervise the departmental employees. She then gave Patty a new and more challenging responsibility—to motivate the sales staff to assist with departmental duties in addition to selling.

The following week, Patty decided to take a more direct approach with the sales associates. She delegated stockkeeping jobs to each person and then offered to work with them on their assignments. The entire atmosphere shifted as the saleswomen began complaining about the additional work. They told her that they were on commission and that their salaries were a direct result of work they did with the customers. They explained that time spent on stockwork and displays would decrease their sales, resulting in unfulfilled quotas and subsequent unemployment. Finally, the sales associates stated that Patty's plan to delegate tasks had been attempted years ago and that it had not worked. Sales volume and employee morale had suffered, they continued, and she would understand this better after she had been with the store for a while. As the day progressed, one of the sales associates actually completed her stockwork assignment, but all the others did not even make an attempt to work on their assigned duties.

Patty was devastated. In a matter of a day, the reactions of the sales staff reduced her from feeling confident about her new management position to feeling inexperienced and ineffective. She thought about the age range and work experience of the saleswomen and felt as though she were telling her mother what to do. Patty felt as though the departmental associates did not recognize her authority and did not respect her as an assistant department manager. She felt unprepared for her new position and unclear about her job expectations. Patty decided to reevaluate her plan and to return the next day with a revised proposal and a refreshed attitude.

1 **If you were in Patty McCoy's place, what would you do?**

2 **If you were in Wendy Cox's position, what would you do?**

Name Sally Tucker

Date 1/15/96   **Case Study Number** XXI

Case Study Title The New Kid on the Block

Immediate Problem Disorganization in the store's children's wear department due to the laxity of its department manager and unclear job expectations by sales associates.

Central Issue How can rules of conduct be established for employees after a previously loose environment has been permitted by management?

Alternative Solution 1 (Patty McCoy's Perspective) The assistant department manager can schedule a departmental meeting for all sales associates to review the past situation, to announce the new regulations, and to outline penalties for failure to comply by the new departmental rules.

Advantages

a The sales associates could possibly appreciate an honest, direct approach. The meeting should bring out problems and show employees the need for improvement.

b This is the fastest route to change.

c It treats the sales associates as a group rather than as individuals, not singling out any one employee.

Disadvantages

a Employees may resent an aggressive approach by a young person who is also a new employee.

b A group meeting may enable mass antagonism to develop — all of them against one.

c If the assistant department manager cannot stand up to the group effectively, she will lose (and may never regain) credibility and confidence.

Alternative Solution 2 The assistant department manager could work individually with each sales associate.

Advantages

a This may set an example for the other employees.

b The assistant department manager may be able to "win over" the employees by this indirect approach as it gives each person individual attention and slowly implements a more balanced workload.

c There would be less resentment to affect morale.

Disadvantages

a It will be difficult to retrain "old hands."

b This plan will take substantial time.

c It may not have a lasting effect. Sales associates may slip back into their former habits when not working individually with the assistant department manager.

Alternative Solution 3 The assistant department manager could contact the human resources director for authorization to terminate the worst offender.

Advantages

a Fear may be a strong motivator for the remaining sales associates.

b The assistant department manager would establish herself as a strong executive with the sales staff.

Disadvantages

a Departmental morale could be destroyed.

b There may be legal implications.

c The remaining sales staff may quit because of fear of being fired at a later time.

d This plan does not promote a spirit of cooperation.

Alternative Solution 4 The assistant department manager could resign and look for another job.

Advantages

a She would not have to deal with the problem.

Disadvantages

a She would avoid responsibility and would establish a poor job record.

b She would have a lapse in salary and benefits.

c She would have difficulty explaining her short-term job to prospective employers and would have little chance of obtaining a positive reference from the department manager.

Alternative Solution 5 The assistant department manager could ask for a transfer to another, more efficient, department in the store.

Advantages

a She could avoid this unpleasant work environment.

b She could remain employed with the store, rather than job-hopping at this early stage in her career.

c She would not have to find a new employer.

Disadvantages

a She would dodge management responsibility and may develop a reputation for this in the store.

b A transfer may not be available.

c She avoids facing and conquering conflict.

Alternative Solution 6 The department manager could direct a departmental meeting during which she would advise the sales associate that the assistant department manager would be assigned the responsibility of delegating stockkeeping tasks to them.

Advantages

a New rules can be implemented immediately.

b Hierarchy is established for management.

c Cooperation is more likely to be provided to the assistant department manager as the department manager's support for her authority is apparent.

Disadvantages

a The sales associates may go over the department manager's head with complaints and dissatisfaction.

b The assistant department manager will have to formulate the plan to improve stockkeeping.

c The assistant department manager has no assurance of employees' cooperation.

Selected Alternative and Justification Alternative 6. This alternative reflects the management chain of command within the department. Training will be provided to implement clearer and more stringent job expectations.

Implementation For the assistant department manager:

1 Develop a list of departmental responsibilities, including: installation of displays; maintenance of fitting rooms; regular stockkeeping of inventory; receipt and set-up of new merchandise.

2 Write a job description for sales associates that contains all duties determined in Step 1, as well as selling.

3 Construct a calendar to rotate responsibilities among sales associates.

4 Establish a training session for each job responsiblity that all sales associates are able to attend.

5 Determine consequences: positive for successfully completed tasks; negative for tasks unfulfilled.

6 Receive approval on all implementation steps from department manager.

Chapter 1
The Nature of the Organization

Business Categories

In an effort to communicate effectively about the various types of organizations in the apparel and soft goods industry, businesses are frequently categorized into seven basic classifications:

- Legal form of organization

- Ownership

- Types of merchandise sold

- Types of services offered

- Level of nonstore selling

- Extent of the organization's departmentalization

- Communication channels

The following are brief discussions of these classifications, all of which provide an overview of the nature of an organization.

The Legal Form

A business may be classified under one of three forms of legal organization, which are:

1 Sole proprietorship, in which one person owns the business and assumes personal responsibility for its debts. An example of a sole proprietorship is a clothing store owned by an individual. Although this person may have received bank loans or financing from family members to open and operate the store, s/he is solely responsible for the retail operation's debts.

2 Partnership, in which two or more people invest their time and money while maintaining liability for business debts. They determine how the business is to be operated, the amount of time each partner will devote to it, and how profits and losses will be divided. As an example, a partnership may consist of three people in which the first has 50 percent legal responsibility, the second has 30 percent legal responsibility, and the third has 20 percent legal accountability. Their individual responsibility for the company's debt is usually in direct proportion to the amount of their legal responsibility.

3 Corporation, in which stockholders invest in the business, but do not necessarily share in management decisions. Major decisions are made by a board of directors, while daily operations are conducted by executives and employees of the organization. Stockholders have limited personal responsibility for the firm's debts, as determined by the amount of their investments. A stockholder owning 50 percent of a company may be responsible for half the firm's debts, yet may not participate in the daily operation of the business.

Ownership

Ownership or control of a business may take one of seven forms, which are:

1 Chain operation, which has multiple outlets under common a ownership whose major functions (i.e., buying, advertising, employment) are often controlled by a central headquarters (e.g., Walmart, Dillard's, Sears).

2 Ownership group, which is a parent corporation that owns divisions of a business (e.g., Federated, Dayton Hudson, Carter Hawley Hale).

3 Manufacturer/retailer, which operates its own outlets, eliminating wholesalers and gaining absolute control of the distribution process (e.g., Kinney Shoes, Esprit, factory outlet stores).

4 Independently owned business, which usually has only one outlet, often owner-managed (e.g., Mother Goosebumps in Gilson,

Illinois, Poppy in Columbia, Missouri, Sun Fun in Orlando, Florida).

5 Leased department, which is an arrangement in which a retailer rents space within the store to another company (e.g., Estée Lauder, Brown Shoes, Consolidated Accessories).

6 Franchise, which is a manufacturer, wholesaler, or service company that sells to a smaller firm or individual the right to conduct a business in a specified manner within a certain period of time, using the franchise organization's name, logo, and so forth (e.g., Merle Norman Cosmetics, Benetton, Hathaway Fabrics).

7 Consumer cooperative association, in which consumers own shares in the operation. While owners determine business policy, actual operations are maintained by a manager (e.g., University Supermarket, Big Bear Resale Company, Kids R Fun).

Types of Merchandise Sold

Types of merchandise sold refers to the company's products. The "merchandise" can vary widely, for example, an object, service, activity, person, place, organization, or idea. The types of merchandise sold by an organization may also predetermine the level or method of nonstore selling a company conducts. Nonstore selling methods include selling techniques that do not require the physical plant, yet are viable components that contribute to the productivity of many retail operations. For example, the owner of an interior design firm may develop an at-home selling plan to present the company's products in the consumer's home, as the sales of home furnishings and related accessories are conducive to this setting. Nonstore selling methods are categorized as direct selling, party plans, mail order retailing, catalog retailing, telephone selling, and electronic selling. The QVC home shopping network illustrates nonstore selling via television—a form of electronic selling.

Types of merchandise sold also affect the organization of traditional store selling. Floor layout is often determined by the store's inventory. For example, a lingerie boutique requires shelving, garment racks, and dressing rooms. On the other hand, a fabric store may need racks to hold bolts of cloth, peg boards for small notions, and cutting tables. Additionally, personnel needs vary with the type of merchandise sold. In a specialty store operation with high-ticket items (e.g., fine jewelry or furs), a large number of sales associates are needed to provided service as well as security because of the expensive nature of the merchandise. In contrast, a warehouse operation requires few sales associates as the merchandise is selected and carted to the cash register by the customer, rung up by the cashier, and checked for payment at the exit door by a either a sales associate or a security guard. The type of merchandise sold also impacts the level of inventory an organization may need to carry. Garments that have definite sizes (e.g., 4, 6, 8, 10, 12, 14) require a higher amount of stock for customer selection than the one-size-fits-all type of apparel.

Types of Services Offered

Some organizations sell services rather than tangible products. Some categories of services sold are:

- Rentals
- Repairs
- Maintenance and custom work
- Personal services

Formal attire and costume rental, alteration service, custom sewing, wardrobe consultation, and fashion show production are examples of services sold by textile and apparel firms. While some businesses are totally service-oriented (e.g., a resident buying office), others provide some services for a fee.

Departmentalization

Many medium-sized and large department stores are organized according to various retailing functions, referred to as "the extent of departmentalization." In 1927, Paul Mazur developed the original concept of "planning by functions." The Mazur Plan divided business activities into four major areas: merchandising, public relations, operations, and control. Later, the National Retail Merchants' Association (now the National Retail Federation) added fifth and sixth functions—personnel and branch division. Merchandising includes responsibility for all the activities involved in buying and selling merchandise. The public relations area is concerned with all nonpersonal selling activities (i.e., sales promotion, advertising, publicity). The major activities of operations are business maintenance, purchasing of supplies and equipment to operate the business, customer services, and security. The control division is responsible for monitoring the firm's financial status through accounting and record keeping, credit and collections, budgeting, and inventory control. Personnel, now commonly called human resources, is responsible for overseeing the company's employees in terms of recruiting, hiring, training, promoting, compensating, and terminating. The branch division takes responsibility for the organization's outlets that are not within the company's headquarters.

Communication Channels

Organizations may also be classified in terms of communication channels. Effective communication assists management with recognition of employee and consumer wants and needs. It also helps employees understand organization objectives, policies, and opportunities. Commonly used channels of communication are downward vertical (manager to employee), upward vertical (employee to manager), and horizontal (manager to manager). Informal communication is the use of vertical and horizontal lines for verbal communication. An unofficial communication network is referred to as a grapevine, usually transporting messages (although often distorted) faster than through official channels. Formal communication involves the use of employee handbooks, suggestion systems, newsletters, bulletins, meetings, and education departments. All types of organizations experience various communication channels. In a "Mom and Pop" operation, for example, the store owner/manager may prepare a memo on holiday store hours for the sales associates. This illustrates a downward vertical, formal communication channel.

In the following pages, you will find a series of case studies that will provide you with an examination of the nature of several different types of organizations.

1 To Buy or Not to Buy

Details is a specialty store chain of eight stores located in college towns across the midwest. These stores carry contemporary women's apparel and accessories. The owners of this partnership, Barbara Ray and Micky Stanley, have recently enlisted the assistance of a major resident buying office in New York through a one-year contract. Although this affiliation is very expensive for the store owners, they both believe that the resident buying office membership will enable them to build their business to higher profit margins. They are particularly interested in the assistance of the resident buyers regarding vendor selection, private label merchandise, quantity discounts on group purchases, and the promotional opportunities that would expand their nonstore selling efforts.

For their first buying trip to New York, Barbara and Micky begin the week with an introductory, informational meeting at the resident buying office. The ladies' sportswear and dress buyers conducted a presentation for a fall catalog that the resident buying office is offering to its client stores. The resident buying office will produce the 12-page color catalog that will feature approximately 36 key items from major sportswear and dress vendors. The merchandise will be exclusive to the resident buying office's client stores and will carry the resident buying office's private label. Additionally, the merchandise will be available at 25 percent below line price (i.e., manufacturer's wholesale price) because of the group purchase, although the regular retail price will appear in the catalog. The catalog will be imprinted with the individual store's name, address information, branch locations, telephone numbers, payment options, shipping costs, and other related information. Although the store is responsible for the expense of mailing the catalogs to their customer list, the resident buying office is not charging a fee for the catalogs because the vendors that will be featured in the catalog are providing cooperative advertising funds to offset the costs of production. This will be done in exchange for having the vendors' names included in the catalog copy.

Barbara and Micky are impressed with both the catalog and the resident buyers' enthusiasm for this project. They spend the next few days in the market, viewing the lines of vendors they have used during past seasons and those of new manufacturers recommended by the resident buying office. At the end of the week, it is time to write the orders for their fall merchandise selection. They review their notes on all of the lines previewed and analyze their options.

Micky analyzes the costs of purchasing merchandise to support the catalog. She is shocked at the end result. To minimally cover their eight stores with an adequate size-range representation of each catalog item, they will need to spend 75 percent of their available open-to-buy funds on the catalog styles only! This would greatly limit the merchandise assortment they could purchase from other vendors; however, at the same time, it provides them with exclusivity, a higher profit margin, and an opportunity for catalog sales. If they spend the large amount of open-to-buy dollars required to support the catalog, they will need to reduce or eliminate orders with vendors they have successfully carried in the past. As many of the manufacturers featured in the catalog have not been stocked at Details in prior seasons, they have no selling track record with those vendors. However, the catalog looks sensational; the initial markup is appealing; and the decision is extremely tough.

1   **If you were one of the owners of Details, would you purchase the resident buying office's catalog?**

2   **Would you develop an alternative promotional/nonstore selling method? If so, what is the alternative method?**

Figure 1.1 *This is an example of a divisional breakdown of job responsibilities for a retail operation.*

GARLAND STORES

Division	Responsibilities
MERCHANDISING	• Merchandise development, selection, pricing, and selling • Controlling inventory (joint responsibility with Operations). • Sets merchandising policies: quality standards, price ranges, fashion leadership position, exclusivity. *The **Merchandising Division** is the only division that generates income for the store.*
CONTROL	• Payroll • Expense planning and control • Credit office • Internal auditing • Accounts payable • Inventory monitoring and reconciliation • Statistical: generates purchase journal *The **Control Division** initiates and monitors all areas covering finance and general accounting within the store.*
PROMOTION	• Advertising, copy, and layout • Catalog, radio, television • Display: interior and windows • Store design and decor • Public relations/Special events *The **Promotion Division** works closely with the **Merchandising Division** to generate customer traffic and a favorable store image.*
HUMAN RESOURCES	• Training • Employee selection and development • Rating and reviews • Termination • Job Analysis • Benefits *The **Human Resources Division** recruits, develops, evaluates, and manages the store's personnel.*
STORE OPERATIONS	• Customer service — sales, service desk • Telephone and mail order • Warehouse • Restaurants • Receiving and marking • General operations activities: security, housekeeping, delivery, alterations *The **Store Operations Division** provides general support services, internally and externally, that allow the store to function.* *The **Branch Store Division** operates as a microcosm of the other divisions — solely for branch store locations.* *Within each branch are offices for **Advertising, Operations, Personnel,** and **Control.** Branch department managers perform the operational and merchandising functions.*

Figure 1.2 *This is an example of a six-month merchandising plan that is used to project sales and inventory levels in terms of retail dollars.*

GARLAND STORES

6-MONTH MERCHANDISING PLAN FOR PERIOD FROM .... **TO** .... **YEAR** ....

Buyer		DIV MGR		GEN MGR			DEPT

Store 1

STORE NO.			NET SALES	FEB/AUG	MAR/SEP	APR/OCT	MAY/NOV	JUN/DEC	JUL/JAN
ACT LY	PLANNED THIS YEAR	ACT TY	LAST YEAR						
	NET SALES		PLAN						
	AV MO STOCK		THIS YEAR						
	STOCK TURN		EOM STOCK / JAN/JUL	FEB/AUG	MAR/SEP	APR/OCT	MAY/NOV	JUN/DEC	JUL/JAN
	MARK DN %		ACT LY						
	GROSS MARG		PLAN TY						
	MAINT M/U		ACT TY						
			MD LY						
			MD TY						

Store 2

STORE NO.			NET SALES	FEB/AUG	MAR/SEP	APR/OCT	MAY/NOV	JUN/DEC	JUL/JAN
ACT LY	PLANNED THIS YEAR	ACT TY	LAST YEAR						
	NET SALES		PLAN						
	AV MO STOCK		THIS YEAR						
	STOCK TURN		EOM STOCK / JAN/JUL	FEB/AUG	MAR/SEP	APR/OCT	MAY/NOV	JUN/DEC	JUL/JAN
	MARK DN %		ACT LY						
	GROSS MARG		PLAN TY						
	MAINT M/U		ACT TY						
			MD LY						
			MD TY						

Store 3

STORE NO.			NET SALES	FEB/AUG	MAR/SEP	APR/OCT	MAY/NOV	JUN/DEC	JUL/JAN
ACT LY	PLANNED THIS YEAR	ACT TY	LAST YEAR						
	NET SALES		PLAN						
	AV MO STOCK		THIS YEAR						
	STOCK TURN		EOM STOCK / JAN/JUL	FEB/AUG	MAR/SEP	APR/OCT	MAY/NOV	JUN/DEC	JUL/JAN
	MARK DN %		ACT LY						
	GROSS MARG		PLAN TY						
	MAINT M/U		ACT TY						
			MD LY						
			MD TY						

Store 4

STORE NO.			NET SALES	FEB/AUG	MAR/SEP	APR/OCT	MAY/NOV	JUN/DEC	JUL/JAN
ACT LY	PLANNED THIS YEAR	ACT TY	LAST YEAR						
	NET SALES		PLAN						
	AV MO STOCK		THIS YEAR						
	STOCK TURN		EOM STOCK / JAN/JUL	FEB/AUG	MAR/SEP	APR/OCT	MAY/NOV	JUN/DEC	JUL/JAN
	MARK DN %		ACT LY						
	GROSS MARG		PLAN TY						
	MAINT M/U		ACT TY						
			MD LY						
			MD TY						

2   **Too Much of a Good Thing?**

Barton's is a prestigious men's wear specialty store that has been family-owned for three generations. The merchandise assortment includes better-priced men's casual and tailored apparel, men's furnishings, and a small selection of active sportswear. The store volume has supported its owners in a comfortable manner for years. Barton's has the reputation for carrying top quality, moderately fashionable men's wear at moderate to better prices. The store is also known for its exceptional customer service, its positive community image, and its knowledgable staff. Business has grown steadily throughout Barton's history. As the family has grown, however, the proprietors have consistently investigated alternative ways of increasing profits for the business.

Donna Virden, one of the owners, has called a meeting of the rest of the family owners to present her plan for generating additional sales volume. Donna begins by describing the current state of the business and punctuates it with two interesting observations: (1) almost exclusively, women accompany and advise the men who are interested in new apparel; and (2) these women actually purchase the majority of men's apparel. Based on this observation and armed with data from the National Retail Federation about the growth of women's career apparel in specialty stores, Ms. Virden offers a proposal to incorporate women's classic fashions into the merchandise mix. She recommends eliminating the men's active sportswear section and replacing it with a women's career clothing department. The men's active sportswear department has the slowest stockturn and lowest maintained markup of all of the men's wear departments within Barton's. Additionally, there are several local, nearby competitors that also specialize in this merchandise classification, including a golf pro shop and a men's sportswear shop. Donna believes that the addition of a women's apparel department will create additional sales volume while also enhancing sales in the traditional men's wear departments. She states that women who choose Barton's for their own apparel purchases will generate multiple sales by also purchasing merchandise for the men in their lives. Donna also notes that the implementation of women's apparel in Barton's merchandise mix will not require the expense of new floor space, if the sluggish men's active sportswear department is eliminated.

The store owners discuss the costs of promoting and stocking a new department. They examine the difficulties of training and hiring new sales personnel for a new department. They debate the risks of entering a merchandise classification with which they have no retail experience, buying expertise, or vendor relations. Two of the senior owners are extremely resistant to changing the merchandise mix and altering the target market of the store, questioning "If it isn't broken, why try to fix it?" Finally, they debate the possibility of blurring their company image by trying to be "everything to everybody."

1 **If you were one of the owners of Barton's, would you advise maintaining the current merchandise mix as it exists?**

2 **Would you recommend expanding the store's inventory to include women's wear? Are there additional alternatives?**

3 **Would you suggest that men's active sportswear be eliminated, remerchandised, or expanded?**

3   **What Do You Want?**

Diane Hunter is employed as the home accessories department manager in a branch store of Garland Stores, a major department store chain. She has worked for the company since her graduation from a nearby state university last year, beginning as a sales associate in the bed linen department. Ultimately, it is her long-term goal to become a store manager for this company. She is a dedicated, hard-working, and enthusiastic employee who is well-liked by her peers and by her supervisor, Mrs. Silverman.

Diane is conscientious about customer service within her department. If a customer is searching for an item that is not currently in stock, she immediately makes a notation of the requested item on the customer want list—a record of merchandise voids that will be forwarded to the home accessories buyer. Diane will then write the customer's name, telephone number, and the item in her personal customer book so that she can quickly and efficiently contact the customer when the merchandise arrives. She is anxious to build a customer following in an effort to increase departmental sales volume and her commission bonus, as well to make herself quickly and eminently promotable.

When the buyer, John Andrews, visits her branch store, he mentions that he has never received a customer want list from her department and is curious about any specific items customers may be looking for that were not in stock. Diane looks surprised, but does not respond to Andrews' comments. John notices that she is hesitant about answering his requests and decides to pursue the cause of this problem at a later date. John quietly checks the customer want list notebook and notices that there are several pages of Diane's detailed notations in regard to unavailable merchandise that had been requested by customers. He realizes that this information would be quite helpful in determining which goods to send to the branch store. Diane is concerned about the possibility of creating problems with Mrs. Silverman by mentioning to Mr. Andrews that the lists have been made, but have not been forwarded. She is surprised that these customer want lists are not being utilized, because she recognizes that they are a worthwhile, if time-consuming, task. Diane is puzzled as to how to respond to Mr. Andrews' question about the want lists. She does not want to create conflict with her immediate supervisor, Mrs. Silverman, yet she realizes that her commission is dependent upon her sales volume. Her sales could greatly increase if she was able to fill her customers' requests. Additionally, Diane recognizes that the performance evaluations of both Mr. Andrews and Mrs. Silverman will be critical in determining when and if she is promoted to a department manager position in the future.

After John has left the store, Diane carefully reiterates to Mrs. Silverman his remarks about not receiving the customer want lists. Mrs. Silverman is apathetic and states that she is too busy to get all of the departmental tasks completed. "Besides," she continues, "many of the customers have ridiculous requests and John doesn't have the time to follow through up with them anyway."

1   If you were in Diane Hunter's position, what would you do?

2   If you were in John Andrew's position, what would you do?

Figure 1.3 *This is an organizational chart illustrating the line and staff divisions of a major retail department store.*

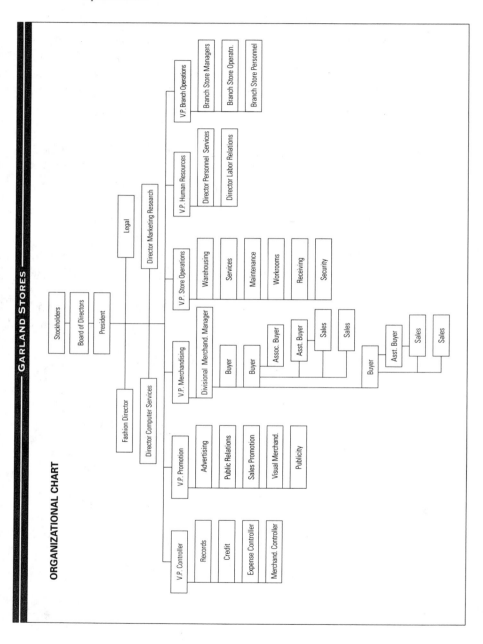

4   Sewing Up the Loose Ends

Katie Lynn is the regional manager for a chain of five home sewing stores, Pins and Needles, located within a 120-mile-wide geographical area in Illinois. The stores, which are extremely profitable for the corporation that owns them, feature a total merchandise mix directed to the home sewer and home decorator. The extensive product assortment includes apparel and upholstery fabrics, patterns, notions, craft products, dress forms, and sewing equipment. In addition to the vast product mix, Pins and Needles offers a large number of customer services: product demonstrations, special order availability, sewing machine servicing, custom sewing, among others.

In her position as regional manager, Katie is ultimately responsible for overseeing the general operations of all the stores. She travels to each of the branch stores weekly to personally work with the individual store managers, assistant managers, and sales associates. Her job duties consist of training new management personnel, designating merchandise transfers and markdowns, communicating directly with the buyers on merchandise needs, monitoring the stores' budgets and sales volume, planning advertising and promotional events, and making certain that the stores look attractive and organized to the consumers. The last duty—store appearance—has been a growing problem for Katie.

Visual merchandising is a critical part of the home sewing business. The customers depend on effective interior and window displays to spark their imaginations for creative uses of the fabrics and other products. Due to the diverse range of goods and the minimal number of sales associates, the inventory must be organized in a way that the customer is able to help herself in merchandise selection. New inventory arrivals must be featured in a predominant location in the stores to encourage repeat visits by the customers and to receive an early reading on possible reorders for the buyers.

Without exception, all the stores are a visual disaster. Often, displays remain unchanged for months. The most effective displays are usually partially disassembled by customers who purchase the featured merchandise and the displays remain in this state of disrepair for weeks. New merchandise receipts are shoved into the racks because the store managers and associates do not have the time to carefully sort new merchandise. As Katie spends the majority of her time in the branch stores installing new displays and reorganizing the inventory, she has little time for all of her other responsibilities, such as personnel training and information gathering. It is an endless task as, when she returns the following week, she must start the display and clean-up process all over again.

This week she decides to develop a plan to resolve the visual merchandising mess and stockkeeping dilemma. She determines that the store managers and sales associates have a full schedule with customer service. The corporation that owns the chain requires a minimal number of personnel on the sales floor in order to keep overhead costs low through a carefully controlled payroll. Business is flourishing. Within the next two months, three additional stores will open in her region. If she does not handle this problem now, she will have real trouble. She decides to construct a proposal to present to upper management.

1   How would you recommend resolving the problem if you were advising Katie about the Pins and Needles situation? Would you recommend placing visual merchandising responsibilities with existing store personnel (managers and sales associates)?

2   Would you advise that Katie accept visual merchandising responsibilities as part of her job description?

3   Would you suggest an alternate course of action? If so, what is your plan?

5   **Changing of the Guard**

Anglers is a twelve-unit department store chain with five branches located in Kansas and seven units in Missouri. It is a third generation family-owned operation that carries hard and soft goods that range from home furnishings to apparel for men, women, and children. The branch stores are located in mid-sized cities throughout Missouri and Kansas. The flagship store is situated in downtown Kansas City and houses the centralized buying offices and merchandise distribution center. The company has experienced considerable growth recently, adding the five Kansas stores over the past year.

The chief executive officer of the company, Kenneth Powell, is beginning to look forward to retirement. He has worked for forty years with the company, starting his tenure with Anglers as a sales associate when the company consisted of two stores under his grandfather's leadership. It has been his desire to pass down ownership of the business to his daughter or son; however, neither is genuinely interested in pursuing a retail career. Mr. Powell's daughter has decided to pursue a career in law, while his son is working in real estate.

Mr. Powell has discussed his concerns about the future of his company with his colleague and friend, Harry Donegal. Mr. Donegal is the owner of a major resident buying office in New York, the office with which Anglers is affiliated. With Powell's permission, Mr. Donegal is spreading the word that Anglers may be for sale in the near future. A specialty store chain owner in Oklahoma—another retail member of the resident buying office—expresses interest in purchasing the entire chain. The Oklahoma chain store owner offers a moderate price for the Anglers' operation. At the same time, the chief executive officer of a major retailing corporation contacts Mr. Powell directly to discuss the possibility of buying the group of stores in Missouri. This corporation is not interested in the Kansas branches as they presently own several stores in competitive areas. On a per store basis, this is a higher offer than the Oklahoma retailer, but Mr. Powell believes it will be difficult to sell the Kansas stores separately. Additionally, he does not want to prolong his efforts to sell Anglers. He is anxious to relax and recuperate from decades of business ownership.

However, both potential purchasers are adamant that, when the sale goes through, Mr. Powell must stay with the company for a transition period as a business consultant. While the prospective purchasers believe that Mr. Powell's participation is necessary to maintain continuity of sales volume and to retain Anglers' dedicated personnel, Mr. Powell questions whether or not he will actually be able to retire in the near future if he commits to a consultation position. He believes that he has waited long enough to retire.

1   If you were in Mr. Powell's position, what would you decide to do with Anglers?

2   If you were the specialty store chain owner in Oklahoma, what would you propose to Mr. Powell?

3   If you were an executive with the major retailing corporation, what offer would you present to Mr. Powell?

6   Lay It Away—Does it Pay?

Sarah Ann's is a small "Mom and Pop" store located in the downtown shopping area of a rural town in Pennsylvania. The specialty store, owned by the husband and wife team of Sarah and John Smith, has a positive image in the community that has resulted in a dedicated customer following. The store features moderately priced apparel in children's wear and ladies' wear. The inventory primarily consists of the following merchandise classifications: sportswear, dresses, intimate apparel, and accessories. Recently, the store owners have decided to add outerwear to the merchandise mix for several reasons: (1) the higher unit price points of coats and jackets should substantially increase the store's overall sales volume; (2) there is no direct competition in coats and jackets within the immediate shopping area; (3) the long, cold winters in their market area are conducive to the sales of coats and jackets; and (4) the owners are working toward their goal of offering a full-service apparel operation for their consumers.

After attending the April apparel market and viewing fall lines in outerwear, Sarah and John learn from the coat and jacket manufacturers' representatives that outerwear manufacturers offer "early bird" pricing for orders to be delivered preseason. Through this "early bird" incentive pricing, the stores receive a substantial discount on new merchandise for placing their orders early and for accepting delivery of the merchandise in July and August. It can be a win-win situation for the store and the vendor as there are benefits for both: the retailer receives a merchandise discount and the manufacturer is able to maintain year-round production by manufacturing and shipping goods each month. Additionally, through preseason discounts, both the retailer and the producer have the opportunity for an early reading on possible reorder items through consumer sales in July and August. The Smiths decide to purchase their entire outerwear inventory through these "early bird" incentive deals.

As they make promotional plans for announcing the arrival of their new outerwear department, Sarah and John decide to add layaway to their previously limited range of customer services. The Smiths believe that the layaway option will encourage their customers to purchase fall merchandise early—particularly such high ticket items as coats. They determine that the layaway policy will include a 10 percent-down payment, monthly installments equal to 20 percent of the garment's price, and a maximum 90-day layaway period. The layaway service is a major part of the outerwear promotion as it is emphasized in the store's newspaper and radio advertising, as well as the store's displays.

The outerwear department debut was a huge success at the retail level and the layaway service was a critical part of the exceptional coat sales. The sales of coats and jackets exceeded the planned sales figure determined by Sarah and John. The store owners were particularly pleased with the results of their promotional efforts. In fact, the majority of customers mentioned the advertisements citing the layaway option as a critical factor in bringing them to shop for a winter coat to Sarah Ann's. Additionally, many customers used the layaway option to purchase other fall items, for example, sportswear ensembles, dresses, and leather handbags. As time progressed, however, the downside of the layaway service began to surface.

The Smiths were spending many hours each week maintaining the layaway bookkeeping records, recording the customer's payments and telephoning customers to remind them of monthly payments. The layaway merchandise was taking up a huge amount of space in the back stockroom. Most significantly, there were the problems associated with layaway merchandise returns. In some cases, customers changed their minds about their layaway choices— weeks or months after they purchased the items—and demanded refunds on their down payments and/or installment payments. In other cases, customers who paid the balances on their layaway merchandise selections at the end of the 90-day layaway period would find that by the time that they paid off their layaway, the identical merchandise had been marked down on the sales floor. These customers now wanted to receive the reduced retail prices on their merchandise and refunds on the differences in price.

The Smiths felt as though they had unknowingly created a monster through the layaway service option; at the same time, however, they recognized the positive impact that the layaway service had on merchandise retail sales. The Smiths were faced with a dilemma. They had to decide whether to discontinue the layaway service, modify the layaway policies and procedures, or to continue the existing service. Sarah suggested converting the office space in the back room into layaway storage. John advised that they increase the "early bird" retail prices in order to build in extra markup to offset later returns and price reductions.

1 **If you were in Sarah and John Smith's position would you decide to continue the layaway service? If so, what changes, if any, would you make in the existing layaway policies?**

2 **If not, in what ways do you believe the elimination of the layaway service will impact the store's retail sales volume?**

Figure 1.4 *This is an example of a layaway inquiry form maintained by a retail operation to track sales and customer payments.*

GARLAND STORES

LAYAWAY INQUIRY

```
----------------------------------------------------------
                          Date: 1/15/97
                       Program: 263.45
                         Store: 03
                    Department: 11
   Men's Shoes and Boots Class: 1 Better
                 Clerk Number: 46 Tina Sherwood
                   Layaway ID: 329471.5B
                    Last Name: Jones
                   First Name: David
                    Address-1: Street
                          -2: 639 West 72nd St.
                          -3: New York, NY
              Zip/Postal Code: 10023
               Telephone-Home: 212-555-1212
                         Work: 212-555-2121
                Purchase Date: November 23, 1996
         Last date for Pickup: January 23, 1997
                     Comments: Customer to pick up by 12/31/96
      Original purchase amount
               (with 8.25% tax): $323.67
       Original deposit amount: $75.00
           Amount paid to date: $200.00
 # of payments to date(incl.dep.): 3
        Amount of last payment: $75.00
          Date of last payment: 12/22/96
                       Action: Send postcard reminder
----------------------------------------------------------
```

GARLAND STORES

LAYAWAY POLICY

Customers may put merchandise on layaway with a 25% down payment on the date of purchase. This deposit/down payment is NON-REFUNDABLE! Every layaway will be given a last date for pickup, which must be adhered to by the purchaser. This date will be available at the layaway desk at all times. This last date for pickup is to be two months from the date of purchase. If the merchandise is not picked up within the two month layaway period, the merchandise will be returned to stock and the deposit/down payment will be forfeited by the purchaser. Layaway merchandise includes all full-price merchandise and merchandise of up to, but not over, 25% off. Purchaser acknowledges that layaway merchandise may be marked down further on the sales floor, but this does not include the purchaser's layaway merchandise. Layaway merchandise will not be marked down any further than those markdowns taken before the layaway period begins. Garland Stores does not agree to match any competitor's markdown price on any merchandise including layaway merchandise. As a courtesy, Garland Stores will send you a bi-monthly reminder about your layaway purchase.

Agreed to on this day_____

Signed_____

Purchaer_____

Address_____

Telephone (day)_____

Telephone (night)_____

7   Kids Act II

Cindy Tobin worked for several years for a market research company while she was completing a Master of Science degree in Business Administration. She then married and spent a number of years as an active homemaker and mother raising her son and daughter. As her children entered school, Cindy began to pursue the dream of owning her own business. She did some brainstorming to analyze her goals, interests, and strengths. Cindy determined that the past decade had provided her with expertise and experience in understanding children, marketing, organization, budgeting, and business. She decided that she would investigate opening a children's wear store in the new strip mall located near her home.

As Cindy researched apparel store alternatives, she became extremely interested in the growth of resale clothing stores. Resale apparel retailers directly purchase and/or accept on consignment quality used clothing from the public (referred to as the consignor) and then resell the merchandise to the ultimate consumers. Consignment merchandise is that which is entrusted to the retail store, but for which the store does not pay until the merchandise is purchased by a customer. In other words, the ownership title of the goods does not pass from the consignor to the retailer until the merchandise is purchased by the resale store's customer. If the retailer elects to carry consignment merchandise, the consignor usually receives 40 to 60 percent of the final retail selling price, while the retailer receives the remaining balance for handling the merchandise and its subsequent sale. Resale apparel stores featuring only consignment merchandise often refer to themselves as "consignment boutiques" and describe their merchandise as "preowned" or "gently worn." It is a business area that is upgrading itself from yesterday's thrift shops to a viable retail alternative for today's apparel and accessories customers.

Cindy visited a large number of resale clothing stores and, in several cases, had the opportunity to discuss the business aspects of resale retail operations with the store owners. She examined the size, fixturing, and general appearance of the stores. She reviewed the various contracts the consignment store owners required of their consignors. She visited with the resale store owners about the positive and negative aspects of their respective retail operations. Without exception, all of the resale store proprietors were extremely satisfied with their businesses. In addition to visiting the stores, Cindy read several articles in apparel trade journals about ladies' apparel and children's wear resale clothing stores.

One of the companies that Cindy read about was a highly profitable children's resale clothing store franchise. She was fascinated as she read of the franchise's exceptional success and was provided with a brief glimpse of the firm's procedures, promotions, and profits. Cindy traveled to another state to view one of the franchise operations and to interview its owner. She was further impressed after this visit. She then immediately contacted the franchisor and requested information about purchasing one of their franchise operations. The franchisor was extremely interested in working with Cindy as there were no direct competitiors near her anticipated location.

When Cindy reviewed the informational materials from the franchise headquarters, she was distressed with the substantial financial requirements. The franchisor required a one-time, lump sum of money in advance as payment for the use of the company's name, logo, and business procedures. There was another substantial amount of money needed to begin the store set-up that included the costs of signs and fixtures. Additionally, the company required that Cindy maintain a minimum balance of funds in a business checking account to ensure payment of such overhead costs as rent, utilities, insurance, payroll, and promotion. Finally, the franchisor was to receive a monthly fee (paid each month of business) based on a specified percent of sales volume—this percent would be renegotiated annually.

In exchange for these expenses, Cindy, as the franchisee, would co-own her business with the franchisor. She would be sharing the risks of opening a new business with an experienced partner, the franchisor. She would be provided with guidance on every aspect of the children's wear resale business including, store set-up, recruitment of merchandise sources, installing a computer system, advertising compaigns, as well as assistance with any problem or question that she might have.

Cindy's mind whirled with such questions as: "Should I open the business on my own and save the start-up costs and monthly fees associated with the franchisor? Do I know enough about retailing to open my own business without assistance? Won't I have an edge by working with a successful, growing company that has ironed out the wrinkles in the children's wear resale business?" She began to weigh the advantages and disadvantages of collaborating as a franchisee versus opening the business on her own.

1   Would you advise Cindy to open the children's wear resale business on her own?

2   Would you recommend that Cindy affiliate with the children's wear resale franchise?

3   Do you have an alternate idea to assist Cindy in reaching her goal of store ownership? If so, what is your plan?

Figure 1.6 *This is an example of a consignment operator/consignor contract. It is used by resale apparel and accessories stores to establish policies and procedures with merchandise sources.*

Resale Consignment Policies

1. Number of Selling Days
There is a 90-day selling period. If, after 90 selling days, the merchandise on consignment is not picked up by the consignor, the merchandise becomes the sole property of this retail store. Unsold items are donated to charity.

2. Merchandise Requirements
All merchandise must be clean and pressed, in good repair, placed on hangers, and fashionably appropriate for the season. Gently worn, well-maintained clothing of 3 years old or less is preferred; however, vintage items may be accepted if in excellent condition. Spring/summer items will be accepted during January through June. Fall/winter items will be accepted during July through December.

3. Receipt of Consignment Merchandise
Consignments are accepted on Mondays and Tuesdays from 9:00 a.m. to 12:00 noon and by appointment.

4. Payment to the Consignor
Only those persons whose names appear on the account will be permitted to collect money from that account. Consignors are paid monthly and may contact the store at the beginning of each month for a current account balance. The retailer will determine selling prices on merchandise, based on current resale prices and the prices of new, similar goods. The consignor's percent on each item is as follows:
$$\text{under } \$10.00 - 40\%$$
$$\$10.01 \text{ to } \$50.00 - 50\%$$
$$\$50.01 \text{ and over} - 60\%$$

5. Markdown Procedure
After 30 days in stock, consignment items will be marked down 20% off the original selling price. After 60 days in stock, items will be marked down an additional 50% off the original selling price. For example, the selling price established on a party dress you consign is $100.00. If it sells at this price within 30 days, you will receive $60.00. If not, it will be reduced to $80. Your payment is now $48. If it has not sold after 60 days, it will be marked down to $50. Your available payment is now $25.

6. Responsibility of Merchandise
This retail establishment is not responsible for theft or damage to merchandise while on the premises. We assure you that we will do everything within our power to prevent loss or destruction of your property. Finally, we retain the right to refuse any items we deem inappropriate.

Signed and executed on this day_____

Consignor's Signature_____

Printed Name_____

Address_____

Telephone Number_____

Consignee Signature_____

Printed Name_____

---

8 **To Hire or Not to Hire**

Sheila Summers is the director of human resources for one of eight branch units of a midsize department store chain in the Southeast. She has been in this position for only six months, hiring three new employees to date and terminating none. She enjoys her new position and believes that she is fair and competent in hiring trustworthy and effective employees.

Recently, the media has given much coverage to certain organizations that have expressed their belief that the company Sheila works for "is racist and hires as few minority candidates as it can get away with." The articles have been circulated in many major newspapers, magazines, and trade journals. Sheila is well aware that the continuation of this negative publicity can and will harm the reputation, and, subsequently also the profits, of the company. She deeply believes that these accusations are false for the company as a whole; she knows for certain that they are incorrect in regard to her limited work as the human resource director of one of the branch stores. She is concerned that the media will continue to focus on this biased perception as long as possible, thus permanently damaging the company's community image which was previously untarnished.

Sheila recognizes that there a only a few minority employees working in her branch store. She questions whether it is purely a coincidence. "Regardless of the reason," she thinks, "this does not reflect my efforts, as I have only been in the position to hire for six months." Sheila, however, is smart enough to know that this situation leaves her store wide open for attack from the press and interested organizations. The owners and executives of the company have made it clear to the human resource directors of all of the branch stores that the future of the company may be in jeopardy and stated that their "hiring habits may need some reforming." The message received by the human resource directors is that they simply must hire more minority employees.

Sheila is currently analyzing vacant positions she will need to fill within the next few months. The manager of the misses' sportswear department has recently submitted a personnel requisition form for an assistant department manager. The department manager is frantic as she desperately needs the help of a competent assistant to meet the tremendous work requirements of the misses' sportswear division, which generates the highest sales volume in the entire operation. Sheila has been interviewing applicants for the last two weeks and has finally narrowed the interviewees down to two final candidates, planning to make a final decision by the end of the week. Under normal circumstances, she would have no hesitation in making her decision. The two finalists consist of a white man who has extensive management experience in retailing and a black woman who has minimal management experience. Both candidates have completed their college degrees; both interviewed quite effectively. Sheila believes that on-the-job experience is extremely important for a future management position and believes that the female candidate may be lacking in this area. While it appears to her that the male applicant is more qualified for this particular position, the unspoken pressure from company executives and the media is contributing to her difficulty in making the final decision.

1 If you were in Sheila's position, would you hire the minority candidate?

2 Would you employ the male applicant?

3 Would you choose and alternate course of action? If so, what is your plan?

9 Honesty vs Loyalty

The Carousel, located in a major mall in Sugar Hill Georgia, is part of a national chain store organization that carries a specialized selection of apparel and accessories that appeal to contemporary young men and women. The company's primary target market is the 13- to 25-year-old student population. The majority of sales associates and store managers are in the 18- to 25-year-old range and can personally relate to the needs and wants of the store's consumers. The store has a reputation for its upbeat and energetic atmosphere, as well as its merchandise assortment of trendy unisex fashions.

Within the Sugar Hill branch store, the store manager, Jennifer Miller, supervises 17 full- and part-time sales associates. With regard to hiring employees, the company has established an interview process that it believes is significant in finding the right person with all of the needed qualifications for the job. During the interview process, a prospective employee must interview with Jennifer, several of the branch store's sales associates, the regional manager, and a store manager from The Carousel branch unit that is nearby. Throughout the multiple mini-interviews, team playing is emphasized as a skill required for employment and future success with the company. Debbie Moss is one of Jennifer's success stories. As a part-time sales associate, Debbie has the highest sales volume and is a valued member of The Carousel team. Jennifer is pleased with Debbie's progress and would prefer to hire more employees that are like her.

A new employee, Nichole Altman, has been hired recently at the Sugar Hill store. She has been selected due to her positive attitude toward being part of The Carousel team, her excellent product knowledge, her merchandise presentations to the customer, her outgoing personality, and her previous retail sales experience. Additionally, Nichole is a close friend of Debbie, with whom she had attended high school. Nichole and Debbie share the same group of friends and often spend social time together. Debbie provided a glowing personal recommendation for Nichole to the company's management staff. Jennifer especially liked Nichole because of her effective leadership qualities and her ability to get along well with others.

Last Friday, at the closing of a busy day of sales, Jennifer was counting the cash drawer and calculated a $10 shortage. Jennifer assumed there had been a simple error in ringing up a sale or returning change to a customer because cash shortages rarely occur; a few nights later, however, there was another cash shortage. Unknown to Jennifer, Debbie had observed Nichole removing money from the drawer during a customer transaction. Debbie could not believe that her friend would do something dishonest. She decides that she will not mention this incident to Nichole now. Instead, she will try to find a way to bring up the subject of the stolen money with Nichole when they are together as friends outside of the store. Debbie is concerned about how she will discuss this issue with Nichole, as she doesn't want to lose their friendship.

On this particular evening, when the cash drawer is being reconciled, Jennifer is faced with a $15 cash shortage. By this time she knows that one of her employees is stealing. Jennifer confronts the store staff as a whole, stating that if someone in the group does not admit to her what has happened, she will confer with each employee individually. Additionally, she continued, she will initiate security checks of each employee's belongings and begin requiring supervision of the cash drawer. She gives the employees until the next day to reveal any information they may possess.

Debbie witnessed Nichole taking the cash from the register. Debbie has been an employee of The Carousel for two years and is working toward a management position of her own Carousel branch store in the future. Nichole is one of her best friends and Debbie is fairly certain that Nichole knows that she is the only person who could have seen the removal of cash from the drawer. After all, they were the only two persons near the cash register at the time! If Debbie shares her observation of the theft to the store manager, she certainly will lose her friendship with Nichole. She also wonders whether or not Nichole would be in trouble legally if the stealing is revealed. On the other hand, Debbie believes that if she confesses her knowledge of the theft the store manager will recognize how honest she is and how concerned she is about the company's well-being. This could be a critical factor in her promotion to store management. If Jennifer learns that Debbie was aware of Nichole's theft and elected not to report it, Debbie believes that her opportunity for advancement with The Carousel would be eliminated. Worse, Debbie is concerned that her own employment may be terminated if the store manager finds out that she had witnessed the thievery and chose to ignore the crime.

1   If you were in Jennifer Miller's position, what would you do?

2   If you were in Debbie Moss' position, what would you do?

10 **Peeling Back**

Banana Anna's has been hit hard by the difficult economic times.
This specialty store—one that has been profitable for the past five
years by catering to a junior clientele with its trendy apparel and
accessories—has shown losses for the past few months. Business is
tough right now for all junior apparel retailers; it is anticipated,
however, that the economy will improve by the start of next year.
The co-owners of Banana Anna's, Cynthia Simon and Mary
Ruppert, plan to tighten their belts by making needed changes and
concessions to cut their losses and stay in the black. The store owners intend to weather the storm with visions of higher profits in the
future.

One of the first changes the owners implemented was to reduce
the inventory level. They decreased the open-to-buy funds they
planned to spend at the next market. To generate sales, they ran a
huge markdown promotion on existing inventory. Next, the owners
examined costs associated with the store's monthly overhead. The
owners carefully reviewed the sales associates' work schedules in an
effort to reduce employees' hours and, subsequently, the payroll
costs. Finally, they eliminated part of the promotional budget by
cutting back on newspaper and radio advertisements over the next
few months.

Cynthia Simon has also suggested that they analyze the operations function of the store to find additional means of reducing
costs. Cynthia has recommended that they reduce some of the
store's services such as free delivery, complimentary alterations,
and gift wrapping. The cost of gift wrap, boxes, ribbons, and tissue
added up to a substantial expense. Additionally, Cynthia has pro-

posed finding a new source for the store's shopping bags—one that would provide a less expensive product.

Mary Ruppert, on the other hand, is extremely concerned about the impact of these operational cutbacks on the store's image. Banana Anna's is well-known by its customers for attention to details and all the "little extras." Mary believes that the customer services—including the unique shopping bags—are an integral part of the store's success to date. She states that they (as the owners) should be simply looking for ways to reduce overhead as an effort to get through the difficult economic times—not to alienate the store's target market. Mary believes that reductions in future inventory levels and payroll costs are adequate concessions to reduce business expenses. She was extremely hesistant about reducing the promotional budget, as she believes that decreased advertising will result in decreasing store traffic. Mary is adamantly opposed to eliminating such store services as gift wrap, alterations, delivery, and the expensive packaging. Cynthia and Mary are at an impasse regarding these operational decisions.

1   If you were in Mary Ruppert's position, how would you "sell" your philosophy to your business partner?

2   If you were in Cynthia Simon's position, how would you persuade Mary Ruppert to accept your suggestions?

3   If you were a business consultant, what other alternatives could assist you in improving the store's profit margin?

11 Charge It!

Taffy's is a better specialty store chain that features children's and women's apparel. The company has seven branch stores located throughout Colorado. Since the company first opened with a single store in Boulder twenty years ago, Taffy's has offered its customers the option of a store credit card. The owners of Taffy's believe that the store credit card is actually a service that promotes customer patronage. Their store credit card records indicate that Taffy's charge card encourages the consumer to make multiple purchases. Additionally, the owners recognize that the company has added revenue through the interest fees collected from the credit card accounts.

As the retail operation has grown from a single store to seven units, the number of store charge accounts has also increased accordingly. The growth of the store credit card holders has required Taffy's to allocate a large space for the control/accounting office, as well as hiring a manager, several associates, and a collection agency to operate the credit division. An expensive computer system was also purchased and installed to facilitate accurate and timely recording of customer charge transactions. Recently, the store owners were approached by an accounting firm with an offer to purchase the store credit card accounts. The accounting firm will literally buy out the credit card debts, relieving Taffy's of the balances due on the existing charge accounts. The accounting company would take over the responsibilities of billing, recording, and collecting payments. Taffy's customers would continue to open accounts at the store locations and would carry the same cards;

however, payments by customers would now be forwarded to the accounting firm.

The store owners are examining this option carefully. They are extremely concerned about the interest fees they would no longer accrue from the credit card accounts. Additionally, the owners of Taffy's are concerned about the company employees in the control division who will be without jobs if the store credit card accounting office is eliminated. On the other hand, they recognize the benefit of receiving payment for the credit card debts in one total amount. This funding would enable them to purchase additional inventory, renovate some of the older stores, and put a little profit away. Additionally, the store owners are aware of the monthly costs that would be eliminated by the removal of the store's accounting department that is currently required to operate the credit card accounts. It is a difficult decision for the store owners, but one that they must make immediately.

1 **If you were one of the store owners, would you recommend maintaining the store's charge accounts as they are currently managed?**

2 **Would you advise selling the store's credit card accounts to the accounting firm?**

3 **Do you have an different idea for the operation of Taffy's credit card accounts? If so, what is your plan?**

12 **Waving the Flag!**

For years, the major discount chain, ThriftMart, has been cited by the newspapers and television stations for promoting its product assortment primarily through a "Made in America" campaign. The merchandise sold in this amazingly successful chain ranges from cosmetics and household cleaners to hardware, from apparel to housewares and appliances. Almost everything that an average American household could need is carried in the giant, warehouse-style ThriftMart stores—at big discounts! The discount chain store's advertisements usually feature merchandise manufactured in the U.S. In addition to specifying the city and state of production, ThriftMart's television, print, and in-store display advertisements always mention the number of jobs that are created for American laborers by the domestic manufacture of this merchandise. This promotional campaign—a flag-waving appeal to the patriotic American consumer—has had tremendous impact on the discount operation's sales volume.

Many of Thriftmart's customers can personally relate to the appeal to purchase American-made goods. ThriftMart stores are located in small to midsize towns primarily in the South and Midwest, (but with a few branches also in the northeast and west) and according to exhaustive market research conducted two years ago, the majority of the discount chain's customers are "blue collar" workers and employees earning lower- to middle-class incomes. A large percentage of their customers are also military veterans or the families of veterans. It is this population segment that has been economically affected by the layoffs and job terminations resulting from offshore production and an influx of imported goods.

ThriftMart's target consumers are loyal to the discount chain because of the perception of the "Made in America" campaign. Then, overnight, all of that seemed to change.

Suddenly, the national newspaper headlines are filled with accusations of corporate greed, misleading advertising, and unpatriotic intentions. Major television news shows are highlighting stories about the company's attempt at public deception, claiming it as a betrayal to the American consumer. Overnight, the nation's most-favored discounter is suddenly on the "hot seat." The newspaper narratives and television commentaries state that the majority of the discount store's products are manufactured outside of the U.S.; however, they suggest that the discount operation chooses only those products manufactured in the U.S. to feature in promotional campaigns. The newspaper reporters believe that the discounter's selective advertising is misleading and deceitful to the American consumer. They insinuate that the discount store chain has become a profitable giant by preying upon the consumer's sensitivity to a declining U.S. labor market and a growing foreign trade market. Major newspapers and television stations are in the process of requesting interviews with the executives of the discount chain store operation, as they are demanding a response to the charges.

You are the public relations manager for ThriftMart. Although you have received a few telephone calls from newspaper reporters asking for information about the selection of imported goods over domestic merchandise, you had no idea that this storm was in the horizon. The chief executive officer of the company was waiting in your office when you arrived this morning. He is extremely concerned about the national negative publicity and wants to know how you intend to handle the problem.

1 As the public relations manager, how would you respond to the press regarding these allegations?

2 If you were the chief executive officer, how would you advise the public relations manager to handle this situation?

3 If you were the chief executive officer, how would you respond to the media in regard to this unfavorable publicity?

Chapter 2
The Customers

Understanding the Customer

Most organizations will succeed or fail according to their ability to analyze and understand their primary customer. The customer's psyche, emotional needs, habits, and purchasing motives internally influence their spending patterns. Economic factors, store location, and parking facilities are examples of external contributions to customer spending behavior. An organization's ability to develop a sound strategy for pleasing their customer requires constant evaluation of the internal and external factors that influence the customer, particularly through analysis of:

- What motivates the consumer to buy?

- How does the consumer move through the stages of the buying process?

- Who is the consumer?

Buying motives are needs or desires that cause a customer to act or to make a purchase. They include:

- Emotional: motives that develop without logical thinking (e.g., love, vanity, anger).

- Rational: motives that involve judgment and logical thinking (e.g., security, value, durability).

- Biogenic: motives that relate to physical needs (e.g., food, shelter, sex).

- Psychogenic: motives that stem from psychological needs (e.g., to enhance the ego, to protect, to provide satisfaction).

- Patronage: motives that cause consumers to choose to shop at one store or business rather than another (e.g., personalized customer service, store credit cards, discounts or giveaways for repeat purchases).

The buying process consists of steps the consumer goes through when deciding what, when, where, and how to buy. The steps in the consumer decision process are:

1 Recognition of a need

2 Search for information

3 Evaluation

4 Purchase decision

5 Post-purchase behavior

After understanding the stages a consumer passes through in the buying process, an organization often will analyze who their customers are—and who they aren't—through the development of a customer profile. This includes an examination of demographics, lifestyles, social classes, reference groups, and cultural influences. Next, you will find a discussion of these consumer profile factors.

Demographics

A demographic refers to the breakdown of the population into such statistical categories as age, gender, education, occupation, income, household size, and marital status. Organizations that are interested in reaching special populations are concerned with market segmentation, which is the total market divided into smaller, homogenous sections. Through market segmentation, consumer groups are chosen that are as similar as possible in their merchandise preferences, tastes, and shopping habits. A section of the consumer market with long-term profit potential that is not effectively served by competition is sought by organizations developing a market segment. Some important market segments are: teenagers, working women, customers with special needs, minority groups, and the elderly.

Lifestyles

Lifestyles are affected by demographic background because age, income, and education greatly influence the way a person may choose to live. A lifestyle is the unique way in which a particular group sets itself apart from others. An analysis of consumer lifestyles requires the examination of social class, reference groups, and cultural influences.

Social Classes

Social classes are homogeneous divisions of families and individuals within a society. A social class division is determined by occupation, source of income, education, family background, dwelling type, and other variables. The six levels of the class system are upper-upper, lower-upper, upper-middle, lower-middle, upper-lower and lower-lower. Groups that are influential in shaping attitudes and opinions are known as reference groups. The family is considered one of the most influential of all reference groups. The members of reference groups who exert influence on consumer decision-making are called opinion leaders. Opinion leaders are found on all social levels and are selected by their followers for several reasons:

- They are regarded as a source of information and advice.

- They possess recognized expertise.

- They are highly visible to the group and are the first to adopt new styles.

Culture

Culture and lifestyle are inseparable. Culture refers to the behavior typical of a group or class. The social meaning attached to a product within a culture is critical in assessing how the product might be accepted. Religious beliefs, nationality, and heritage are several key aspects of culture. The work ethic, a need for security, and a drive for status are examples of cultural influences that spark the competitive drive to purchase products that can be identified with success; for example, designer apparel, fine jewelry, and status wristwatches. Additionally, some products that can be identified with cultural influences are those related to ethnicity (e.g., kente cloth, mola, or tartan).

An accurate consumer profile can be determined through an extensive analysis of demographics, lifestyles, social classes, reference groups, and cultural influences. Next, you will find a series of case studies that examine the interrelationship of the customer with the manufacturer, merchandiser, and manager.

13   **Who is in Charge Here?**

Shane Randolph is a manufacturers' representative for a group of moderately priced, children's wear apparel lines. Shane has built a lucrative business in his territory with a variety of accounts that include major department stores, discount chains, and specialty stores. In addition to travelling to work with the buyers in their retail store offices, Shane rents temporary booth space at several regional apparel markets each season to show his lines to the buyers. The regional markets are located in such cities as Kansas City, Dallas, Chicago, and Minneapolis and primarily attract the owner/managers of small "Mom and Pop" retail stores.

Individually, the "Mom and Pop" store owners place small orders in terms of dollar volume as compared to the orders of the large department store buyers; however, the specialty store operations are greater in number than the major department and discount stores, causing the total "Mom and Pop" orders to add up to a substantial portion of Shane's sales volume and subsequent commission payments. Additionally, the small specialty stores are critical in circulating the manufacturers' names to a broader, ultimate consumer base.

At the recent regional apparel market in Dallas, Shane was preparing to present the new back-to-school lines to Heather Woods, the owner of a small children's wear shop. Heather was a long-time customer of Shane's and had an excellent track record in selling the merchandise he carried. Throughout past seasons, Heather had relied upon Shane to guide her regarding style and color selections. During their past appointments, Shane previewed the lines with Heather, recommended the top-selling styles, and assisted her in determining color and size quantities. Heather believed that Shane knew his lines thoroughly and that he had the experience and insight to identify the key styles each season. Although Heather usually worked the lines independently with Shane, this time she was accompanied by a new store employee, Mary Smith.

Mary was hired as a full-time sales associate several months ago and had become the top-selling employee. She was an excellent addition to the sales staff as she consistently doubled or tripled her sales quotas. When Mary expressed a desire to attend the market, Heather was delighted to have a second opinion on merchandise selection from a colleague who was an expert regarding the store customers' wants and needs. Because Mary had daily, personal contact with the store's customers, Heather believed that she could receive effective guidance in regard to customer merchandise preferences from Mary. Heather introduced Mary to Shane and together they began to preview the new lines.

Much to Shane's surprise, Mary was extremely and immediately vocal with her opinions about the line. She openly disagreed with Shane's suggestions regarding style and color selections. She recommended the styles in the line that had no past-selling performance. She discussed the merchandise carried by other manufacturers' representatives as preferable. Heather was quiet as she watched Shane and Mary disagree time and time again. As Heather simply observed the exchange between Shane and Mary, Shane became perplexed. He worried that he might lose Heather's business, which was an account that he had been able to depend on season after season.

1 **If you were in Shane's dilemma, what would you do to keep Heather's business?**

2 **If you were in Heather's position, how would you react to Mary's involvement in the line showing by Shane?**

Figure 2.1 *This is an example of a sales and inventory report used by a manufacturers' representative to monitor selling performance of a line by a retail store account.*

Manufacturers' Representative's Analysis of Retail Account Sales Performance for Intimate Apparel Department

Account Name _____

Outlet Location _____

199_ Actual Sales _____
Stock Turns _____
Average Basic Stock _____

199_ Planned Sales _____
Stock Turns _____
Average Basic Stock _____

Retail Merchandising Plan

	February			March			April			1st Quarter			May			June			July			2nd Quarter			6 Months		
	Last Year	Plan	Actual	Last Year	Plan	Actual	Last Year	Plan	Actual	Last Year	Plan	Actual	Last Year	Plan	Actual	Last Year	Plan	Actual	Last Year	Plan	Actual	Last Year	Plan	Actual	Last Year	Plan	Actual
Monthly Basic Opening Inventory																											
(Plus) Purchases																											
(Equals) Total Available Inventory																											
(Minus) Sales																											
(Plus) Returns																											
(Equals) Closing Inventory																											
Percent of Year Sales																											
Comments: Note Ads or Special Promotions by Month																											

14 May I Help You?

Jennifer Jones is a new sales associate in the home accessories department of a major department store. Her salary is based on an hourly wage of $7.50 with an additional 10 percent commission for sales volume exceeding her sales quota. The sales quota for the home accessories department is $100 for each hour worked on the sales floor. Because she believes she has the opportunity to earn a substantial amount of additional income through her commission plan, Jennifer is eager to become an effective salesperson with the profitable goal of building an extensive customer following.

At the start of her employment with the department store, Jennifer attended a workshop for new employees directed by the company's human resource division. During the seminar, sales associates received training regarding use of the computerized sales terminal, forms to use for customer returns and exchanges, interpretation of merchandise ticket codes, and basic selling procedures. Additionally, Jennifer read several books on sales techniques in an effort to strengthen her selling skills. As part of the department store's training program for new sales associates, Jennifer participated in a mentoring program, in which new employees are teamed with top-selling, senior sales associates. The new employees "shadow" their mentors for a two-week period. It is the primary objective of this program that the new salesperson will learn firsthand about selling skills, closing a sale, operating the cash terminal, and handling customer returns and exchanges. The department store executives believe that the company's most effective teachers are its most successful employees.

During her first week on the job, Jennifer was the only salesperson assigned to the home accessories department on weekday mornings. Early Tuesday morning she worked with a customer who was looking for accessories to furnish her new apartment. Jennifer approached the customer and began to inquire about the type of merchandise for which she was looking. The woman was extremely pleasant and was interested in finding several lamps, framed prints, and bed linens. Jennifer spent over an hour with the woman, coordinating the bed sheets and a spread, pillow shams, a dust ruffle, table lamps, and two prints. The customer looked satisfied as she reviewed the selection, then hesitated while Jennifer briefly waited on another customer. While Jennifer rang up this other purchase, the first customer interrupted Jennifer to say that she would look around and possibly return later to purchase the items. Jennifer was confused as she thought she had landed a sale of over $500, resulting in a $40 commission for that purchase alone. The woman never returned to purchase the merchandise she and Jennifer had selected.

1 **If you were in Jennifer's position, what would you have done differently?**

2 **If you were the customer with whom Jennifer had coordinated the home accessories, what would you have preferred Jennifer to do?**

15   Fighting a Losing Battle

Maude's is a major retailing corporation that operates a number of large specialty store chains located throughout the nation. The seven chain store divisions are individually named and each features a specific merchandise classification including contemporary men's wear, bath and cosmetic products, ladies' lingerie, large-size women's apparel, children's wear, contemporary junior fashions, and misses' fashions. The latter division of misses' apparel, Miss Maude's, has gradually declined in sales volume over the past two years. The management team of Maude's has recently completed an in-depth examination and analysis of its misses' fashions division with the ultimate objective of reversing the downslide in sales performance.

After conducting extensive market research on Miss Maude's sales data, analyzing the customer listing, and interviewing employees and consumers, the research team has determined that the loss of sales volume is primarily attributed to the following four problems and perceptions:

- Many former customers are now shopping at the contemporary junior specialty store division of the corporation because they believe Miss Maude's merchandise selection is unfashionable.

- Other former customers are now patronizing mass-merchandise and discount outlets because they are able to find similar-quality apparel that is more updated fashion-wise at lower prices.

- Currently customers are waiting to purchase the Miss Maude's merchandise they prefer when it has been reduced to sale prices

- Employees and customers have pointed out that many of the major fashion trends featured at Miss Maude's are also heavily stocked at the "sister store", which carries large-size fashions that are quickly copied by mass-merchandisers, thus creating an oversaturation of these fashion looks in the misses' market.

The research team is meeting with the corporate executive team of Maude's retailing corporation and the upper management staff of Miss Maude's division. The objective of the meeting is to determine the future of Miss Maude's. The corporate executives are open to the option of eliminating the misses' apparel division; however, they are also receptive to suggestions that would quickly turn around the sales volume decline. Some of the corporate executives are supporting the concept of downsizing by closing the Miss Maude's chain; other executives believe that this division has potential for vast improvement. The upper management staff of Miss Maude's is in unanimous support of maintaining this division. Their jobs are dependent on the future growth of Miss Maude's chain! The regional store director also has several ideas to stimulate business within this chain store operation.

1   **If you were a member of the corporate management team of Maude's, would you recommend eliminating the Miss Maude's division?**

2   **Would you advise continuing the Miss Maude's division? If so, what changes in the division would you suggest?**

3   **If you were the regional store director of the Miss Maude's branches, how would you advise the corporate management team to reverse the sales volume decline in your division to make it a profitable corporate entity?**

Figure 2.2 *This is an example of a client profile form used by retail sales associates to record the merchandise preferences of a personal customer.*

GARLAND STORES

Client Profile

Department Design Studio

Name Ms. Lily Barnett   **Title or Nick-name** Lee

Date entered 3/22/96   ○ **Cash** ⊗ **Charge**

Garland Stores account 160 01 7892 (Silver Card)

Other charge account 1000 2000 3000 4005

Charge type: ○ **AE** ○ **MC** ⊗ **V**   **Valid/Exp. date** 9/98

Address (billing address) 1000 Broadway

City San Francisco   **State** CA   **Zip code** 94109

Second address 2600 Park Avenue

City Palm Desert   **State** CA   **Zip code** 92260

Home phone (415) 555-1212   **Office phone** (415) 555-2121

Occupation Interior designer

Contact preference ○ **Phone** ○ **Home** ⊗ **Work** ○ **Mail**

Preferred contact times 10-12:00 am (M-F) at work   **Birthday** 9/16/52

Other special dates 7/23 Anniversary, 2/28 Daughter's birthday

Size information
Size 6: Jacket, Pant, Skirt, Dress   Size 4 or 6: Shirt or Blouse

Vendor and style preference
Likes updated, stylish looks, nothing "over-the-edge"
Lightweight, quality fabrics
Subtle, pulled together combos
Colors: Natural, off-white, and earth tones; also black and teal

Personal information
Approx. 5'6", slender
Age: Early 40's; looks much younger
Personality: Can be demanding, but has a good sense of humor

Other
Ask about her daughter, she just became an attorney in San
Francisco

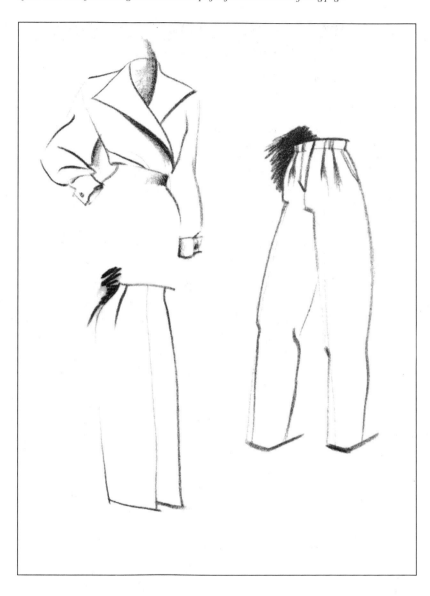

16 **Creating a Campaign**

The promotional division of a major catalog company specializing in fashion apparel and home accessories for the entire family is determining the focus of its holiday promotional campaign. The mail order firm carries moderate to better merchandise that appeals to middle class consumers. Those attending the meeting include the staff of the advertising department (i.e., the advertising director, copy writer, photographer, and several artists), as well as the visual merchandising director and the general merchandise managers for the women's and men's apparel divisions. The primary objective of the meeting is to begin the selection of a holiday promotional theme based on the determination of a particular consumer buying motive. As the image of the catalog company is contemporary and fashion-forward, the theme must reflect the company's personality.

The meeting attendees discuss emotional buying motives versus rational motives. They debate appealing to the customer from the perspective of the joy of holiday giving or from the viewpoint of purchasing the best values and quality for the most reasonable prices. They investigate the possibility of using psychogenic motives in the advertising campaign by appealing to the customer from an ego perspective by emphasizing a sophisticated and up-to-date company image. Finally, the team members examine the use of patronage motives as a foundation for the holiday advertising campaign. As they analyze the various buying motives, the advertising staff and visual merchandising director suggest techniques for implementing each through various themes. The merchandise managers discuss how the projected fashion trends would fit into the suggested themes.

At the conclusion of the meeting, each team member is assigned the task of selecting a buying motive and formulating a corresponding theme for the holiday advertising campaign. The group will meet again during the following week to select the most effective campaign concept.

1   If you were a member of the promotional division, what concept would you propose if you selected the approach of an emotional buying motive?

2   If you were part of the promotional team, what theme would you develop if you chose a rational buying motive?

3   If you determined that an approach based on a psychogenic motive would be most effective, what would be your campaign concept?

4   If you elected to use a patronage motive for the holiday promotional campaign, what would be your theme?

Figure 2.3 *This is a timing calendar used by retail buyers in women's apparel to approximate weeks of the month for introduction and promotion, peak sales, price reductions, and close outs of seasonal merchandise. Source: National Retail Federation.*

Buyer's Timing Calendar

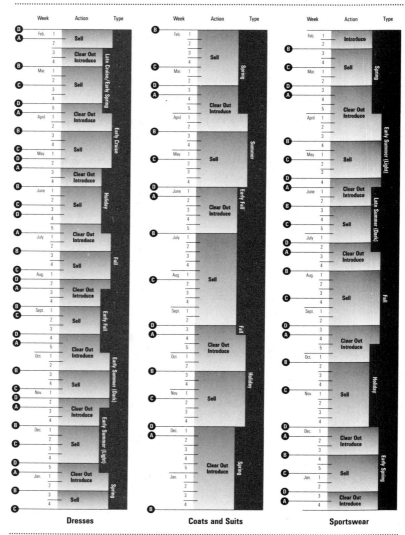

Dresses

Coats and Suits

Sportswear

Ⓐ Begin receiving for new season
Ⓑ Major fashion promotion before this point
Ⓒ No reordering past this point
Ⓓ Begin markdowns

17 A Value Decision

Renee Kennedy is the assistant manager of a trendy clothing boutique in a large mall. The store, part of a chain, caters primarily to
juniors, teens, and contemporary women and its sales have
increased steadily over the one year since its grand opening. Renee,
a 23-year-old woman, grew up in the area and is well-acquainted
with many of the customers. She attended elementary school
through college in this town and then married her high school
sweetheart. Renee is an effective assistant manager, a fashionable
young woman, and a devoutly religious person. Her husband is a
minister and they are active in the community through church-
related activities. Although she feels she is an open-minded individual, Renee stands very firmly for the values and morals in which she
believes. She is extremely pleased with her position at work and is
optimistic about her future with the company. Renee has an
extremely cooperative relationship with Kathryn King, her store
manager, and, although some of the sales associates believe that
Renee is a bit on the conservative side, they respect her and enjoy
working for and with her.

After a year of smooth sailing on the job, Renee is faced with a
situation that causes her much concern. As she checks in new merchandise that has arrived at the store, she unpacks a large shipment
of new T-shirts. Every shirt is imprinted with a statement that has a
sexual connotation and a correlating cartoon illustration. Although
the intention of the designs is humor—Renee is not smiling. "There
is just no way that I can sell these things," Renee reflects. "How
could I possibly allow myself to be a part of this?" She also thinks

about the store's clientele and how many of them will find these garments offensive and in extremely poor taste.

Renee decides to discuss the problem with her manager, Kathryn. She tells Kathryn that she finds this merchandise offensive and that the store's customers will also find it to be distasteful. She suggests that they return the merchandise to the company's central distribution center immediately. Kathryn does not agree and replies, "Renee, these T-shirts may raise some eyebrows, but they are not X-rated. I wouldn't buy one myself. If the customers don't approve of them, they won't purchase them either. Eventually, they will be transferred to another store or marked down." Kathryn is concerned that Renee is allowing her personal beliefs to interfere with the ultimate goal of the store, which is to generate a high sales volume. She questions whether the store's customers will actually find the merchandise offensive or whether Renee is projecting her individual taste level. On the other hand, Kathryn values Renee as a dedicated, hard-working employee and friend. She knows that Renee is her "right arm" and that her position as store manager would be extremely difficult without Renee as her assistant. Kathryn wants Renee to be happy and comfortable with the job, yet she does not want to "make waves" with the store's merchandising staff.

Renee is in a dilemma. She wants the company to prosper and does not wish to be perceived as a difficult person to work with. She hopes to build a profitable sales volume for the store, but she needs to remain true to her personal beliefs.

1   **What would you do regarding your personal values and your career potential if you were in Renee's position?**

2   **What would you do regarding Renee's concerns if you were in Kathryn's position as her store manager?**

18 **Wishing Wells**

For years, Dawn Wells has been an active volunteer and spokeswoman for people with special needs. She participates annually as the mistress of ceremonies for the Children's Miracle Network during the organization's television fundraiser. She is deeply committed to enhancing the quality of life for those with physical disabilities—from infants to senior citizens. Dawn has recently discovered yet another way to support the well-being of the special needs population.

Through her work with Children's Miracle Network, caring for her grandmother who has had a severe stroke, and her volunteer visits to hospitals around the country, Dawn has recognized that many of these people have great difficulty finding clothing that is comfortable, functional, attractive, and that fulfills their need to preserve their dignity and quality of life. She realizes that the physically disabled person has a lifestyle that requires specific apparel needs, which are not being met by garment manufacturers. From a functional standpoint, the clothing must be easy to put on, comfortable to wear, and simple to care for. From a design perspective, the garments must be adaptable to accommodate such devices as wheelchairs, braces, and medical apparatus. The garments must also fasten easily for those who have difficulty in dressing themselves. Also, from an aesthetic outlook, the apparel should be comfortable, fashionable, and attractive.

As Dawn analyzes this market segment, she acknowledges that there are three key issues relating to her customer's lifestyle that will determine her marketing plan. First, she will require assistance with the fabric sourcing, garment costing, and the actual production of the apparel line. Dawn decides to contract an existing apparel manufacturing company to purchase fabrics and to produce the line. She will work with the company's operations manager to develop pricing on the line. Dawn develops a business plan, a portfolio of design sketches, and a promotional theme for her company and then contacts several garment manufacturers to discuss the opportunities for production of Wishing Wells Collections Inc., her new line. She is able to locate several manufacturers who are anxious to produce her apparel collection.

Second, she will need help with the actual design of the apparel line. She concludes that she will offer the project of developing the line to the fashion design students of a college with which she is affiliated. Additionally, she will collaborate with a free-lance designer regarding garment illustrations and the "flat sketches" (mechanical drawings) needed for pattern construction. She also intends to actively solicit style suggestions from potential special needs clientele and their medical professionals (e.g., physical therapists, physicians, and nursing personnel).

Third (and most important), Dawn is faced with the question of how to promote and distribute her apparel line. How will she reach her target market? While many of her prospective customers are living in traditional residences, others are located in nursing homes, assisted-care facilities, and hospitals. Some may find it difficult to shop in stores because of physical constraints.

1   If you were in Dawn's position, what would be your plan for marketing and distributing this new apparel line?

2   If you were a manufacturers' representative interested in carrying Wishing Wells Collection Inc., what types of retail accounts would you identify as potential clients for this new line?

Figure 2.4 *Below is a customer questionnaire developed by Dawn Wells to generate a detailed consumer profile, to assist with garment designs, and to determine a preferred channel of distribution.*

Questionnaire

I really care about you and what you want, and as my company grows, I'd like to keep you with us. How you feel is important to me. I'd like to know more about you; what you prefer—and what you don't; what your needs are. *I value your opinion,* so take just a moment to fill out the questionnaire below and return it to me, with or without your order. I would really appreciate any input and ideas you might have.

Thanks!

1. Where do you currently purchase specialty clothing? _____

   _____

2. Are you purchasing for ☐ yourself ☐ friend ☐ relative ☐ patient ☐ other
3. Is the above recipient ☐ male ☐ female
4. Is the recipient living ☐ at home ☐ retirement center ☐ long term health facility ☐ other
5. What is the age of the recipient? ☐ 20 and under ☐ 20–30 years ☐ 30–40 years ☐ 40–50 years ☐ 50–60 years ☐ 60–70 years ☐ 70–80 years ☐ 80–90 years ☐ 90+ years
6. What is your age? ☐ 20 and under ☐ 20–30 years ☐ 30–40 years ☐ 40–50 years ☐ 50–60 years ☐ 60–70 years ☐ 70–80 years ☐ 80–90 years ☐ 90+ years
7. Are you ☐ health care professional ☐ sole caregiver ☐ shared responsibility caregiver ☐ relative ☐ friend ☐ other
8. What garment features are most important? (check all that apply) ☐ pockets ☐ monogram ☐ short sleeve ☐ long sleeve ☐ high neckline ☐ low neckline ☐ long garment length ☐ short garment length: ☐ above knee ☐ below knee ☐ 100% cotton ☐ 100% polyester ☐ poly-cotton blends ☐ fabrics in prints ☐ fabrics in solid colors : list favorite colors _____

   _____

9. What types of garments are needed? ☐ sleepwear ☐ loungewear ☐ robes ☐ casual housewear ☐ streetwear ☐ career clothing ☐ headwear
10. What are your special needs in clothing? _____

    _____

Please feel free to expand on a separate sheet of paper.
THANK YOU!

Figure 2.5 *Below is a page of photographs from the Wishing Wells Collections, Inc. catalog.*

LEFT: Dawn modeling one of her spring collection's reversible garments.

BELOW: Always concerned about quality and details, Dawn develops some new looks for spring.

BELOW LEFT: Associate Janice Olson fitting headwear on Dawn. Janice is also the designer of the catalogue.

© 1989 Wishing Wells Collections, Inc.
Photos by Foto-Look International. Garment photos by Janice Olson.
Printed in USA by Craig Printing. Catalogue design by Janice Olson.
Public Relations: Freeman and Sutton Public Relations.
All of Los Angeles, California

19 Trading Up

Anne's is a specialty store in New Orleans, Louisiana, which carries bridal wear and special-occasion apparel for women. The retail operation is located in a section of town that is undergoing dramatic changes. The neighborhood has recently been rehabilitated primarily through two sources of funding: (1) city funds designated to renovate its historic buildings; and (2) the investments of local contractors interested in developing a new, fashionable residential area. Old brownstone structures have been converted to elegant townhouses and storefronts have been restored to reflect the illustrious historical past of the locale.

As a result of the physical and economic improvements in the area, a new residential population has emerged. Young, single executives and career couples are relocating to this part of the city, bringing with them a higher expendable income than that of past consumers. Previously, the area attracted low-income customers from the heart of the city and had little consumer traffic from the more prosperous residents living outside of the close proximity of the city. Now, there is a "live-in" clientele with money to spend. The merchants are thrilled with the changes taking place in their neighborhood shopping district.

In the past, the owner of Anne's, Joyce Gillespie, has been very concerned with the pricing of the merchandise carried within the store. Because the previous customers were extremely cost-conscious, Joyce located goods from budget to mid-priced special occasion and bridal wear vendors. She often purchased off-price and close-out goods to provide her customers with the types of merchandise at the price ranges they were seeking. Presently, she is rethinking her merchandise assortment as she believes that this is the ideal time to trade-up, to carry a higher quality, higher-priced product mix. She could offer more exclusive styles and more personalized services. Joyce is concerned that it may take some time to attract the new, more affluent clientele. She worries that she should not totally alienate her current customer base.

Trading up her merchandise assortment will require a huge amount of changes. Joyce anticipates that the store will need some remodeling and that she will need to locate new vendors that carry a higher level of bridal and special-occasion goods. Joyce also determines that she will have to re-evaluate her promotional plans, focusing on style and selection rather than price. She will need to identify the advertising and promotional vehicles that will most effectively reach the new clientele. As she studies all of the challenges involved with changing her previously successful business, Joyce questions whether or not she should maintain her existing operation, rather than reacting to the recent changes in her shopping area.

1   **If you were Joyce Gillespie, the owner of Anne's, would you maintain your business as it has operated successfully since its start up?**

2   **If not, what would you do to adapt to the changing environment in your business area?**

Chapter 3
The Company Mission

The Mission Statement

The members of a business organization are able to effectively coordinate their individual efforts in a united direction through the development of a company mission statement and a plan describing the company's objectives and goals. An organization's formal mission statement answers four questions:

1 What is the existing business?

2 Who is the customer?

3 What is value to the customer?

4 What potential opportunities exist?

An effective mission statement motivates company personnel through a shared sense of direction, opportunity, significance, and achievement. Under the company mission statement, widely dispersed employees can work independently, yet collectively, toward realizing the organization's potential.

Goals and Competition

A typical mission statement includes a detailed set of supporting company objectives and goals for each level of management. These objectives can be turned into specific quantitative goals for both planning and control, for example, "Nordstrom will increase its market share in children's wear by 20 percent within a six-month period." Goals describe objectives that have been made specific with respect to magnitude and time.

Market positioning refers to locating a clear, distinctive, and desirable place that a product occupies in the market and in the minds of target customers. When positioning itself in a market segment, an organization will identify all the competitive products and brands currently serving customers. Companies seek out marketing opportunities in which the firm would enjoy a competitive advantage.

Every business faces a wide range of competitors. An organization must understand its direct competition, while still recognizing that there are other ways of competing to satisfy the customer's needs. These direct and indirect alternatives for a firm's customers become the company's competitive environment. For example, a specialty store may directly compete with other local specialty stores; however, it also could be competing indirectly with discount operations, home sewing firms, mail order catalogs, a television home shopping network, and department stores.

An organization's mission statement and the resultant goals and objectives provide direction for the company's employees to position the firm in a place of growth within a competitive environment. In the following pages, you will find a series of case studies concerning issues that relate to mission statements, goals, and objectives.

20 Crossing the Bridge to a New Market

With much consideration, the owners of a better designer dress company, Maggie Paris, are deciding whether or not to open a bridge division of the corporation. The bridge market caters to clientele who want designer looks at lower prices than those of designer apparel. This means:

- The prices are a step higher than those of moderate apparel.

- The styling is more fashion-forward than mid-priced apparel.

- The fabrics and construction details are lower in cost to produce than those of designer lines.

As many designer styles are "knocked off" by moderate-priced apparel manufacturers, several key designers have opened their own lesser-priced divisions and have created bridge versions of their own top-selling designer styles. Most important, the designer name frequently has status appeal to the consumer—in either a bridge or designer line. The designer can use this ego allure to generate substantial sales volume through the addition of a new product line and the subsequent recruitment of a new target market. Because Maggie Paris has been extremely successful in the designer dress division, the company's owners are eager to increase the firm's revenues by using their designer name to appeal to a new market.

The corporate executives are discussing the advantages and disadvantages of opening a bridge department dress line. They examine the cost of producing and promoting a new line, the possibility of oversaturating the market with the designer's name, and the risk of losing designer customers to the proposed new bridge line. They analyze the number of bridge dress lines available in the market and the success or failure of these potentially competitive lines. Finally, the executives review the prospective sales volume that may be generated, the production capabilities of the firm's design staff and contractors, as well as the potential target market in terms of retail store accounts and ultimate consumers.

Maggie Paris' management team learns that they do have the manufacturing capabilities to produce an additional line. Also, they can obtain the funding to support a new division. However, the executives believe that they need to examine alternatives other than a bridge line in order to completely explore expansion opportunities.

1 **If you were a member of the executive staff of Maggie Paris would you recommend adding a new bridge dress division?**

2 **Would you advise an alternate means of increasing the company's revenues? If so, what is this alternative?**

21   **Times are Changing**

In the city of Ocala, Florida, the downtown shopping district is a beautiful and lucrative area. There is a wide variety of stores, including many women's and men's apparel shops, a children's wear boutique, a card and gift store, several restaurants and coffee shops, and an active sportswear store, among others. The storefronts are edged with canopy-covered sidewalks and flower boxes and metered parking spaces line the streets facing the retail stores. All of the retail operations are sole proprietorships or partnerships and many have been family-owned for generations. The majority of the retailers do not own the buildings in which their stores are located; rather, they rent the store space from several local businessmen who own have owned the buildings for years. Additionally, there are three strip centers located on the perimeter of the city that feature some specialty stores and a few mass merchandise and discount operations—however, most of the apparel retail stores are located in the downtown shopping district. Also, there are three colleges in the city and all are within walking distance of the downtown business district.

Recently, a large parcel of land on the south side of the city has been purchased by a retail mall development company. This will be the only enclosed mall in the city and will initially open with over 100 retail operations, including major specialty store chains, department stores, boutiques, and sole proprietorships. Consumers in town are excitedly anticipating the opening of the new mall. The local newspaper is filled with classified advertisements seeking management and sales personnel for the new mall stores.

The mall ownership group is promoting the opening of the new mall in a big way. Giveaways, promotional events, and special discounts are featured in newspaper and television ads weekly. Billboards announcing the grand opening of the mall have been erected at most major thoroughfares. Local news shows are applauding the economic growth Ocala will experience as a result of the mall opening. The public relations efforts are effectively seducing the city's consumers to the mall.

Several months prior to the grand opening of the mall, the downtown merchants' association held a meeting to discuss the impact of this new competition on their businesses. At the start of the meeting, many of the downtown store owners were in a panic. Several of them stated that some of their key employees had secured new jobs with mall stores, leaving them with vacant sales and management positions. Other downtown store owners mentioned that customers shopping in their retail establishments were discussing the convenience of an enclosed mall and its extensive parking. A few merchants were questioning whether they should renew their downtown leases or pursue reopening their businesses in the mall, although the monthly rental fees would be twice as costly. They discussed the extensive shopping hours the mall would offer customers, including Sunday openings. By the time the meeting came to a conclusion, nearly all of the downtown merchants were panicking about their new competition—the mall.

1 **If you were the owner of one of these downtown businesses, what would you do to ensure the continuing profitability of your business?**

2 **If you were the real estate owner of the building leased by several of the downtown business owners, what would you do to ensure continuing revenue from your property?**

Figure 3.1 *Below is an example of a retail department store's mission statement, which is used to provide direction and unity of purpose to its employees.*

GARLAND STORES

Mission and Objectives Statement

Garland Stores mission is to be the premier quality department store in all our locations and to be the fashion leader for our target customers. To be the first store that our customer thinks of and goes to when shopping and to offer our customer the finest quality fashion merchandise in the upper-moderate to better price range. Our longest term goal is to achieve not only more profit, but to be the number one fashion department store in the United States. To achieve these ends, our objectives include such factors as: target customers, positioning, merchandise, value, service, promotion, and expansion. These factors are outlined below:

Target Customers
Garland Stores target customers are middle, upper-middle, and upper-level income consumers who shop for fashionable, well-made apparel, accessories, and home furnishings. Our focus is on consumers who want fashionable, well-made lifestyle merchandise of identifiable worth.

Positioning
We want our target customers to perceive Garland Stores as having the most timely and competitive selections of fashionable, quality merchandise. We believe that one of the keys to our future growth is the consumer between the ages of 18 and 55, who shops for fashionable, updated merchandise; therefore, our focus will be on an appropriate balance of updated and traditional merchandise, with an emphasis on updated, fashionable apparel, accessories, soft goods, and home furnishings of recognizable worth and value.

Merchandise
Garland Stores' will present a balanced selection of fashion apparel, accessories, soft goods, and home furnishings in a variety of colors, fabrications, styles, and brands. Because our focus is on updated goods, fashion merchandise must be timely, offering the newest colors, styles, and fabrications that are just beginning to gain our target customer's acceptance. Our merchandise must be of the finest quality available, in the moderate to better price range.

To create a sustainable competitive advantage, the merchandise focus in most lines will be on Garland Stores private labels and on recognizable name brands of excellent quality. Consistency and longevity in the private labels will build brand acceptance, which will encourage repeat purchases, and thus will increase profits in both the short and long terms. In the fashion apparel lines, recognizable designer bridge and better lines will also be offered in limited quantities, but in sufficient numbers to satisfy our upper-end target consumer's needs. An adequate supply of these designer goods will not only augment our private labels, but will keep our fashion offerings on the cutting edge and will sustain our long-term goal of being the fashion leader in the United States.

Because Garland Stores buying offices are centralized, our merchandise is consistent from store to store (with regional and specific needs taken into account for each branch). We want our customers to know that when they enter a new or different Garland Store, they will be met with the same excellent quality, price, and service that they have received in any other Garland Store.

Value
While Garland Stores wishes to be the fashion leader, we also want to offer our customers the best available price on all offered goods. Because our buying offices are centralized,

Figure 3.1 (Continued)

we have the opportunity to buy top-quality merchandise in large quantities, which will assist in keeping the prices in the moderate range. Our buyers have been instructed to purchase those goods that are not only fashionable, but also are well-made and of obvious value. Our private label merchandise will assist us in achieving this end as the majority of merchandise will be of a caliber that we can control, while the bridge and better designer lines will help us to achieve an important balance between the moderate and upper-end prices and consumers.

Service
In keeping with our overall goal of leadership, we wish to offer our customers the finest possible service available. Our sales staff must be courteous, caring, and knowledgable about our merchandise and the current fashions. Above all, our sales staff must be available to our customers, and be willing to help our client achieve the look they want. To accomplish this, we require a regular updating of our computerized client profile lists, and we encourage all our sales staff, buyers, and department executives to actively call our listed clients to advise them of new merchandise shipments that would be of interest to those clients.

Also in keeping with this level of courteous, caring, knowledgable, and comprehensive service are such other services as: a variety of low-cost gift wrap is available year-round (free Garland Stores logotype gift wrap is available during the Holidays); free home delivery on purchases over $200; low-cost alterations; layaway; mail-order; Garland Stores credit cards. Our credit accounts are one of our most important services, as it not only encourages more sales by offering our customers an easy way to shop with easy payments, but it also garners profit for the store through the interest payments.

Promotion
To reach our target customer, to gain new clients, and to promote our image as a fashion leader, Garland Stores will continue to present our merchandise in a variety of formats and locations. In addition to our semi-annual fashion shows (Fall and Spring), we sponsor several fashion design contests and bridge trunk shows that are presented in Garland Stores locations throughout the United States. We actively seek cooperative advertising agreements with major brands and designer bridge lines, while at the same time presenting frequent television, radio, and print media ads for our private label brands. Our nationally advertised quarterly sales (Fall, Winter, Spring, and Summer) and our monthly one-day sales also help us to gain new, value-minded customers, while also keeping our merchandise stock fresh and updated. Because Garland Stores strives to remain open to all new merchandising promotion avenues, we are currently pursuing a Garland Stores home shopping club, a CDRom catalog, and selling on the Internet and the Web. Our long-term, highly profitable billing inserts will also be continued, as this is one way to definitely reach our established, credit clients with our best merchandise and values.

Expansion
In our overall goal of being the number one fashion leader in the United States, Garland Stores is actively pursuing new locations and new markets. While the concentration of the majority of our stores is in the Midwest and Southeast, last year's opening of two new branches in the Northeast and three branches on the West Coast has made Garland Stores an up-and-coming force in these two all-important markets. Next year, the further expansion into these two markets will ensure our overall growing leadership in the United States.

22 Mission Impossible?

Susan Gooden, a junior in college majoring in fashion design, has secured an internship position with a sportswear manufacturer in Portland, Oregon. Susan is thrilled to receive on-the-job training as an assistant patternmaker, as well as the opportunity to earn an income provided by the internship's summer salary. Because she is earning college credit for the internship as part of her degree program requirements, she is required to complete an internship workbook assigned by the fashion design department of her university. Through completion of the workbook, she will analyze the total company and document her work responsibilities as an assistant patternmaker.

A section of the workbook indicates that she is to investigate the firm's mission statement. She schedules an appointment to meet with the sportswear company's owner, Bill Leon, to discuss this topic. Much to her surprise, Mr. Leon informs Susan that the company executives have never formulated a mission statement. "However," he continues, "This is the perfect time to develop a mission statement and it is an ideal project for you." Susan is hesitant and a little overwhelmed by the challenge, but agrees to develop a mission statement proposal by the end of the following week for Mr. Leon's perusal.

Susan begins by analyzing the criteria that provide the foundation for a mission statement:

1 A description of the existing business.

2 An analysis of the customer.

3 The customer's perception of value.

4 An understanding of potential business opportunities.

She meets with the firm's designers, the operations manager, some of the sales representatives, and several of the buyers of key retail accounts to collect their views on the business and its customer profile.

Based on these discussions, Susan determines that the company produces active sportswear apparel for male and female amateur and professional athletes primarily participating in running, aerobics, and cycling. Susan is perplexed by the variety of opinions that she gathers from the different constituencies of the sportswear firm. It seems that each person she asks has a unique perspective on the company's clientele and product line. The sales representatives believe that the company's customer is more interested in quality, durability, and comfort than in fashion trends. The designers believe that forward styling, color selection, and fit are extremely important to the company's clientele. However, both agree that price is not as important to the customer as quality. She receives diverse opinions about the line from the retail buyers—some reflect the designers' viewpoints, while others duplicate the sales representatives' perspectives.

1   Develop a mission statement for the sportswear firm from the viewpoint of the designer.

2   Construct a mission statement for the sportswear manufacturer from the perspective of the manufacturers' representative.

3   Create a mission statement for the sportswear company from the point of view of the retail buyer.

23   Super Sales Without Super Service

Angela Murphy was aggressively recruited to fill a full-time sales associate position from a competitive designer apparel store by the human resource director of Garland Stores. Angela came to Garland Stores with extensive sales experience, an impressive customer following, and an excellent knowledge of designer apparel fit and styling. She quickly understood store procedures, programs, and policies and almost immediately started to exceed her sales goals on a daily basis. The human resource director was thrilled with the success of Garland Stores' newest sales associate.

About three weeks after Angela began her employment with Garland Stores, the company's "mystery shopper" was scheduled to assess the sales associates on how effectively they serve the customers. The "mystery shopper" is a business consultant hired by the human resource director to analyze each salesperson's accomplishment of the company's Friendliness Program. This program consists of five elements, which are:

1   Smiling

2   Greeting the customer promptly

3   Being helpful

4   Using the customer's name whenever possible

5   Thanking the customer

The salesperson is evaluated on each component of the program by the unidentified mystery shopper. An assessment report summarizing each sales associate's performance is then forwarded to the human resource director, who then distributes the reports to the department manager.

The department manager of designer apparel was shocked when she received the assessment report from the human resource director. Angela received the lowest rating in every category and was the sole sales associate in the department to earn an unsatisfactory score. In response to the report, the department manager began to observe Angela's interaction with the customers. She noticed that Angela tended to "zero in" on her personal clientele or those customers who looked as though they would spend a great deal of money while ignoring other customers. Although Angela gave exceptional service for her "big spenders," the store's policy and standard procedure are to provide this type of service to each and every customer.

Angela is a highly productive sales associate who was actively recruited from a competitor's sales floor. While her personal contribution to the department's sales volume has been substantial, her level of customer service is erratic and inconsistent with the store's procedures. The department manager is concerned about confronting Angela with her unsatisfactory evaluation. She is worried that Angela may become angry and terminate her employment with Garland Stores. Angela's sales volume has greatly increased the designer department's sales figures. The department manager questions, "Why not leave well-enough alone? Angela is accomplishing the ultimate goal of excellent sales. Should the other sales associates take care of the Friendliness Program while Angela generates sales?"

1 **If you were the department manager, how would you work with Angela to help her maintain or increase her sales volume while providing a high level of service to all customers?**

2 **If you were the human resource director, what would you do to assist the department manager in helping Angela eliminate this problem?**

3 **If you were the human resource director and you were responsible for resolving this problem directly with Angela, what would you do?**

Figure 3.2 *This is a shopping report used by retail managers to evaluate the performance of sales associates regarding effective customer service.*

GARLAND STORES

SHOPPING REPORT

SHOPPING REPORT NO.	STORE BRANCH	DEPARTMENT

DATE	DAY	TIME

SALESPERSON'S NAME	SALESPERSON'S NUMBER

DEPARTMENT TRAFFIC	DEPARTMENT CONDITION
☐ BUSY ☐ AVERAGE ☐ SLOW	☐ EXCELLENT ☐ GOOD ☐ FAIR ☐ POOR

ADDITIONAL COMMENTS

WHAT WAS SALESPERSON'S SALUTATION?

	RATING
I. APPROACH TO CUSTOMER	
A. Was salesperson prompt in approach? ☐ Yes ☐ No ☐ N/A (20 pts.)	
If store was busy, did salesperson acknowledge customer? ☐ Yes ☐ No ☐ N/A (20 pts.)	
B. Was salesperson pleasant in approach? ☐ Yes ☐ No ☐ N/A (20 pts.)	
II. MERCHANDISE KNOWLEDGE	
A. Was salesperson able to answer specific questions? ☐ Yes ☐ No ☐ N/A (10 pts.)	
If unable to answer, did salesperson seek assistance in answering? ☐ Yes ☐ No ☐ N/A (10 pts.)	
B. Did salesperson offer additional product information? ☐ Yes ☐ No ☐ N/A (10 pts.)	
III. SUGGESTION SELLING	
A. After closing the original sale, did salesperson suggest item(s) in addition to the original merchandise customer selected? ☐ Yes ☐ No (5 pts.)	
B. Did salesperson explain the features and benefits of the suggested item(s)? ☐ Yes ☐ No (5 pts.)	
IV. CREDIT SOLICITATION	
A. Did salesperson offer to put original and/or suggested item(s) on the store's charge account? ☐ Yes ☐ No (5 pts.)	
B. Did salesperson offer to open a store charge account? ☐ Yes ☐ No (5 pts.)	
V. CLOSING THE SALE	
A. Did salesperson thank customer for shopping at our store? ☐ Yes ☐ No (5 pts.)	
B. Did salesperson tell customer to "Enjoy the rest of the day?" ☐ Yes ☐ No (5 pts.)	
VI. FINAL EVALUATION	
Based on the above, would you as a shopper return as a customer? ☐ Yes ☐ No (10 pts.)	
Total Available Points: 100	

SHOPPER'S ADDITIONAL COMMENTS

FOLLOW-UP INTERVIEW

DATE	EMPLOYEE SIGNATURE	SUPERVISOR SIGNATURE

24 The Customer is Growing Up

Polly Finders is a children's wear manufacturer that has built a respectable customer following by specializing in traditional girls' dresses from sizes 4 to 14. The garments feature specialty construction details that include smocking, ruffles, bows, and petticoats. The styles are traditional and feminine, while the retail prices are upper-moderate. These frilly dresses are affectionately referred to in the industry as "grandmother bait." Due to the superior quality, timeless styling, and the higher retail price, a Polly Finders dress is an ideal gift for a grandmother to purchase for her granddaughter. Additionally, matching dresses are offered in the 4 to 6X size category as well as the 7 to 14 range, allowing a mother or grandmother to purchase look-alike garments for sisters in both size ranges. Although this market niche has been successful for the company for years, recently, Polly Finders has seen a decline in sales volume within the 7 to 14 size classification.

It appears that this young customer is becoming more sophisticated in her apparel preferences. The average 8-to-14 year-old girl now prefers to dress similarly to her teenage friends and role models, rather than to wear the smocked-front, tie-back dresses that her grandmother would select. Although the management of Polly Finders has decided to maintain the selection of the traditional girls' dresses, the company executives have formulated a new goal and a corresponding objective for the upcoming year: to introduce a selection of contemporary dresses that will appeal to the size 7 to 14 clientele, and, subsequently, to increase the annual sales volume in this size category by 20 percent.

The design staff has been assigned the goal of creating a collection of new styles that have a contemporary junior look. The merchandise manager has been directed to identify major trends emerging in the contemporary junior market. The marketing division has been requested to develop a promotional plan to introduce the collection to both the retail buyers and the ultimate consumers. The manufacturers' representatives have been asked to generate a list of retail accounts that would be an appropriate target market for the new collection. All have been advised that the new garments will be shown to the retail store buyers for the first time during the January markets in both New York and Dallas. The executives of Polly Finders remind the staff that there are two key issues to keep in mind regarding the new product line. They identify these issues as:

- Maintaining the current customer following for the traditional line while adding a new target market for the new line.

- Creating an identity that clearly separates the new collection from the traditional line and that maintains a customer base for both lines.

1 **If you were a member of the marketing division of Polly Finders, how would you promote the company's new division?**

2 **If you were a manufacturers' representative for Polly Finders, how would you debut the new line to your retail accounts?**

3 **If you were the company's national sales manager, how would you introduce the new line to the sales representatives and retail store buyers during the January markets?**

25   **A Tough Decision**

Marie Wilson is a student majoring in fashion merchandising at a small state university in Florida. As part of the university's requirements for graduation, she must complete an internship in her prospective field of employment during the summer between her junior and senior years. The university, in conjunction with the textile and apparel department, has established these guidelines for the internship requirement:

- The student must complete a minimum of 140 work hours on-the-job during the summer of the internship.

- The internship must be directly related to the student's anticipated field of employment.

- The student must fill out the internship workbook approved by the department.

- The student, academic internship sponsor, and employer must jointly approve the internship initally and then communicate regularly throughout its duration.

Six months prior to the anticipated start of her internship, Marie begins to prepare for securing a summer internship position. She constructs her resumè and drafts a letter of application with assistance from the university's Career Planning and Placement Center. She discusses internship possibilities with senior-year students who have completed this requirement. She attends the departmental internship workshops and reviews the bulletin board for available internship openings. Through these announcements, Marie obtains information about several internship opportunities with retail operations that appeal to her and are located near her summer residence.

After completing initial interviews with six prospective employers, there are two positions that interest Marie equally. In both cases, the employers have offered her an internship position. She is now at the point at which she will have to make a decision in regard to which opportunity will meet her goals and objectives most effectively.

The first position is with a small, heavily travelled specialty store operation. The store owners are extremely enthusiastic about the prospect of working with a student intern and are particularly impressed with Marie's past experience in retail sales. They have offered her full-time employment for the entire summer at minimum wage plus commission. Although her primary job responsibility would be assisting customers on the sales floor, the owners have offered to expose Marie to their total retail operation by taking her with them to the regional apparel market, allowing her to participate in advertising meetings, encouraging her to work on in-store displays, and permitting her to assist them with accounting and receiving duties. Marie genuinely likes the store owners and the store itself and she believes that she would learn how a specialty store operation functions—inside and out.

The second internship position that Marie is considering is with a major department store. The store has a formal internship program in which ten student interns participate. The interns are paid $2 per hour over minimum wage for the program's duration. There is also the possibility of employment after the conclusion of the internship program if an opening exists at that time. During the six-week program, the group of interns receives one week of in-class training and five weeks of working in all of the major divisions of the store from the advertising department to the human resource division. Actual on-the-floor selling is a minimal part of the job description. The department store is well-known and has branch stores located throughout the Southeast. As approximately 100 students have applied for the company's internship program, Marie is thrilled to be one of the top 10 invited to participate. She believes that she would receive in-depth exposure to a department store operation.

Both internship opportunities meet the requirements of the university and department. As Marie evaluates the pros and cons of each position, she becomes more and more confused about which job she should accept.

Because Marie is at an impasse in regard to her internship decision, she consults with one of her favorite college instructors, Dr. Jean Hamilton. Dr. Hamilton is a professor in the Textile and Apparel Department; she is also the academic sponsor for the department's internship program. Marie tells her that she does not know which position would be best for her in terms of her long-range career plans. Dr. Hamilton suggests that Marie carefully evaluate three areas: her goals and objectives for an internship, her goals and objectives for a career, and her prior work experience. After thinking about these three issues, Marie discovers that she would like to understand how a retail business operates from top to bottom and that she would like to gain hands-on experience in as many of the functional divisions of the business as possible. She also recognizes that her career objectives may change, but right now her ultimate goal is to own a successful retail store. As to her prior work experience, Marie was employed as a waitress during her high school summers and during college, she worked as a student assistant in the Textile and Apparel Department. She was also a resident advisor in the university dormitory where she lived. Marie is looking forward to her summer internship, as it will actually be her first retail store work experience.

If you were in Marie's position, what would you do?

26 A Brandmart for Berryville?

In the small town of Berryville, Arkansas, the majority of retail organizations are owned and operated by members of the community. From grocery stores to clothing boutiques, some of the businesses have been family-owned for years—all are owned by people living within the general area. The town features a quaint downtown consisting of specialty shops and restaurants. Additionally, there are several strip centers in the community where other specialty goods and service retailers are located.

There is big news in Berryville. A major discount chain operation, Brandmart, is planning to open one of its "super store" outlets in town. This huge facility will provide a full-service approach to shopping: a hypercenter that offers groceries, fabrics and notions, lawn and garden equipment, apparel for the entire family, sporting goods, home accessories, pharmaceutical products, automobile products and services, and many other product lines. You name it— the "super store" carries it. Nearly every merchant in town will be in direct competition with this new store. The merchants are well-aware of this new competitor because one of these "super stores" opened last year in an adjacent town just 40 miles away. They all felt the impact of this distant competitor in their sales volume.

The local store owners have researched this company and have some disturbing news. In many cases, the opening of Brandmart super stores in communities similar to Berryville has correlated with the closing of many of the small specialty stores and the subsequent vacancy of flourishing downtown areas. Some of the store owners are concerned that many of the young people who had intended to eventually take over these family businesses would end up leaving Berryville. Additionally, the merchants learned that if the "super store" does not generate the sales volume planned by the corporate executives, the company will close the operation and vacate the building. In several communities in which the "super store" did not meet the sales quotas, the townspeople were left with "ghost town" downtowns, a large vacant store facility, little local shopping, and serious levels of unemployment.

On the other hand, Brandmart is able to offer the community residents exceptional prices on a wider range of merchandise assortments. The "super store" additionally provides a large number of employment opportunities at substantially higher wages and benefits than the small store owners can provide. Many residents believe that the competition will be healthy in regard to the types and prices of merchandise offered in town and that there are plenty of customers for both the specialty store and discount operation businesses.

1 **If you were a local merchant who has been asked to advise the town's mayor, what would you recommend?**

2 **If you were the new store manager of Berryville's Brandmart, how would you develop positive community relations for the new "super store?"**

3 **If you were a member of the Berryville community seeking employment (e.g., a new college graduate), what would you recommend regarding the potential opening of Brandmart?**

Chapter 4
The External Environment

Macroenvironments

No organization operates in a vacuum. Rather, there are many influences and events, which are outside the organization, that affect its life. These influences and events are sometimes referred to as the external (or macroenvironment) of the organization. Because these particular influences and events cannot be manipulated or affected by the management of the organization, they are also called uncontrollable variables. Although these variables are uncontrollable, management must be constantly sensitive to them in terms of their impact on the organization, which result in patterns of decision-making.

The macroenvironment is often broken down into six subsets or environments, which are:

1 Economic environment

2 Social/demographic environment

3 Political/legal environment

4 Natural environment

5 Technological environment

6 Competitive environment

Each of these environments affects organizations in an industry, but in different ways and to differing degrees. This depends on where that organization is in the channel of distribution and how that organization relates to its clients. A closer look at each of these subsets makes this clear.

Economic Environment

A single organization cannot do anything about the general economic state of the world, the nation, or the local community; however, these economic conditions certainly affect the economic environment of the organization. The important question is, "How do changes in the economy and economic policy affect this particular organization?" Do not assume that a depressed economic environment will be bad for all retailers. While general merchandise retailers may suffer under such circumstances, others (for example, do-it-yourself retailers, home sewing stores, discounters) may thrive as never before.

Social/Demographic Environment

The social/demographic environment encompasses the wide range of characteristics of the consumer population that can be interpreted statistically. Examples of social/demographic factors include age, income, education, career choice, race and ethnicity, family size, religious preferences, and residential location, to name a few.

Changes in population growth, geographical residence patterns, attitudes about having children, attitudes about appropriate gender roles and age appropriate behaviors, and changing commitments to religious expression are some of the many factors that can change the social/demographic environment. A social shift toward increased education could result in a larger market for a museum An increase in the number of professional working women might result in a men's clothing store experiencing great success by adding a line of women's tailored suits and accessories. A trend toward smaller family size by two-income families might alter spending patterns that have repercussions all the way back down the channel of distribution to retailer, manufacturer, and designer.

Political/Legal Environment

The overthrow of a South American government, import quotas on merchandise manufactured in Asia, the prevailing attitude of the courts on acquisitions and mergers, a local community's change in laws regarding Sunday openings—these are only a few of the issues that comprise the political/legal environment for any business. One of the current issues in the apparel and soft goods industries pertains to country of origin in terms of product manufacturing. This particular political issue has impacted textile and apparel import and export quotas as well as consumer purchasing.

Natural Environment

Most homeowners' insurance policies do not cover the many diverse components that comprise the natural environment (for example, wind, rain, hail, and snow). These elements can also affect retail sales. Cold, snowy weather is generally believed to lead to depressed sales, but this effect is not just on the behavior of customers; it also causes late shipments, late openings of stores, and employee absenteeism. Rainy weather, on the other hand, can spur an increase in sales for the direct mail merchandiser as the consumer prefers to shop at home. More subtle and gradual are such issues as the erosion of top soil from prime agricultural land that affects, for example, the production of cotton. The concern over the world's supply of oil, the trend toward ecological issues, and an increase in the cost of petroleum have a dramatic impact on the production of most manufactured fibers, energy costs in factories and stores, and how far customers are willing to drive to shop.

Technological Environment

The computer has revolutionized all segments of nearly every industry, from retailing to design. Advances in the technological environment have altered the way information is transmitted, stored, and used. New low-soiling carpets reduce cleaning expenses; new materials speed the manufacture of clothing; new manufacturing equipment results in changes in labor costs and in employee morale within the organization.

Technological advances also affect businesses throughout the distribution channel. Recent advances on the information superhighway have greatly impacted the response time between the retailer and the manufacturer in reordering merchandise preferences for the consumer. Just-in-time (JIT) and Quick Response

(QR) refer to computerized programs between the retailer and the manufacturer that reduce the amount of lead time between placing an order and receiving the merchandise in the retail store. Technology has influenced pricing, sales tracking, and inventory control through the use of the Universal Product Code (UPC) scanning. Computer programs are available to assist with computer-aided design, computer-aided manufacturing, merchandise planning and control, and merchandise promotion. The impact of technology is influencing virtually every aspect of the apparel and soft goods industry!

Next, you will be presented with a group of case studies that examine how the external environment can impact an organization through economic, social, political/legal, natural, and technological influences.

27 The Blackout Causes Manufacturers to See Red

The spring ready-to-wear market in New York City is a seven-day period in January that produces a substantial portion of the annual sales volume for the apparel manufacturers and sales representatives in the garment industry. The representatives spend weeks prior to the market dates telephoning their key retail accounts to schedule appointments for the buyers to preview the new lines in the Manhattan showrooms. It is critical for the sales representatives to meet with their buyers during this time period for several reasons, among which are:

- Buyers have calculated their open-to-buy projections and are prepared to place orders for new seasonal merchandise.

- Buyers are comparison shopping the market and may not allocate adequate funds for lines they do not view during market week.

- Buyers are determining placement of their largest orders at this time as they select promotional merchandise to introduce the new season's trends to their customers.

- When buyers visit the New York showrooms to preview the various lines, sales representatives are saved the cost of traveling to the buyers' office locations within the rep's territory to show the line.

This particular spring market began as expected with buyers arriving in New York from all parts of the country, flooding the airports, and filling all the Manhattan hotels. The manufacturers' representatives had arrived the weekend prior to work with the lines' merchandise managers regarding style and color assortments, fashion trends, delivery schedules, and promotional packages. Sample lines were organized, models were hired, catered lunches were ordered, and it was time to begin the show. Unfortunately, two days after the market week opened, an unanticipated disaster occurred.

The garment district was hit with a blackout, a total power failure. Elevators were halted, showrooms were dark, computers and even some telephone systems were shut down! Many of the hotels in which the buyers and manufacturers' representatives were staying were also affected by the blackout. It was not only difficult to conduct business in this environment, but security was an additional serious issue. It was impossible to determine when the blackout would end—one day to a whole week were the predictions announced through the news media. Many of the out-of-town buyers felt extremely unsafe in the darkness of Manhattan's garment district—others were concerned about the time and financial costs of "waiting out" the blackout.

Many of the buyers made plans to return home immediately. As the majority of regional apparel markets were scheduled to follow the debut of the New York market, some planned to work the lines closer to home at one of these markets. Other buyers patiently waited to receive instructions on what to do next from their key sales representatives.

1   If you were a sales representative during the market week of the New York blackout, what would you do to keep your buyers from leaving the city before viewing your new lines?

2   If you were a sales manager for a group of manufacturers' representatives, what alternative plan(s) would you make to be certain that your representatives met with their store buyers to show and sell the new lines?

3   If you were a retail store buyer, what would you do in this situation in regard to reviewing the new lines of the sales representatives?

28 Cutting Their Losses

Calhoun's is a mid-sized "Mom and Pop" store located in a small suburb. The owners, Jean and Andrew Daverin, primarily run the store with limited assistance from three part-time sales associates. The extensive inventory consists of men's, ladies', and children's apparel, fabrics and notions, accessories, and footwear. Jean and Andrew have owned the store for one year, purchasing the business from its previous owner with savings and a Small Business Administration loan. Although they are enjoying the freedom and independence derived from owning their own business, they are amazed at the tremendous amount of work hours required to operate a retailing establishment. One of the most time-consuming, yet critical, activities to date was the completion of the store's physical inventory.

When the result of their annual physical inventory was contrasted with that of the book inventory, the Daverins were completely shocked. The difference was a shortage of thousands of dollars, representing almost seven percent of the retail operation's annual sales volume! Although they recognized that the shrinkage could be attributed to shoplifting losses, employee pilferage, and/or clerical errors in bookkeeping, the bottom line was that they had lost a substantial amount of potential profits. As they realized that their anticipated vacation funds had been eliminated because of this shortage, the store owners were determined to reduce the store shrinkage to half of this year's percentile by the following annual inventory.

Because of the large merchandise assortment, it is difficult for the Daverins to determine whether or not the shortage can be attributed to theft. They feel certain that their employees are honest and that they are observant of customers' activities in the store. Jean is responsible for the store's accounting procedures. She maintains the records for all merchandise receipts, calculates the payroll and taxes, submits payments for merchandise and store overhead costs, and places the orders for the store's merchandise. It is a full-time responsibility that keeps Jean off the sales floor much of the time. Andrew, on the other hand, is responsible for managing the store's selling staff. He spends the majority of his time as the primary full-time sales associate. Additionally, Andrew is the company's merchandiser, as he takes care of all buying, purchase order follow-ups, receiving, pricing, and visual merchandising. Andrew, too, has a full work load.

As the Daverins discuss the disastrous results of the store inventory, they evaluate several options for managing inventory control. They discuss purchasing a computer system to assist with maintaining the accounting functions, but it may be difficult to install, hard to understand, and costly to buy. They examine investing in a security system that would enable them to tag merchandise with alarm devices that must be removed by a sales associate. Again, they recognize the time and financial constraints of this option. Finally, they investigate the alternative of hiring an additional employee or two to cover the sales floor more thoroughly. The additional costs of payroll and benefits, the time required to train a new associate, and the underlying question regarding employee honesty were then reviewed by the Daverins.

If you were one of the owners of Calhoun's, what would you decide to do to stop the shortage problem in their store?

Figure 4.1 *This is an example of a physical inventory count sheet that is used to record the number of pieces and prices per unit of the merchandise assortment.*

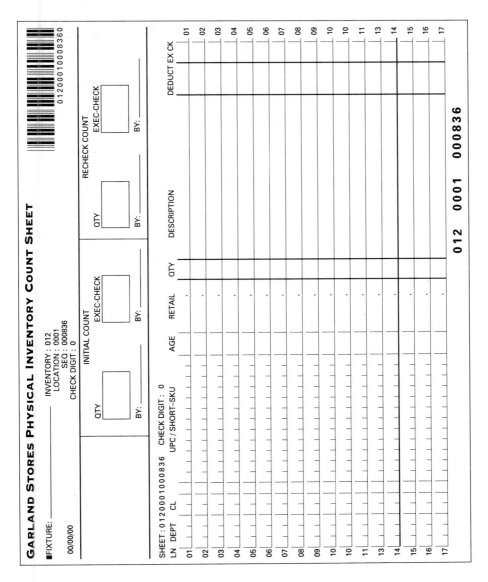

Figure 4.2 *This is a quotation form utilized by retail merchandising and manufacturing companies to calculate the landed cost of imported merchandise.*

GARLAND STORES

QUOTATION FOR OFF-SHORE OR OVERSEAS PURCHASE

Vendor

Street

Country

Commodity

Mfrs. Item

Total Quantity Ordered

Ex-Factory Cost, per _____

Foreign Inland Freight

F.O.B. Dock Origin

Agent's Commission

Master Pack

Duty % (   )

Ocean Freight

Insurance Rate

Broker's Fees Conference

Wharfage and Handling

Non-Conference

Cartage

U.S. Port Landed Cost

Inland Freight

Total Charges Per _____

GENERAL INFORMATION

Is label or other identification of merchandise required:
City & State

Pre-Ticketed: ☐ YES   ☐ NO

PACKING:

1. Unit Pack

2. Units per Inner Pack

3. No. of Cartons

4. Weight per Master Pack

5. Dimensions

6. Cube

7. Ocean Freight Rate

(a) Contract
(b) Conference
     Non-Contract

(c) Rate

8. Latest Shipping Date

9. Cancellation Date

10. Approx. U.S. Arrival Date at

11. Quantity

12. RN Number

MARKS:

Dept. No.

Order No.

Code No.

U.S. Port

Numbers 1/up

29 Foreign Intrigue

The misses' sportswear buyer for a major specialty store chain, Jordan Maze, is preparing to leave her office for two weeks on an overseas trip to China. The primary objective of the trip is to evaluate the potential of foreign sourcing for the production of basic merchandise for her department. Jordan's company is interested in importing exclusive merchandise that can be purchased at a lower cost price than the basic stock offered by domestic manufacturers. Through the specialty store's resident buying office and a trade organization operated through the Chinese government, Jordan was able to make contact with several apparel manufacturers in China. She has made appointments to personally meet with the principals of the production firms and to review her merchandise needs as they relate to the manufacturing capabilities and costs of the Chinese apparel companies.

After two days of long and exhausting travel, Jordan arrives at her first appointment. Through an interpreter the manufacturing company has provided, Jordan learns that the manufacturer can produce the goods she needs for her chain of over 100 stores. The basic pants, turtlenecks, skirts, and cardigan sweaters can be produced in the exact color assortment she has previously determined at wholesale prices that are approximately 35 percent below the cost prices offered by the American manufacturers. The Chinese manufacturer is prepared to use any apparel sizing specifications that the store prefers (e.g., skirt and sleeve lengths, waist sizes).

Jordan continues her investigation of the foreign apparel producers over the next few days. She finds the manufacturers to be fairly competitive in their merchandise offerings, delivery schedules, and pricing. She then works with her store office by fax, telephone, and computer and with the various representatives of the Chinese apparel manufacturing firms to calculate the landed costs on the goods. They determine the additional fees associated with foreign and domestic inland freight, ocean transport, wharfage and handling, insurance costs, and duties on the merchandise. After they have computed the costs associated with importing the goods, Jordan develops quotations for the overseas purchases with each of the Chinese manufacturers.

Jordan decides that—if she decides to use the foreign sourcing—it would be best to work with a single manufacturer in order to have color and sizing consistency in the merchandise assortment, rather than to choose sweaters from one manufacturer, skirts and pants from another, and turtlenecks from yet a third. She concludes that—if she decides to import merchandise—she would select the first manufacturer she worked with based on the company's pricing structure, its production quality, and its prior experience in manufacturing for other major retailers in the U.S. The single purchase with this manufacturer will represent 40 percent of her total department inventory for the start of the fall season. This is a critical decision for Jordan as a professional buyer and for the profitability of the company as a whole.

Next, Jordan evaluates the pros and cons of importing merchandise from overseas. She determines that the primary advantages include: merchandise exclusivity, an opportunity for private label goods, lower prices, higher markup potential, and the opportunity to have merchandise made to the store's specifications. She then carefully examines the disadvantages of importing the goods and decides that they include: the requirement for a large quantity purchase, lack of control during the merchandise production process, difficulties and delays in communicating with the resource, and—most important—the potential for delayed shipments because of unpredictable problems relating to quotas, governmental constraints, and shipping difficulties. Additionally, she questions her customer's political position on "Made in America" goods as opposed to imported merchandise.

Jordan is faced with a difficult dilemma. She must immediately decide whether or not she will purchase nearly half of her inventory from a foreign manufacturer or from domestic producers. The pros and cons need to be weighed; the advantages and disadvantages must be evaluated.

1   If you were in Jordan's position, what would you decide to do in this situation?

2   If you were an overseas apparel manufacturer, what would you do to secure Jordan's order of your merchandise?

3   If you were a U.S. apparel manufacturer, what would you do to keep Jordan as a primary customer of your merchandise?

4   If you were the chief executive officer of Jordan's specialty store chain, how would you advise Jordan in this situation?

30 **Layoffs Lead to Losses**

This & That is a gift store located in Blue Springs, a suburb of Green Bay, Wisconsin. The store is a sole proprietorship that has been owned and managed by Kim Etlinger for the past five years. Kim's business has gradually grown over time, presently supporting Kim, a staff of five part-time sales associates, and an accountant. In her store, Kim carries a selection of papergoods that includes gift wrap, stationery, and cards. This store also has an assortment of jewelry, a variety of bridal gifts that includes specialty dinnerware, and such home decorating accessories as candleholders, candles, and picture frames. As the only retail gift shop in town, This & That was a profitable business until the economy was hit by an economic bombshell.

For many years, Blue Springs has been the home of a large electronics manufacturer, which is a significant supplier of electrical components in the worldwide market. After much consideration, this electronics company has recently allocated the production of a large portion of its product line to an offshore contractor. This corporate decision has literally crippled the town's economy. Hundreds of company employees have been either laid off or terminated. Others—in anticipation of further work force reductions—are looking for jobs elsewhere. The unemployment rate has never been higher in Blue Springs.

The electronics manufacturer's sourcing decision is also having a substantial financial impact on the business of This & That. As the electronics manufacturers' employees have been released, Kim's business has declined with each layoff. Her clientele no longer has extra money to spend on gifts—gift-buying is one of the first luxuries her customers discarded as their incomes dropped. Kim is concerned about the future of the business she dearly loves and has worked diligently to develop. She is worried about her own income and the continued employment of her staff. Several of her sales associates now need their positions at This & That more than ever, as their spouses have been laid off by the electronics corporation.

At this point in time, Kim is scheduled to attend the regional gift market in Minneapolis, Minnesota. She is concerned about spending her open-to-buy allocation for the upcoming season with the economic disaster that is affecting her community. On the other hand, she concludes, it would create an additional loss of sales volume if This & That has a minimal, aged inventory. Initially, Kim believed that she had time to ponder the future of her business; however, the upcoming market dates require that she make a preliminary decision immediately.

1   If you were in Kim's position, what would you do about this dilemma?

2   If you were one of the sales associates of This and That, what would you recommend to Kim if she asked for your input about the future of the company?

3   If you were the manufacturers' rep of a key vendor for This & That, how would you advise Kim regarding the upcoming market?

31 Flooded with Business Decisions

The Country Club Plaza in Tucson, Arizona is a beautiful open shopping district designed with a Spanish flair. The gorgeous fountains, exquisite hotels, moderate- to better-priced specialty stores, specialized boutiques, art galleries, and unique restaurants combine to create an ambiance that is not soon forgotten by both tourists and consumers. Interiors by Olga is one of the most successful specialty shops located in the Country Club Plaza. The store features personalized interior design services, uncommon home accessories, unusual furnishings and paintings, and custom upholstery/drapery services. Its lucrative business is dependent upon its established customer following, as well as the extensive traffic generated by the Plaza location.

Interiors by Olga is also well known for its exceptional service and the breadth and depth of its stock. Every nook and cranny of the shop is filled with an inventory of incredible interior accessories and furnishings. The stores' sales volume has grown steadily over the years under the direction of its effective owner, store manager, and its dedicated sales and design staff. That is, it grew until Mother Nature decided to change the course of the business.

For three weeks, The Country Club Plaza has been besieged by torrents of rain, which have resulted in floods that have destroyed bridges, made the streets impassable, and damaged many of the businesses in the Country Club Plaza. Because Interiors by Olga is located on the perimeter of the Plaza (the area most affected by the floods), it is one of the retail operations that has been most seriously impacted as the streets and bridges surrounding the store have been heavily impaired.

In addition to the accessibility impasse created by the floods, the store's interior and inventory have also been damaged by the flooding. The roof has leaked because of the torrential rains, staining the wallpaper and destroying some of the electrical outlets and lights. The store's carpet is covered with muddy water several inches deep. The inventory is damaged in various degrees; some of the merchandise is completely ruined, while other parts of the stock are unaffected. A complete physical inventory is necessary to determine the actual fiscal loss in merchandise.

The owner of Interiors by Olga is faced with a difficult decision. She questions whether she should call it quits and close the operation completely or attempt to recoup her once thriving business. Thoughts of relocation also enter her mind.

What would you do if you were in the store owner's predicament?

Figure 4.3 *Below you will find an example of a flood sale advertisement featured in a newspaper by a retailer.*

WALL-TO-WALL'S

Final Closeout
Flood Salvage!!!

All Carpets and Rugs in Tent
at the Front of Our Store
Juniper City, 345 Cedar Street
Selling begins at 8:00am sharp
Saturday June 15

Some of the Great Bargains You Will Find:

Shag Carpet ....from $10 sq ft
Sculptured Carpet..from $12 sq ft
Wool Worsted Carpet...from $15 sq ft

Braids (ovals and rounds , all sizes)...from $5 to $20 ea
Dhurries (4' x 4' to 12' x 16')..from $5 to $30 ea
Persian Rugs (all sizes)..from $20 to $300 ea

And Many, Many More Styles and Sizes All Drastically Reduced!

All Carpets and Rugs are Undamaged by the Flood!
Must Move Them Out to Build Our New Store!
Come In and Make Us a Deal!

Inquire about our truckload of carpet padding that was slightly damaged by the flood, starting at $1 sq ft!!!

WALL-TO-WALL CARPET CENTER

Look for our new store — we reopen in September!

Figure 4.4 *This is an illustration of an advertisement created by a retailer to offset the impact of a disaster of the natural environment, the flood.*

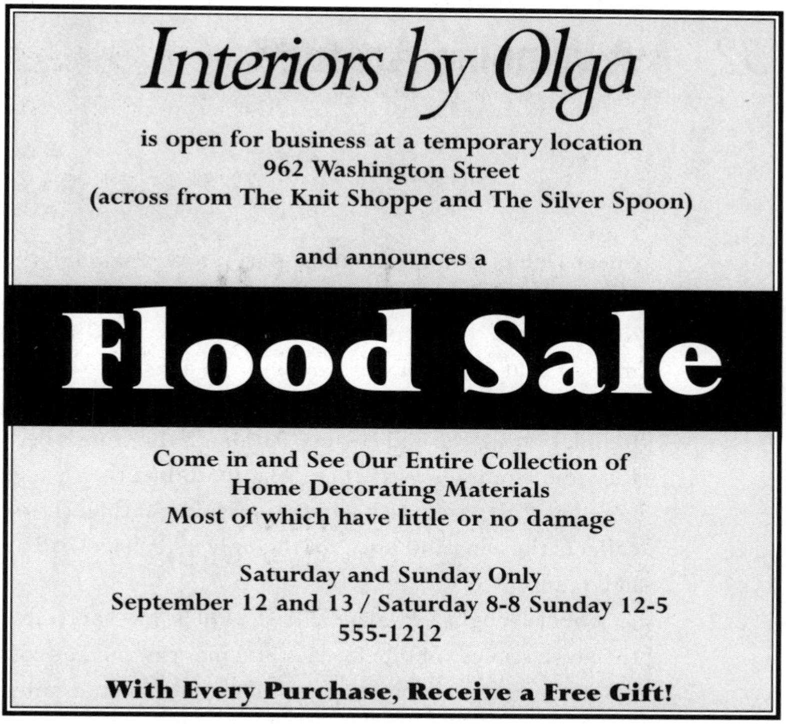

Interiors by Olga

is open for business at a temporary location
962 Washington Street
(across from The Knit Shoppe and The Silver Spoon)

and announces a

Flood Sale

Come in and See Our Entire Collection of
Home Decorating Materials
Most of which have little or no damage

Saturday and Sunday Only
September 12 and 13 / Saturday 8-8 Sunday 12-5
555-1212

With Every Purchase, Receive a Free Gift!

32   A Winning Attitude

Sheer Delight is an intimate apparel store located in the downtown shopping district of a college town. The boutique is within walking distance from the large university and caters to a specialized target market that encompasses women from ages 18 to 50. The merchandise assortment includes daywear, exercise apparel, sleepwear, foundations, gifts, and hosiery. Although the store's decor, its inventory, and its target market are very feminine, the weekend sales volume has fluctuated with a more masculine influence—one that reflects the wins and losses of the university's football and basketball teams.

Sheer Delight's manager, Trisha Giles, has carefully analyzed the store's sales volume by days and months and has correlated the results with the community calendar that indicates university and local events. Additionally, she has observed the numbers and types of store clientele shopping in her place of business both on weekdays and on weekends. She has come to the conclusion that the business is dramatically impacted by the traffic generated by the external influences of community and college activities. On football weekends, when the football team is on a winning streak, the attendance to home games increases as does the sales volume within the store. When there is a concert at the local auditorium, the store sales volume reflects the increase in downtown activity. When the sports teams are playing away from home or are on a losing streak and there are no community events, the sales volume is at its lowest level.

Trisha has attempted several strategies to improve Sheer Delight's overall sales volume over the past few seasons. Trisha has spent a large amount of her promotional budget on weekly advertisements in the local newspaper. Additionally, she has created monthly in-store promotions that feature specific merchandise classifications at discounted prices. For example, she will offer sleepwear at 25 percent off one month and foundations at 15 percent off the next month. Also, Trisha has mailed newsletters to the personal customers in her files to announce the arrival of new merchandise receipts. These efforts have been mildly successful. She feels, however, that she needs an overall, recognizable strategy to increase sales significantly. To this end, she has also developed a mailing list through customer registration, which she feels will help her in the drive to increase sales.

1 **If you were in Trisha's position, what would you recommend to increase the overall sales volume of Sheer Delight?**

2 **If you were a business consultant hired by the owners of Sheer Delight, what type of promotional campaign would you develop?**

3 **If you were the director of the downtown merchant's association, how would you advise Trisha to increase Sheer Delights' sales volume in relation to the downtown activities?**

33   Four Hundred Wedding Gowns and a Fire

The big, beautiful, white wedding dress is the center of nearly every bride-to-be's dream. With so much anticipation riding on one garment, it is no surprise that hundreds of New England soon-to-be brides awakened to a nightmare on May 25. During the previous night, a suspicious fire gutted The Bridal Boutique, destroying over 400 gowns that had been special ordered for weddings in the coming month. Not only were the brides-to-be in trouble, but the mothers of the brides and the bridesmaids were also without their finery for these most important occasions. Many of the clients had ordered their dresses months prior to the wedding dates; they thought that they were well-prepared and ready to relax before their big days. No one—particularly the store owners—expected the boutique's thriving business would go up in flames overnight.

The boutique owners were devastated and were ready to call it quits. The owner stated to the local newspaper and television news, "Can you imagine? When we have just one dress missing, the entire shop goes nuts! Can you imagine losing all of them?" After the fire was reported in the newspaper and on television, many of the store's customers came to the site of the burned building in a panic. They were shocked to learn that very few of the gowns could be salvaged by firemen and those dresses and gowns not burned to ashes were pungent and soiled. Some of the store's customers were so busy with wedding preparations on the day of the fire that they were not aware of the problem until they arrived at the boutique to pick up their dresses for their planned celebrations. It was an emotional scene for the shocked owners, discouraged store employees, and their broken-hearted brides-to-be.

While nearly all of the boutique's inventory was destroyed, there was one salvageable area remaining within the store's embers. The bookkeeping department in the rear of the store was least affected by the flames. The majority of store's customer records, order forms, and accounting ledgers were smudged and tattered—however, most were legible. The store owners were somewhat relieved to know that they had records to document most of the current inventory, on-order log, and their invaluable customer listing. This would be critical information in regard to insurance and customer adjustments.

The store owners are faced with a dilemma. Should they throw in the towel, close the business, and attempt to recoup some of their losses and reimburse their customers' expenditures through the store's insurance? Or should they try to salvage their business? If so, how should they attempt to meet their customers' needs at this critical time?

1 **If you were one of the owners of The Bridal Boutique, what would you do?**

2 **If you were a bridal gown manufacturer, what would you do to try to help the Bridal Boutique stay in business and fulfill its customers needs?**

34 Surfing the Internet

Wearable Products, Inc. is a progressive company that manufactures moderate to better misses' apparel. The line features classic designs with contemporary twists that appeal to the updated misses' customer who has a large expendable income. Examples of the line's hot sellers include: cashmere sweaters in the latest silhouettes, fitted man-tailored separates in worsted woolens, and knit silk T-shirts with dyed-to-match drawstring pants. The company owners are convinced that there is a new world of marketing opportunities available through the information superhighway. As a company that has built its reputation by leading on the cutting-edge, Wearable Products, Inc. wants to be among the first apparel manufacturers to sell its merchandise in cyberspace.

The Internet is the largest computer network in the world, providing instant access to unlimited resources and millions of people. The owners of Wearable Products, Inc. have researched the Internet and learned that while the explosive growth of the Internet thus far has been phenomenal, experts predict that the number of users will grow exponentially on into the next century. The owners believe that the Internet promises to be one of the most powerful business tools of tomorrow. Through a workshop they attended on understanding and using the Internet, they have learned that Wearable Products can be marketed to millions of potential customers for a service provider fee of less than $50 a month. To surf the Internet, all that is needed is a computer, a modem, and a phone line. The owners of Wearable Products, Inc. believe that the vast audience of consumers sitting in front of their personal computers is a dream come true to apparel manufacturers. In fact, they believe that the Internet may very well be the most important business tool ever invented.

The company principals have definitely decided to procure an Internet on-ramp, to invest in a service provider membership, and to secure a national server. To generate new promotional ideas and to keep the entire team up-to-date on marketing opportunities, the executives intend to provide training for key employees in marketing and public relations on the Internet. Although the company will continue to promote its product line through more traditional avenues of television, billboard, and print media, they believe that supplementing the current promotional strategies with the Internet will provide a more forward approach (and possibly a more cost effective approach) to marketing in the future. The company owners are anxious to get started down the information highway and up to speed—fast!

1   **If you were one of the owners of Wearable Products, Inc., how would you begin marketing your company and/or product line through the Internet?**

2   **If you were an employee in the marketing division of Wearable Products, Inc., what suggestions would you offer to the company owners in regard to the company's debut on the Internet?**

3   **Do you believe that the Internet is a viable promotional vehicle for the apparel and soft goods industry? If so, why? If not, explain the disadvantages to marketing apparel and soft goods on the Internet?**

35 **Scented Sourcing**

Sally Genena has been looking for a business opportunity and believes that she has now found the product niche she has been seeking. While recently visiting her relatives in Egypt, Sally purchased some beautiful perfume bottles for her own use and to give as gifts to friends at home in the U.S. The gifts were such a huge success that Sally is considering marketing the perfume bottles as a business. She wants to import, sell, and distribute them under her own company name, Genena Imports International, after she has determined that there is sales potential for the fragrance receptacles.

Sally has worked in the fashion industry since her graduation from college in 1988. At that time, she moved to New York City where she began a successful career in fashion retailing and wholesaling. Since her arrival in New York, she has been variously employed as an apparel buyer for a major department store on Fifth Avenue, a manufacturers' representative for an accessories firm, and, most recently, as the product development director for a specialty store chain based in Manhattan. Throughout the years that Sally was employed in these positions, she has been focused on her long-term goal of eventually owning her own business. It has been her intent to find a business niche that would combine all of the skills and knowledge gained from her work in these fashion occupations. Wholesaling the perfume bottles would seem to be the ideal entrepreneurial opportunity as it would unite her prior work experience in buying, selling, and marketing. Additionally, this business alternative would utilize her contacts, language, and cultural understanding of her birthplace—Egypt. It would appear to be an opportunity that would maximize all of Sally's attributes, abilities, and past experiences. She is thrilled with the concept of opening her new business.

First, Sally decided that she must test market her concept by presenting the merchandise to a number of selected retailers. She wanted to measure the retail buyers' interest in the product and their corresponding wholesale prices. Sally scheduled appointments with buyers for key specialty and department stores—some with a merchandise assortment emphasis on apparel and others with a focus on home accessories and home furnishings. Without exception, the buyers were ecstatic about the perfume bottles. They were thrilled with the products, the prices, and the exclusivity. In all cases, the buyers were eager to place large orders for the perfume bottles. A few buyers discussed placing the bottles in bed and bath departments, others suggested positioning them in gourmet food departments to use as wine and salad dressing containers, and still others recommended locating them traditionally in cosmetic and fragrance departments. Sally walked away from her appointments with the retail store buyers full of new ideas with which to market the products. She was delighted to realize that her target market was much broader than she had anticipated.

Based on her test market success, Sally then began working to secure a large quantity of the fragrance bottles to fill her initial orders. She contacted the producer of the perfume containers in Egypt and was dismayed with the manufacturer's response. He stated that he was unable to export this quantity of merchandise to an American wholesale business. Egypt's quota policy indicated that the manufacturer could directly ship abroad to retailers, but not to a wholesaler. Apparently, the Egyptian government is concerned that foreign businesses would profit from Egyptian products, rather than the Egyptian manufacturers themselves. Restricting quantities of exports enabled the government to monitor situations in which revenue for the country might be lost because of interception by foreign industry. Sally was crushed as she was certain that she had found the ideal business opportunity. But rather than cancel the orders with the New York retailers, she decided to evaluate her options and to develop a plan that would enable her to move forward with her dream.

If you were in Sally's position, what would you do to make your business plan a reality?

36   In My Own Fashion—Over Here or Over There?

IMOF is a contemporary misses' sportswear manufacturer based in New York City. IMOF, an acronym for In My Own Fashion, produces fashion-forward designs for the modern woman with a merchandise emphasis on casual wear for non-office hours. The line is well-known for its creative, relaxed designs that reflect a predominantly athletic influence. Form-fitting silhouettes trimmed with racing stripes provide the company's signature look. IMOF primarily uses spandex, french terry, and sweathirt fabrications to manufacture its sportswear line. IMOF has become a key resource in the sportswear industry because of its innovative styling, excellent prices, superior quality, attention to detail, and its exemplary sizing and fit.

The owner of IMOF, Tammy Parrish, is actively involved in every facet of the business—from design conception to retail outlet sales. She manages to design the line with the help of two design assistants, while overseeing the production aspects of the business with the support of an operations manager, a quality control director, and a production manager. Prior to the major market weeks, Tammy introduces the new line to the manufacturers' representatives of the firm. During the market weeks, she supervises the showroom and directly works with the retail buyers of IMOF's key accounts by showing them the new collections and later utilizing their feedback to edit and improve the lines. Tammy believes it is imperative that she has constant exposure to every aspect of her business to stay on top of it. Although she delegates work responsibilities, she believes it is her primary job—as the company owner—

to oversee the general operations of the firm. Tammy's attention to detail and her involvement in all of the company's functions are prime factors in the business's success.

Since the origin of IMOF, Tammy has hired regional contractors to manufacture the company's line. She visits the contractors weekly as they are located in New York and New Jersey. During her trips to the contractors' facilities, Tammy personally checks the production schedule, inspects the quality of the finished garments, and examines the merchandise in the shipping departments. She is able to oversee the delivery schedule of the merchandise by knowing the specific styles that will be produced in each location at various times.

Recently, Tammy's production manager has been contacted by several overseas contractors who are interested in procuring IMOF's manufacturing business. The production manager has done his homework by compiling a report for Tammy that summarizes the offers the foreign contractors have submitted. Upon perusing the summary, Tammy is amazed at the variance between the price quotes provided by the domestic and foreign contractors. The overseas manufacturers are quoting landed costs of over 20 percent less than the merchandise prices of the American contractors IMOF currently utilizes. Tammy immediately realizes that she could either pass these savings on to the consumer or use the price reductions as additional profit for her company. She analyzes the quality and detailing of the finished garment samples the foreign contractors have provided and determines that the quality is as good as—if not better—than that of her domestic sources.

On the other hand, Tammy is concerned that she will not have the production control she has enjoyed in the past if she utilizes foreign contractors. Currently, Tammy knows first-hand how the finished garments look immediately upon production. She can react to and correct problems that arise during the production phase of the garment. She is able to view how and when the garments are shipped to the retail accounts. She can respond to problems associated with apparel construction, fabric selection, and garment fit as soon as they emerge. If she decides to work with the overseas contractors, the opportunities for proactive problem-solving in the line's production could be greatly minimized.

Additionally, from a personal standpoint, she has been an advocate of supporting U.S. commerce by employing domestic manufacturers. She truly does not want to impact the jobs of the employees of her American contractors by withdrawing her company's production business and sending it abroad; however, the hourly wages of the contractors' workers have risen steadily over the years and continue to increase. Such additional employee benefits as health insurance have also added to the costs of using domestic contractors. She anticipates that the wholesale prices of her line will have to increase as the labor costs of manufacturing the merchandise in the U.S. continue to inflate. Tammy questions whether or not the inevitable higher prices will affect retail sales of the IMOF line.

1   **If you were in Tammy's position, what would you decide to do in regard to the decision between foreign and domestic production?**

2   **If you were the production manager of IMOF, what recommendations would you make to Tammy in regard to the decision between foreign and domestic production?**

3   **If you were a domestic manufacturing source for IMOF, what would you do to keep the business that Tammy has traditionally had with your company?**

Chapter 5
Product Identification

Product Levels

A product is anything offered to a market for attention, acquisition, use, or consumption. A product is capable of satisfying a consumer's want or need and can be an object, service, activity, person, place, organization, or idea. A product can be further defined in terms of its three distinct levels, which are:

1 Core, which is the main benefit or service.

2 Formal, which includes packaging, brand name, quality, styling, and features.

3 Augmented, which incorporates installation, delivery, credit, after-sale service, warranty, advertising, and promotion.

As an example, The Limited offers apparel items (e.g., dresses, blouses, pants, skirts) as its core product. The garment styling, labels, hangtags, color assortment, and brand name are parts of the formal level of the product. Finally, attention to customers, guaranteed product satisfaction, and credit availablility are elements of the augmented product level. If you are working for a service-oriented business, the product is the service. For example, a hair salon may feature hair styling, makeup application, and nail care as its products.

Packaging (a part of the formal level of a product) is defined as the activities of designing and producing the container or wrapper (i.e., the package) for a product. Labeling is part of packaging and consists of printed information appearing on or with the package that contains or holds the product. Several factors that have contributed to the growth of packaging as an effective marketing tool are: convenience, value, consumer affluence, company and brand image, and innovational opportunity. An example of a company that has utilized packaging as an effective marketing tool is Fossil, which packages its unusual watches in collectible tins that coordinate with the watch collection.

Product Classifications

To develop marketing strategies for individual products, marketers have devised several product classification schemes based on product characteristics. These product classifications are:

- Nondurable goods: tangible goods that are normally consumed in one or few uses (e.g., shampoo, fragrance, cosmetics).

- Durable goods: tangible goods that normally survive many uses (e.g., clothing, bed linens, kitchen towels).

- Services: activities, benefits, or satisfactions that are offered for sale (e.g., alterations, delivery, gift wrap).

- Convenience goods: items that the consumer usually purchases frequently, immediately, and with minimal effort in comparison and buying (e.g., pantyhose, underwear, socks).

- Shopping goods: this type of product is usually compared to others by the consumer on basis of quality, price, fit, and style (e.g., sweaters, dresses, sportcoats).

- Specialty goods: this type of goods has unique characteristics and/or brand identification, for which a significant group of consumers is willing to make special efforts to buy (e.g., Guess jeans, Esprit sweaters, Escada blazers).

- Unsought goods: these products are the type that the consumer does not know about, or knows about but does not normally think of buying; a consumer may be made aware of the product through advertising (e.g., TopsyTail™, Wonderbra™, Turn Around™ facial cream).

From a merchandising point of view, products also can be classified as:

- Fashion goods, which are items that are popular at a specific time.

- Staple goods, which are items that are constantly in demand and are infrequently influenced by fashion changes.

- Hard goods, which include tools, large and small appliances, and home furnishings.

- Soft goods, which refers to both textile and apparel products.

Products can also be categorized according to price with "high end" meaning the upper price range and "low end" meaning the lower price range. Finally, the category called "general line" refers to a wide variety of goods while the term "limited line" specifically refers to goods within a particular product category.

Brands

A business may also decide that the product should be given a brand name. Branding can add value to a product through status and prestige associated by the customer with the brand. It can be an important element of the product marketing strategy. Branding terminology includes:

- Brand: a name, term, sign, symbol, design, or any combination of these. A brand is intended to identify the goods or services of one seller or group of sellers and to differentiate their products from those of competitors'.

- Brand name: the part of a brand that can be vocalized.

- Brand mark: the part of a brand that can be recognized, but cannot be spoken.

- Trademark: a brand or part of a brand that is given legal protection because it is capable of exclusive rights to use the brand name and/or brand mark. ™ or ® indicates either a trademark or a registered trademark.

- Copyright: the exclusive right to reproduce, publish, and sell the matter in form of a literary, musical, or artistic work.

- Brand sponsor: the owner or manufacturer of the brand; may also license the brand to manufacturers.

The brand sponsor must also decide what type of brand to use. The three types of brands are:

1 Manufacturer's brand, which is also referred to as a national brand; this type of brand is owned by the manufacturer.

2 Private brand, which is also called middlemen, distributor, or dealer brand; the private brand is owned by the distributor and but may be manufactured by a different company.

3 Private label, which is a brand that is exclusive to the distributor.

To follow, you are presented with several case studies pertaining to product identification as it relates to various organizations at different industry levels.

37 **What is in a Name?**

The department store's dress buyer, Rose Knight, is working out the details of the full-page newspaper advertisement with the company's advertising director, Sharon Clark. Rose has recently negotiated a special purchase with Liz Claiborne, Inc. for a selection of misses' dresses representing the line's top-selling styles in an excellent assortment of colors and a full range of sizes. She is delighted with the purchase as she is able to retail the dresses at 30 percent off their regular prices and still receive a full 50 percent markup on the merchandise for her department. Because the purchase is exceptional, Rose's merchandise manager has allocated a full-page advertisement to her department to promote the goods.

When she was working on this particular purchase with the manufacturers' representative for Liz Claiborne, Inc. Rose asked for cooperative advertising funds to promote this special purchase. The rep, however, declined to provide coop monies on this order because of the bottom-line prices Rose had negotiated. Rose was not surprised at his refusal, but believed that it was part of the responsibility of her job to ask for cooperative advertising funds even if she knew he would decline. She felt certain that her merchandise manager would come up with the advertising support—which she did.

Rose realizes that she is faced with a dilemma as she collaborates with Sharon on the specifics of the newspaper advertisement. It is the store's advertising policy that the manufacturer's name will not appear in the advertisement's copy if cooperative advertising monies are not furnished by the manufacturer. In this case, Rose believes, the manufacturer's name will have substantial influence on the consumer's response to the ad. She states that the advertisement will generate significantly greater traffic if the Liz Claiborne name is featured in the headline and copy. Sharon responds that the store advertising policy is to use the words "famous maker" as a blind identifier for non-coop ads, rather than to promote the manufacturer's name at no cost to the vendor.

Rose is in a difficult position. She understands that Sharon must adhere to the policies that govern the procedures of the advertising department, yet Rose believes that the tremendous cost and value of the advertisement will be dissipated if the manufacturer's name is not featured. She feels that the total store will benefit from the advertisement if it carries the Liz Claiborne, Inc. name through increased customer traffic and the positive image resulting from featuring a key vendor. Both women believe that their different positions are correct. They are at a stalemate in regard to the full-page advertisement, which must be submitted to the newspaper's advertising office by the end of the week.

1 **If you were in Rose's position, what would you do in regard to this newspaper advertisement?**

2 **If you were in Sharon's position, what would you do?**

38 **Hanging on to a Top Seller**

Episodes, a new manufacturer in the contemporary misses' dress market, looked sensational on the models as they glided up and down the runway at the Dallas Apparel Mart's spring show. Following the fashion show, the company was flooded with orders, particularly for the group of bateau-neckline, blouson dresses featured in the show. The silhouettes were fresh and timely for the updated misses' dress customer; the knit fabrications were ideal for travel because of their ease of care and packability; and the color assortment was right on target with the fall season's trends.

The fledgling dress manufacturer was inundated with orders. New contractors were hired to assist with the unanticipated increased level of production. Additional yardages of the knit fabrics were purchased from the piece good manufacturers. After these negotiations were completed, the bateau dresses were scheduled to hit the selling floors of the retail stores in eight weeks.

Episode's owners eagerly visited the factory as the initial orders of dresses flowed off the production line. As the shipping crew was preparing to pack the merchandise for transport to the retail operations, the owners were shocked with what they observed. When the dresses were placed on hangers, the bateau neckline dresses literally fell off the hangers! The blouson waistlines dropped to approximately hip-height and the weight of the falling blouson silhouette was certain to stretch the knits into unflattering shapes. It was not that the dresses were manufactured incorrectly—in fact, they were perfect. It was that these dress styles had no "hanger appeal." And if they did not look appealing on the hangers in the retail stores, the customers would not be likely to try on the garments. It was a disaster waiting to happen.

The owners of Episodes determined that the blouson dresses would definitely be shipped to their retail accounts. The company could not afford to pull the garments from the line due to the investment the firm made in hiring new contractors and procuring additional fabric. Additionally, this group of dresses was so well-received by the retail buyers that it could singlehandedly make Episodes a major player in the misses' dress market. Many new retail accounts were opened due to the buyers' positive reception of the blouson dress group. The company owners have determined that they must make some creative and suitable packaging and shipping decisions to effectively market this product grouping. They decide to brainstorm to find a solution to this "hang-up" in their business.

If you were one of the owners of Episodes, what would you do about this problem?

39 **A Timely Decision**

A Girl's Best Friend is a specialty store that is divided into four separate boutique departments:

1 Fine jewelry

2 Unique gift items

3 Better costume jewelry

4 Watches

Over half of the business's annual sales volume is generated by the better costume jewelry and watch departments. The retail operation is well-known for its inventory of unusual necklaces, earrings, bracelets, and rings. These are artfully designed, many of which have top-quality imitation diamonds and semi-precious stones. Additionally, the store is reputed for its tremendous selection of budget to better watches.

It is the watch department, however, that is creating a problem for the owners of A Girl's Best Friend. The store carries approximately 20 different watch lines. Each line provides a different servicing and product warranty agreement on its watches. Some vendors guarantee performance on their goods for one year, while others offer a five-year warranty. A few of the manufacturers reimburse the retailer for repair services, while other vendors require the merchandise to be returned to them for repair work. Providing service for their watch customers is a confusing, costly, and time-consuming process for the store's employees.

The store owners are evaluating their current policy in regard to watch sales, repairs, returns, and exchanges. Presently, the store handles all returns and servicing on watches for the customer by offering exchanges, collaborating with a watch repair person, or directly handling all return or repair shipments to the manufacturers. The watch department's sales personnel are required to maintain a file of customers with the warranties for their individual watch purchases. They must also contact the customer when the repaired or replaced watch is returned by the manufacturer or repair person to the store.

The store owners are concerned about the expenses involved with contacting the watch manufacturers and shipping the watches needing repairs. Additionally, there are substantial costs involved with paying the watch repair person. Finally, there are less obvious costs associated with providing hourly wages to the salespeople for the hours they spend recording the watch transactions, documenting shipping and repairs, and contacting customers when the watches are repaired. They decide to evaluate the current policy and to explore alternative possibilities that may reduce costs while still accommodating their substantial number of watch customers.

1   If you were one of the owners of A Girls's Best Friend, what would you decide in regard to the company's current policy on watches?

2   If you were a watch customer, what would you prefer as watch policy for A Girl's Best Friend?

Figure 5.1 *Below you will find an example of a product warranty offered by a watch manufacturer.*

MOONSTRUCK Limited Warranty

Coverage: This Moonstruck Quartz analog timepiece (not including battery, crystal, band, or strap) is warranted to the owner for a period of two years from the date of purchase against defects in manufacture by the Moonstruck Corporation. This timepiece is not warranted by the dealer from whom the timepiece was purchased.

Service Guarantee: If this timepiece develops such a defect in which the said timepiece will not keep accurate time (or date if there is a calendar feature), it will be repaired (i.e., a new and inspected movement will be installed) or replaced (a timepiece of equal value and similar appearance will be furnished, if defective timepiece model is no longer available, or with the same model if available) at our (Moonstruck Corporation) discretion, if owner provides proof of purchase and date of purchase.

This Limited Warranty Does Not Cover:
1 Moonstruck will not repair defects related to service or repairs not performed by the Moonstruck Corporation or its Authorized Dealers or Service Centers.
2 Moonstruck will not provide any warranty service if the timepiece exhibits any indication that it has been misused, abused, altered, or tampered with, as in:
  · Moisture damage sufficient to affect the proper function of the timepiece (if timepiece is not water-resistant).
  · Damage to the case.
  · Cracked or broken crystal.
3 Moonstruck reserves the right to charge owner for a replacement battery, if the battery in the timepiece is expended. No additional charge will be made unless the two-year warranty period has expired or if service is necessary for reasons beyond the control of Moonstruck, in which case a reasonable, moderate fee will be charged, as well as any shipping charges.
4 Moonstruck is not liable for incidental, special or consequential damages. Some states do not allow the exclusion or limitation of incidental, special, or consequential damages, therefore the above exclusion or limitation may not apply to owner.

Your Rights Under Implied Warranties and State Law: This limited warranty is in lieu of all other expressed warranties, obligations, or liabilities. Moonstruck limits the duration of any warranty implied by state law, including but not limited to the implied warranties of merchantability and fitness for a particular purpose, to one year from the date of original purchase. Some states do not allow limitations on how long an implied warranty lasts, therefore, the above limitation may not apply to owner. This warranty gives the owner specific legal rights, and the owner may also have other rights, which vary from state to state.

Caring for the Timepiece:
  · Avoid exposure of the timepiece to water, steam, or other forms of moisture if the timepiece is not water-resistant.
  · If the crystal becomes cracked or broken, or in any way damaged, replace it immediately to avoid further damage to the timepiece movement.
  · When the battery is expended, replace it immediately. The required battery type is listed on the caseback. These batteries can be obtained from your local Moonstruck retailer or from a Moonstruck Authorized Dealer or Service Center.

Service of the Timepiece: If your Moonstruck timepiece should ever need service and you are unable to take it to a Moonstruck Authorized Dealer or Service Center, please mail it to the Moonstruck Corporation, addressed in the following manner: Moonstruck Hotline Repair Service, P.O. Box 8732, Springfield, Illinois 62703. Because we cannot guarantee delivery by the Post Office, we advise the owner to insure your timepiece, return receipt requested, when mailing the timepiece to Moonstruck Corporation. If you do not receive a receipt within a reasonable time, trace the package through the originating post office. Never include any article of personal value (e.g., a special watchband) in your shipment. Please note that we may substitute a timepiece of equal value and similar appearance in exchange for mailed-in timepiece on both in-warranty and out-of-warranty repairs.

For your convenience, all Moonstruck Authorized Dealers will provide a postage-paid, pre-addressed Timepiece Repair Mailer.

MOONSTRUCK is a trademark and service mark of Moonstruck Corporation. Reg. U.S. Pat. & TM. Off.

40   The Name Game

Priscilla Anderson is the buyer for the misses' sportswear department of a multiple-unit specialty store. She is currently attending the Chicago apparel market to purchase fall merchandise for her department. During this market trip, Priscilla has decided to investigate the possibility of securing private label merchandise for her store. She believes that there are several advantages to carrying private label goods which are:

1 They offer exclusivity to the merchandise assortment as the label is retained solely by the store.

2 They can provide the opportunity for additional markup on the merchandise as the goods are not carried by competitors.

3 They can be advertised with the confidence that competitive stores will not be promoting identical merchandise.

4 They can enhance the retail operation's image by featuring the store's name.

As Priscilla is working the sportswear lines with her vendors, she realizes that many of the manufacturers offer the option of private label goods. The first prerequisite for purchasing private label merchandise is not a problem—the store must provide the manufacturer with the label logo or the actual garment labels. However, the second prerequisite is causing Priscilla much concern. A large minimum order is required for a private label purchase. All the private label manufacturers state that it is not cost-effective for them to produce and individually label small quantities of merchandise.

Priscilla determines that she will have to eliminate ordering from some of her regular suppliers to be able to allocate adequate open-to-buy money to accomodate the quantities required for a private label purchase. She questions whether or not her clientele would find large amounts of the same style unappealing as her target customer is a specialty store shopper. On the other hand, she considers, the private label merchandise is exclusive to the store and will provide the opportunity for competitive pricing.

1 If you were in Priscilla's situation, what would you decide?

2 If you were one of the private label manufacturers, what would you do to solicit Priscilla's business?

41   **The Bare Foot**

Jade and Barry Scholz have decided to open a new shoe store—The
Bare Foot—based on a unique concept. It is not unusual that the
store will carry footwear and related accessories for the entire family; this retail operation, however, will fill a merchandising niche
that the Scholzs believe has tremendous market potential. They
intend to promote the store as a discount operation with limited
services featuring brand-name shoes, socks, hosiery, and handbags
at the lowest possible retail prices. Jade and Barry believe that the
one-stop shopping concept of purchasing shoes for men, women,
and children at a single location with the added emphasis on lower
prices rather than customer service will generate a large consumer
following. They feel that today's customer is willing to sacrifice service for a price/value benefit as illustrated by the success of general
merchandise hypermarkets and warehouse club stores.

The store will be merchandised in a warehouse format with the
full merchandise assortment on the sales floor. A sample pair of
each style and color will be displayed in front of the corresponding
inventory of sizes. The store will be minimally staffed with just a
few sales associates and a cashier. It will be designed to accommodate self-service shopping with signs and fixtures indicating the various departmental locations and special purchase or promotional
merchandise offerings. The focus will be on the core product—the
excellent quality and exceptional price of the shoes.

Because the Scholzs intend to price the merchandise assortment
at the lowest possible markup to keep their retail prices at a minimum, they must watch costs related to promotion, customer service, and monthly overhead very closely. They question and examine

every decision they must make in regard to store policies and procedures in terms of the impact on operational costs. They have decided to eliminate delivery from their customer service mix based on the added expense. Packaging will be limited to inexpensive plastic tote bags featuring the store's logo. They have developed a stringent customer return policy in an effort to offset the costs of writing off defective merchandise that cannot be returned to the manufacturer. Now, they are faced with determining whether or not to accept major credit cards at the store. It is a decision that they did not realize they would need to consider and one that will greatly impact their business.

The Scholzs have learned from their bank that the major credit card companies charge a substantial initial fee to permit the retailer to accept their cards on top of a monthly percent of all sales transactions conducted with their respective credit cards. Jade and Barry estimate that offering the customer the option of using a major credit card could cost the store several hundreds of dollars monthly. On the other hand, they also recognize that they may lose a significant amount of business by not accepting major credit cards.

1   **If you were Jade or Barry, what would you determine in regard to this augmented product decision?**

2   **If you were a potential customer, what would you prefer regarding payment by major credit card? Would the lack of this service encourage you to shop elsewhere?**

42 The TopsyTail™ Tale

Tomima Edmark, a 32-year-old Dallas-based computer salesperson, thought her long, blonde ponytail could use a little lift. An avid knitter, Tomima started thinking about manipulating hair into attractive variations when she saw a girl in a movie theater with an interesting hairstyle, a French-rolled ponytail. She immediately wondered if she could turn a ponytail inside out. First, she placed a paper clip on the end of a pencil. Next, she fitted an elastic band to the end of a toothbrush. Finally, with a modified circular knitting needle in hand, she went to a luncheon and wove the needle-like device through her girlfriends' long hair. They loved the effect! It was then that Tomima realized she had invented an innovative and marketable tool to create novel hairstyles. The product, which she named TopsyTail™, is a plastic device that can be used to create numerous hairstyles by threading and twisting a ponytail into various configurations. It is simple and quick to use, and produces dramatic results. Her next step was determining how to manufacture the hair product.

First, Tomima paid $500 for technical drawings and an additional $5,000 to patent the hair tool. Assuming that major companies marketing combs, brushes, and hair accessories to retailers would want to buy ideas for new hair gadgets, she then called on the two largest manufacturers of hair products located on the East coast. Both turned her down flat, declaring they did not see a need for the item. Using her background as a saleswoman, Tomima transformed these rejections into challenges and decided to produce, market, and distribute the plastic gadget on her own while still working full-time for the computer company.

Tomima took $5,000 from her savings to pay for a plastic injection mold. She then secured a plastics maker who would produce as many TopsyTails as she needed for approximately 50 cents each. Her next step involved packaging the product for retail sales. The ultimate challenge loomed ahead. Tomima had to determine distribution channels needed to effectively market the product to the ultimate consumer.

Tomima was faced with three major obstacles to marketing the new product. First, the item could be classified as "unsought goods." As there was nothing comparable to the TopsyTail™ available in the hair accessory market, customers would not be seeking a product they did not know existed. Second, TopsyTail™ is an item that requires a certain level of product demonstration. The customer must be shown how to effectively use the TopsyTail™, to achieve successful results from the product. Finally, Tomima has a limited budget with which to promote her new invention. As she has used the majority of her savings to manufacture the TopsyTail™, she has a minimal amount of funds remaining to promote the TopsyTail™, to the ultimate consumer.

If you were Tomima, how would you promote the TopsyTail?

Figure 5.2 *The effective packaging of TopsyTail™ is a significant factor in the tremendous retail sales of this innovative product.*

Figure 5.3 *A promotional vehicle by the manufacturer of TopsyTail™ provided the consumer with the opportunity for communication with the company's management staff.*

For More Information

The TopsyTail™ Hairstyling Tool is your key to many unique and attractive hairstyles. We are continuing to develop new TopsyTail hairstyles. If you would like to be on the TopsyTail mailing list, please send your name and address to:

The TopsyTail Company
P.O. Box 671269
Department R
Dallas, Texas 75367-8269
or call:
(214) 353-0884.

For External Use Only

Ask for TopsyTail™ Hair Jewelry, Hair Ornaments and Instructional Videos wherever TopsyTail™ Hairstyling Tools are sold.

TOPSYTAIL™
Hairstyling Tool

U.S. Patent No. 5,036,870 & Foreign Patents Pending.
Made in U.S.A.

Please Recycle

Chapter 6
The Product and the Customer

Customer Service Mix

In delivering the product to the consumer, the importance of customer relations is significant. To analyze the customer service mix of an organization, the types, levels, and forms of services should be examined. The way the operation handles customer complaints is often critical to the company's future success in terms of creating customer patronage.

Businesses offer varying types of customer services, which often reflect the price ranges of their products. For example, high fashion boutiques that carry expensive designer garments will usually offer a wide range of customer services from low-cost alterations to free home delivery. On the other hand, such discount retail operations as Sam's Wholesale Club, will provide minimal customer services in an effort to maintain low retail prices that are below those of its competitor's prices. At Sam's, the customer is not provided with dressing room facilities, packaging, or delivery. The bottom line is that the customer pays for the services offered by the business in two ways: (1) the services are financed through the high markup margins reflected in the retail prices of the products; or (2) the services are sold as entities separate from the products, as in a fee charged for gift wrapping.

Types of services that apparel and soft goods companies may offer include:

- Advertising services
- Technical advice

- Promotional assistance
- Discounts
- Exclusivity arrangements
- After-sales service
- Fixture availability
- Replacement guarantee
- Convenience of location
- Credit
- Ease of contact
- Delivery service
- Delivery reliability
- Gift wrap
- Alterations
- Personnel training
- Freight allowances
- Layaway availability
- Ease of payment
- Special order availability

The owner of a business predetermines the amount of service(s) that particular business will provide to its ultimate consumer. Also, the level of each service often varies with the type of business. For example, Pay-Less Shoes offers a low level of service while Donegar and Associates resident buying office offers an extremely high (or total) level of customer service. Businesses choose to offer their varying levels of services in many forms. One apparel manufacturer may elect to send a merchandise coordinator to a retail outlet to set up displays, train sales personnel, and direct a trunk show. Another manufacturer may prefer to send direct mail brochures, fliers or videotapes that feature new lines to the retail buyer, rather than providing personnel to preview the lines. Additionally, the identical services can be provided in a multitude of ways. For example, Vanity

Fair intimate apparel manufacturers may hire DuPont sales representatives to contact Vanity Fair's retail store accounts in regard to a national sales promotion for a new fabric innovation by DuPont.

Some business operations have an organized, separate division that has the primary function of assisting the consumer—the customer service department. Others divide the customer service responsibilities into several divisions, for example, maintenance, credit, and adjustments. Finally, there are organizations that handle the customer service responsibilities informally through management and personnel who have direct contact with the customer. Customer service department responsibilities include:

1 Handling customer complaints and adjustments.

2 Offering product maintenance to the consumer.

3 Providing customer credit.

4 Obtaining information for the customer.

These services can be used by organizations as tools to create consumer satisfaction and loyalty.

Product Lines and the Product Mix

A product line (or product classification) is a group of products that are closely related, either because they function in a similar manner, are sold to the same customer groups, are marketed through the same types of outlets, or fall within given price ranges. For example, several product lines are manufactured under the Calvin Klein name, among them are: ladies' sportswear, dresses, men's wear, and fragrances.

A product mix is the set of all product lines and items that a particular seller offers for sale to buyers. It is also referred to as the product assortment. For example, Amway's product mix consists of five major product lines: apparel, skin care and cosmetic products, jewelry fashions, cleaning products, and household items from towels to brushes. Each product line consists of several sublines. Cosmetics break down into lipstick, nail polish, powder, and so forth. In total, Amway's product mix consists of over 5,000 items. Product mix dimensions include:

1 Breadth: the number of different product lines the organization carries (e.g., a department store carries apparel, soft goods, and home furnishings).

2 Assortment: the total number of items in the product mix (e.g., a men's wear department carries furnishings, shirts, tops, pants, jackets, and suits).

3 Depth: the number of variants are offered in each product of the line (e.g., a blouse is carried in six colors with four sizes within each color).

4 Consistency: how closely related the various product lines are in end use, production requirements, distribution channels (e.g., a fabric store carries fabric, notions, and thread).

Customer service is a critical factor to the success or failure of a business. Managers are faced with major decisions relating to the levels and forms of service they can provide to the customer while maintaining profits. Merchandisers are also confronted with essential decisions regarding the product mix. Next, you will find an assortment of case studies that examine the delicate balance between the product, its related services, and the consumer.

43   Is the Customer Always Right?

Michelle Norman has been hired this week as a customer service representative for one of the branch store units of a major discount store chain. Michelle received a crash course in training for the position because the store management staff is always very busy. She was quickly shown how to operate the cash register, briefed on employee policies and procedures, and handed a store policy manual to read. Because she attends the local college as a full-time marketing student during the week, Michelle works night and weekend shifts. As the store manager and assistant manager usually are not working during the evening hours, Michelle is primarily learning the job—on the job.

Because this particular weekday evening is very slow, Michelle decides to use the time to review the employee and store policy manuals. After a few minutes, a customer approaches the customer service department with a large parcel. Several weeks ago, the customer explains, she purchased two Ralph Lauren bedspreads at the store. She indicates that the packages are unopened and that she has the receipt with her. She also has with her a copy of a newspaper advertisement in which a retail competitor is featuring the identical bedspreads at 30 percent off the price she paid for the items. The customer wants to keep her purchases, but she expects a refund on the difference between the competitor's selling price and the price she paid for the merchandise.

Michelle has just finished perusing the store policy manual and is certain that there is no policy statement for this customer issue. She discusses the problem with several of the sales associates who have worked for the store for longer periods of time, but no one seems to know how to handle the situation. The customer is becoming impatient as Michelle tries to locate assistance. After Michelle asks her if she could return the next day to work with a member of the management staff, the customer becomes very irate. She states that she has driven 90 miles to take care of this issue and then threatens that she will return the merchandise and never shop at the store again if the problem is not resolved to her satisfaction immediately.

As the only customer service representative currently in the store, Michelle realizes that it is her responsibility to handle the customer's dilemma now. She questions whether or not she has exhausted all the possible resources. She realizes that she must resolve this situation immediately because the customer is becoming disgruntled.

1   **If you were in Michelle's situation, would you refund the customer's full purchase price and accept the merchandise return?**

2   **Would you refund the price difference between the competitor's retail sale price and her store's merchandise price?**

3   **Would you come up with another solution to this problem? If so, what is your alternate solution?**

Figure 6.1 *This is an example of a retailer's sales ticket featuring a customer's return of promotional merchandise.*

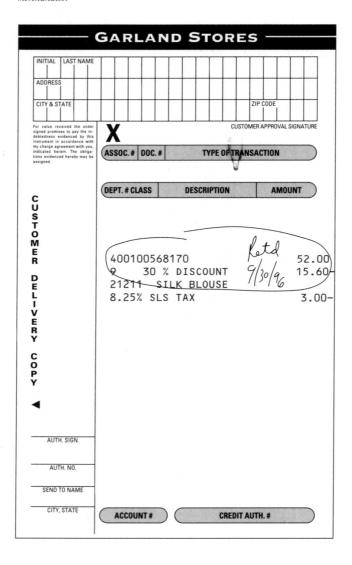

44   **Diving into Deep Water**

As the buyers of The Clothes Horse are seated in the conference room, the new merchandise manager of ladies' apparel, Carl Bedell, is sharing both his assessment of the chain store's current marketing strategies and his suggestions to improve the company's bottom line through more effective merchandising techniques. Mr. Bedell believes that the merchandise assortment has been too fragmented and too diverse in the past. He states that the buyers have been overly cautious by purchasing small quantities of an excessive number of styles from an overabundance of vendors. "The breadth of the inventory has been too extreme," he asserts.

"The resulting stock," Bedell continues, "looks like an end-of-the-year closeout at the beginning a new season." He recommends that the buying staff jointly determine important seasonal trends in advance and take a stand on these looks through more in-depth purchases. He explains that the customer decision-making process is simplified with more consistent stock. "When the consumer sees a clear fashion statement in quantity, she concludes that she must have that look to be fashionable," Bedell summarizes. He adds that an inventory with greater depth makes visual merchandising and advertising efforts clearer and more effective. Finally, he suggests that quantity purchases give the buyer more negotiating power with the reduced number of chosen vendors.

Virginia Nelson has been the misses' swimwear buyer for The Clothes Horse for the past ten years. Although she likes Carl, she is wary of his new approach to merchandising the store. Virginia suspects that Carl's merchandising philosophy is a result of his years of working with mass-merchandising chains, rather than specialty store organizations. Because of her long-term experience with The Clothes Horse, Virginia believes that her customer is extremely selective and does not want to see others coming and going in the same garment. "This will be a turnoff to our customers—it's for a mass-marketing operation, not for a specialty store," she thinks. She decides to continue writing her orders the way she always has done, but she now must receive approval from the new merchandise manager before actually placing an order.

Mr. Bedell slowly reviews the stack of orders that Virgina has prepared and then leans back in his chair. "Virginia, you must not have heard what I said about in-depth purchasing. I see nothing in this pile of orders that reflects a major trend statement. You will need to revise these before I can approve them," he declares. Virginia leaves Bedell's office in frustration.

1   If you were in Virginia's position, what would you do next?

2   If you were in Mr. Bedell's position, what would you do in regard to convincing Virginia that in-depth purchasing will be a successful change for the buyers of The Clothes Horse?

Figure 6.2 *This open-to-buy report facilitates the retail buyer's planned spending for each month by individual department.*

			-SALES	-SALES	-SALES	-SALES	-SALES	-SALES	-SALES	-SALES
					GARLAND STORES					
					OPEN-TO-BUY REPORT					
		(a) SALES	-SALES	-SALES	-SALES	-SALES	-SALES	-SALES	-SALES	-SALES
(a1)	APR	PERIOD PLN	13.9	10.6	21.6	27.9	12.2	11.5	17.9	2.7
(a2)	MAR	PTD TY	17.4	13.0	32.3	27.3	18.9	14.6	19.8	3.0
(a3)		LY	19.4	14.9	25.3	29.0	15.0	14.0	21.6	3.1
(a4)	MAR TY-LY	%CHG	-7.7	-12.8	58.6	-5.9	26.0	4.3	-8.3	-3.2
(a5)	YR TD BOP	MAR TY	12.3	12.0	23.1	19.1	10.2	9.8	13.9	2.3
(a6)		LY	12.4	9.5	8.5	15.0	8.1	6.5	9.9	1.6
(a7)	YR TY-LY	%CHG	-0.5	26.3	171.8	27.3	25.9	50.8	40.4	43.8
(b)		STOCK	STK	STK	STK	STK	STK	STK	STK	STK
(b1)	MAR AUDIT	OH BOP	62.6	65.0	74.8	80.2	58.4	47.6	71.0	23.5
(b2)	MAR -MEMO-BNJ	BOP	23.1	5.9	17.0	14.9	4.9	7.2	10.0	1.1
(b3)	MAR NET RCPTS	PTD	37.5	34.2	60.0	76.8	50.1	36.3	53.1	14.3
(b4)	MAR TRANSFERS	IN	0.2	0.8	12.1	2.4	0.3	1.0	3.1	0.2
(b5)		OUT	-3.2	-5.4	-0.7	-2.4	-5.8	-2.6	-5.6	-0.2
(b6)	LAST WK ON HND	TY	81.8	82.4	105.1	126.3	72.1	64.8	92.4	32.9
(b7)	APR BOP STOCK	PLN	95.3	49.4	86.0	77.0	47.9	59.8	67.8	15.2
(b8)	THIS WK ON HND	TY	88.0	81.6	114.0	129.7	84.1	67.7	101.8	34.8
(b9)		LY	108.7	57.8	104.3	89.2	54.9	67.5	79.8	17.3
(b10)	TY-LY	%CHG	-20.7	23.8	9.7	40.5	29.2	0.2	22.0	17.5
(b11)	MAY BOP STOCK	PLN	105.5	51.4	91.2	77.2	51.7	56.4	70.0	18.0
(c)	OUTSTANDING	OTB	OUTST	OUTST	OUTST	OUTST	OUTST	OUTST	OUTST	OUTST
	MAR	OUTST	1.6	6.3	19.3	12.1	4.8	11.7	15.8	8.6
	APR	OUTST	34.9	16.8	22.7	21.3	5.1	17.1	20.0	9.4
	MAY	OUTST	14.0	11.5	17.5	17.5	13.0	10.1	14.7	7.0
(c1)	JUN	OUTST								
(c2)	AFTER JUN	OUTST								
(d)	APR OP-TO-BUY	BAL	-3.6	-42.1	-41.5	-54.7	-28.4	-27.4	-43.9	-32.1
(e)		MARKUP								
(e1)	FEB	ACT %	47.2	47.1	48.4	51.1	47.1	46.9	47.1	47.3
(e2)	FEB	PLAN %								
(e3)	MMU—SEAS TD	TY								
(e4)	BOP MAR	LY								
(f)		MARKDOWNS	MKD	MKD	MKD	MKD	MKD	MKD	MKD	MKD
(f1)	MAR	PTD								
(f2)	MAR	PLN	0.9	0.8	1.3	1.0	0.9	1.2	1.0	0.4
(f3)	YR TD BOP MAR	TY$	0.2	0.2	1.0	0.4	0.4	0.5	0.4	0.1
		TY%	1.6	1.7	4.3	2.1	3.9	5.1	2.9	4.3
			DEPT	DEPT	DEPT	DEPT	DEPT	DEPT	DEPT	DEPT
			04-02-	04-02-	04-02-	04-02-	04-02-	04-02-	04-02-	04-02-

45 **The Personal Shopper**

In an effort to serve its customers more efficiently, Cooper's Department Store has created a new employee position—the personal shopper. Although Cooper's has a reputation for exceptional service, the store management team believes that the complimentary service of a personal shopper will build business through multiple sales and will generate repeat customer visits. Penny Irving has been hired as company's first personal shopper. There are two primary differences between her position and that of the other sales associates. First, she is the only salesperson within the store's apparel division who works exclusively on commission. Second, she has no departmental boundary lines. She is able to assist customers and ring up merchandise in any of the apparel and accessories departments in the store. Because her salary is solely based on a percent of her sales volume, she strives to assist as many customers in as many departments as possible.

Penny's office is located in the Designer Salon because this is where the store's management believes the potential for a personal shopper is the greatest. When traffic is minimal in the Designer Salon, however, Penny has the option of moving to other departments, throughout the store to assist customers. She searches for those customers that she has previously helped or those that she believes will spend a great deal of money. Although Penny has the freedom to sell throughout the store, the regular sales associates are assigned to a specific area and must remain there. On busy days, it can be difficult for a sales associate to stay within the assigned area, especially when a customer is roaming through several departments in an effort to coordinate items from each one.

On this hectic Saturday, Jane Sheets, a full-time sales assoicate in the Career Sportswear department, is assisting a personal customer, Mrs. Brown. Although Mrs. Brown has worked with Penny in the past, she has also worked with Jane on prior occasions. On this particular day, she walks up to Jane requesting assistance with linen separates featured in an advertisement for the Career Sportswear area. Jane assists Mrs. Brown for over an hour, coordinating the sportswear separates and carrying various garments in and out of the fitting room. Mrs. Brown decides to purchase seven pieces and leaves the fitting room with the items in her hands. At that moment, Jane is ringing up a sale at the cash register while a second customer stands in line. Jane waves to her and says, "I'll be with you just as soon as possible, Mrs. Brown." Mrs. Brown replies that it is no problem as she is not in a hurry.

Seconds later, Penny enters the Career Sportswear department and spots Mrs. Brown loaded down with her garment selections. She greets her by name, takes the merchandise from her hands, and guides her to another cash register. "Let me ring you up down here, so that you won't have to wait in line," Penny remarks. Mrs. Brown smiles and follows Penny to the next register. Penny rings up the purchase under her sales associate number, bags the merchandise, and thanks Mrs. Brown for her business. Jane notices Penny ringing up the sale for Mrs. Brown. Jane is extremely upset because she has spent a substantial amount of time working with Mrs. Brown.

As the personal shopper, Penny's salary is based on her sales volume. Although regular sales associates receive an hourly rate, they are required to meet weekly sales goals to receive hourly wage increases, promotions, and, ultimately, continued employment.

1   If you were in Jane's position, what would you do to recoup Mrs. Brown's sale from Penny?

2   If you were the store manager of Cooper's, how would you remedy this situation? What would you do to prevent this from happening again?

46   Cashing in on the Name Game

Paper White is an elegant boutique located in the Country Club subdivision of a Los Angeles suburb. The shop offers exclusive bed and bath accessories with an inventory emphasis on exquisite European bed linens and bathroom towels. Most of the merchandise assortment is imported and the majority of the goods are featured in white or such shades of white as ecru, beige, ivory, and pale taupe. Paper White caters to an affluent clientele, consisting primarily of female homeowners, interior designers, and brides-to-be. The store is well-known in the community for its unique and high quality merchandise mix, its informed and pleasant staff, and its special efforts toward excellence in customer service.

Within the last two months, the two owners of Paper White have been deluged with customer requests for monograms on their purchases. It is the holiday season and many of their customers would like to add a personal touch to the merchandise they are buying at Paper White. They want to personalize the towels, sheets, pillowcases, robes, and pillow covers with embroidered names or initials for themselves or their gift recipients. In the past, the owners have recommended to customers that they take the merchandise to a local sewing store that offers a monogram service. Lately, however, problems have developed in regard to this alternative.

It appears that the sewing store has been an unreliable recommendation. Customers are complaining to the owners of Paper White that the merchandise is returned to them later than promised; the quality of the monograms is poor, and, in several cases, there have been spelling errors or the wrong initials in the monograms. In fact, a couple of customers believe that Paper White should provide a replacement or refund for their incorrectly monogrammed purchases because the boutique owners made the referral to the sewing store. It is fast becoming a serious problem that must be resolved immediately.

The owners of Paper White are discussing their options. They must do something quickly in an effort to maximize holiday sales. Both are extremely concerned with how this issue will impact sales, the store's image, and repeat customer business.

If you were one of the owners of Paper White, would you discontinue using the monogram service at the local sewing store? If so, what alternatives would you recommend?

47 **High Tech Highway**

A nationally known mail order company located in Chicago has
recently decided to examine alternative ways of reaching the customer through the fast-paced electronic highway. The costs of producing and mailing three major catalogs and twelve supplementary
catalogs annually are skyrocketing. The expenses associated with
hiring models, photographers, art assistants, advertising directors,
and publishing houses in conjunction with the costs of owning and
operating the corporation's buying office and central distribution
center are becoming astronomical. The company believes that its
merchandising niche is nonstore shopping in soft goods, apparel,
and home furnishings for the moderate to upper-moderate consumer. It has determined in the corporation's long-range plan that
it will remain a nonstore retailer that allows the customer to shop
at home, but the company has decided to take a long, hard look at
alternative forms of offering its service to the consumer.

The corporate executives are investigating the technological
advancements in reaching the customer at home. They realize that
a number of alternatives to the paper catalog have developed over
the past couple of years. First, the corporate team examines the use
of video cassette tapes to provide a catalog to the firm's target market. They determine that they could literally videotape the printed
catalog and forward it to customers preferring this option. The
executives also discuss preparing a videotape of the merchandise
with live models and room settings to provide an actual film of the
merchandise offerings. They debate the costs of production and
shipping, then explore the failed attempts of competitors to utilize
this format for at-home shopping.

Next, the executives discuss using the consumer's home computer as a channel of communication. Prodigy, America On-Line, and the Internet are examined as possible routes of reaching the consumer. The corporate team also investigates the possibility of promoting the company's extensive merchandise assortment through a daily or weekly television show, similar to QVC and the Home Shopping Network. Finally, they debate the alternative of presenting the former catalog to the consumer through the use of CD-Rom. They have received reports that CD-Rom is projected to be the most popular family computer accessory. In all cases, they prepare requests to their marketing consultants to have research conducted in regard to cost, time limitations, and accessibility from both the company's and the consumer's perspectives.

If you were a member of the executive team, what would you recommend in regard to the corporation's first attempt to offer an alternative to the traditional catalog? After you have determined a new method of reaching the consumer, you will be requested to take your proposed solution one step further by determining alternative ways to implement your selection.

48 **Adding Shoes to the Closet**

The store owners, Kirstin Matteo and Shelby Sheiner, have finally heard enough; now, they are going to do something about it. Throughout the five years that they have owned My Secret Closet, their customers have repeatedly asked them why they do not carry shoes. The boutique features a beautiful selection of vintage-influenced women's apparel, coordinating jewelry and hosiery, and a large collection of antique-looking hats and handbags. As the store's merchandise assortment is unique with its old-fashioned twist on today's fashions, it is difficult for their customers to locate footwear that harmonizes with My Secret Closet's apparel assortment.

Kirstin and Shelby want to build their business. In fact, they are considering opening a second location in an adjacent city. And they have finally decided to add a shoe salon to their existing retail operation. If it succeeds, they intend to open the new store with a footwear department. There is one major obstacle facing them. Neither Shelby nor Kristin have any experience with the wholesale shoe industry. They are unsure of how to locate footwear merchandise resources, when the shoe markets are scheduled, where these markets are located, and whether or not the manufacturers require minimum purchases. Because their merchandise selection is unusual, Shelby and Kristin assume that they will need to purchase a small number of styles from several vendors. They presume it is unlikely they will find a single shoe manufacturer that produces the range of styles that they will need to specifically coordinate with their vintage-influenced apparel lines. Shelby questions whether locating the type of footwear they prefer will be like finding a needle in a haystack.

Kirstin is concerned about integrating the shoe department within the store. She knows that they need to determine the placement of the shoe salon and its related back stock in the boutique. They will have to purchase appropriate fixtures or have custom ones built. She recognizes that there will be additional personnel requirements for staffing the new department. Additionally, Kirstin must create a plan to incorporate the shoe department into the store's accounting procedures. Shelby and Kirstin have determined that they will add a shoe salon to the store, but they are uncertain about how to implement this expansion.

1   **If you were one of the owners of My Secret Closet, what plan would you implement to add the merchandise classification of footwear to the store?**

2   **What alternatives are available to Kirsten and Shelby if they determine that opening the new shoe department on their own is not a good option?**

49 **Television Reruns**

You are the proud owner of a home shopping channel that is nationally televised throughout the U.S. (congratulations, your net worth exceeds several million dollars!). You are currently working with the manager of the customer service department in regard to his concerns about product returns. According to the customer service manager, merchandise returns are presently sent by consumers directly to the manufacturer of the product. Customers indicate the reason(s) for the merchandise return on an adjustment form; customers also specify whether they would prefer product replacements or merchandise refunds through a charge account credit. Copies of these adjustment forms are forwarded by the manufacturers of the merchandise to the customer service department of the home shopping channel. The accounting office of the home shopping network then credits the customer's account for the dollar amount of the return. Shipping costs to the manufacturers are paid by the customer.

The customer service manager reports to you that the primary reasons cited by the consumers for returning products include:

- Defective product

- Incorrect sizes

- Colors and/or styles are not as expected

- Poor quality

- Does not fit

He addresses his concerns relating to the customer service department to you. According to the return summary report generated by the company's controller, it appears that certain manufacturers are showing extremely high rates of returns. Customers are contacting the customer service department employees to complain about the quality of the products or late shipments on replacement requests. The customer service manager is worried that the network's consumers are avoiding making purchases from the channel based on their dissatisfaction with the products from these manufacturers. Additionally, he continues, the influx of customer returns is extremely costly when calculating both the wages of employees in the accounting office (because of bookkeeping time needed to process the customers' return credits) and the customer service department (because of telephone time needed to console distraught customers).

You then review the list of manufacturers with the highest rates of returns and are surprised to find that two of the top three offending manufacturers are the home shopping network's best resources in terms of sales volume. The third manufacturer is lower in terms of sales volume, but provides an above-average initial markup. This is not going to be a simple to resolve as you had thought. Do you eliminate a key resource due to its high level of customer returns? If so, how will you offset the potential void in sales volume? You have worked closely with both of these manufacturers to develop strong vendor/buyer relationships that have been profitable to both sides. You, however, are losing customers based on their dissatisfaction with these products.

You ask the manager of the customer service department to develop alternatives to reconcile this problem. After thanking him for bringing this issue to your attention, you let him know that you will also come up with a solution by the end of the next business day. You then sit back with pen in hand to evaluate the options.

1 If you were the owner of this home shopping network, how would you reconcile this situation?

2 If you were in the position of the manager of the customer service department, what would you recommend to resolve the problem?

3 If you were an owner of one of the "high return" manufacturing companies, what would you suggest to eliminate this dilemma?

Chapter 7
Pricing

Pricing Decisions

Regardless of an organization's product and profit orientation, pricing is central to the decisions that must be made. An object or a service is defined as a product, and that product is offered to the consumer at a particular price. Normally, we expect that the recipient of the product will pay the price. In some cases, however, institutions like the government may either completely or partially pay the price for the consumer. For example, a city or state museum may have free admission either some or all of the time because the city or state bears either all or part of the burden of covering the costs of its operation. Other illustrations are such trade organizations as the Cotton Council or the Wool Bureau, which offer free services of trend forecasting and fabric sourcing to its retail and manufacturing clients. These services are subsidized by the trade organization's members—the cotton or wool producers.

Many factors must be taken into account when an organization is making a pricing decision. These factors include:

- Costs.

- Characteristics of the target market(s).

- Number and characteristics of the various distribution channel members.

- Nature of the competition.

- Standard trade practices in a particular industry.

- Organizational habit of using the same distribution channel members repeatedly.

- Legal restrictions.

These factors are explored in the following sections.

Legal Restrictions on Pricing

The government is central to the issue of legal restrictions in the establishment of prices. A primary concern of the government is price fixing. The Robinson-Patman Act prohibits price discrimination (i.e., providing different prices for the same services or products) to channel members unless the discrimination can be defended on the basis of savings to the seller. Additionally, individual states may have laws that prescribe the minimum price for which a product may be sold. Finally, consumer legislation, for example, the legislation banning "bait and switch" pricing tactics, protect the consumer and reflect the government's ongoing interest and control in pricing issues.

Competition, Demand, and Pricing

Demand is also important to understand pricing. Demand is elastic because changes in price result in changes in demand (e.g., when prices go up, demand decreases, and vice versa). Competition is also relevant. If your prices go up, but those of your competitor remain stable, customers are likely to move from your establishment to your competitor's. If, however, prices for everyone in your industry go up and there is no competitor offering a cheaper price, demand is more likely to remain stable. In addition to these factors, psychological pricing (e.g., even dollar prices versus prices with decimal endings) is important for organizations to understand when setting prices. Psychological pricing assumes that bargain buyers are more attracted to a price with a decimal ending (e.g., $7.95) than to an even dollar price (e.g., $8.00) because the odd number infers a sale or bargain price. Prestige pricing can also influence a customer psychologically as it may assume that a customer infers a relationship between higher price and better quality. This customer may not buy a product if the price is too low or if it appears to be a sale item.

Customary pricing, which is also psychological, assumes that customers expect a certain product to be available at a certain price and that a significant deviation in either direction from that customary price will result in decreased demand.

Pricing Strategies

There are a number of pricing strategies that can influence customer demand. A loss-leader, for example, is a product offered at an extremely low price, thereby generating little or no profit and perhaps even a loss just to attract customers and generate consumer traffic. A promotional pricing policy is one that attempts to keep prices at a minimum in the belief that there are some customers who are always more attracted to low prices. Penetration pricing is a strategy that is designed to capture a large mass market by offering the product at a low price.

Generally, pricing strategies are focused on increasing market share by:

1 Increasing sales.

2 Increasing profits regardless of changes in sales.

3 Maintaining market share (e.g., maintaining your position in relation to the position of your competition).

Usually the established price for a product is expected to cover all the costs associated with the product and to provide some amount of profit for the organization.

Rate methods for pricing include a standard initial markup, for example, simply doubling the cost of a product to determine the retail price. This is referred to as a keystone markup. The objective is to cover all the costs of production and selling and have something left over for profit. Many retailers set retail prices by using a cost-plus pricing strategy. Doubling the cost price and adding a dollar or two to establish the retail price is an example of this method. Other business organizations use demand pricing to determine the retail price. This method assumes that there is a relationship between the selling price of an item and the amount of that particular item that can be sold. A demand-oriented organization first assesses the demand and then determines whether or not it can afford to incur the costs it will take to meet the demand. When the demand for a product is elastic, the organization must determine whether or not it is better to sell many units of a product at a lesser price or to sell fewer units at a higher price. By using break-even analysis, it can be determined how many items will have to be sold at a certain price to cover all the costs.

The following set of case studies will assist you in understanding more thoroughly an organization's decision-making in regard to pricing strategies.

50   Does She Throw in the Towel?

After the buyers of Smith's, a major department store, presented their interpretations of major fashion trends for the season to the merchandise manager, they then met with the advertising director to develop specific plans for the store's promotional campaign of the next two months. They examined the possibility of sponsoring a special event, for example, as a community marathon to raise funds for the local schools. They discussed institutional advertising efforts that would include a series of television and radio spots created to enhance the store's image, provide shopping hours and locations, and educate the consumer on the store's selection of major fashion trends. Finally, it is time for each buyer to propose items for newspaper advertisements that are intended to feature specific merchandise within that particular department.

Jasmine Young is the new buyer for the Bed and Bath Shop of Smith's. She is a nervous wreck this morning, as she has been warned by the senior buyers that the advertising meetings are extremely competitive and stressful. Apparently, the buyers vie for as much of the total newspaper advertising budget as they can possibly be allocated. A buyer knows that the more advertisements featuring merchandise from that department, the greater the likelihood of higher customer traffic in that department, which often results in increased sales volume. If the buyers believe that an item presented by one of their colleagues is not viable for an advertisement, they do not hesitate to speak out. Additionally, the merchandise manager is extremely selective about those items that will be featured in the ads, as he is ultimately held responsible for the cost/benefit results of the promotional expenditures. Running a newspaper advertisement is expensive; the featured goods must pay off through direct sales and increased customer traffic.

Jasmine's hands are shaking. She is second in line to present her selection of proposed advertising items! When it is her turn, she shows the group a selection of cotton bath rugs, a collection of designer bed linens, a new line of ceramic bath accessories, and a set of embroidered towels. As the buyers, merchandise manager, and advertising director appear impressed with all but the bed linens, Jasmine believes that she has conquered the challenge of her first advertising meeting. She is not off the stage yet, however, as the merchandise manager wants to spend a little more time evaluating how to advertise the set of embroidered towels.

"Jasmine," he begins, "these towels are terrific—a great color selection, nice weight, and a major brand name that the customer will associate with quality. I have an idea—let's run a full-page advertisement and promote these as a loss leader." He goes on to say that the towels should be advertised at their cost prices to generate a high level of customer traffic. He suggests that the towels should not be made available through phone and mail orders in an effort to encourage customers to come into the store. It is his theory that, once in the store, the customer will make additional purchases in the Bed and Bath Shop, as well as other departments within Smith's.

The advertising meeting continues while the remaining buyers present their departmental items. Jasmine can barely concentrate as she analyzes the prospect of advertising the towels as a loss leader. The manufacturer of these towels is well-known and respected by regular-priced merchants for maintaining its pricing structure. The company does not sell its line to discount or off-price operations. At the end of each season, it offers all of its retail accounts price reductions on merchandise representing discontinued colors and styles. In regard to exclusivity and pricing, the towel manufacturer has worked diligently to focus on the needs of its target market—the mid-to-upper-price retailer.

When Smith's competitors see the newspaper advertisement for these towels at cost prices, they will undoubtedly contact the manufacturer to complain. Jasmine has a positive working relationship with the manufacturer's representative for this company. He resides in the city and will obviously see the ad in the newspaper himself. She is concerned that the manufacturer's rep will not sell the product line to her in the future if she reduces the manufacturer's suggested retail prices so extremely. Jasmine is worried that she may lose this important product line for her department if she promotes it as a loss leader. This particular line produces the largest sales volume for her department in the bath towel classification.

From a personal perspective, Jasmine is troubled that she could gain a reputation among the manufacturers and their representatives for "not playing fair." She realizes that her professional reputation will follow her wherever she works—whether or not at Smith's. On the other hand, this is Jasmine's first buying job and she wants to succeed. She reflects that the merchandise manager is an experienced executive and knows what he is doing. The advertised merchandise could greatly impact sales and make her a hero in the store. "Perhaps it will not be a major issue with the vendor," she also thinks. Jasmine is confused and concerned about how to handle this dilemma.

1   **If you were in Jasmine's position, what would you do in this situation?**

2   **If you were in the bath towel manufacturer's position, what would you do if the merchandise is advertised as a loss leader?**

51 Even Manufacturers Have Garage Sales

When Sam Holland, the owner of a large lingerie manufacturing firm, reviews the sales figures for the current season, he realizes that the company's sales performance is running behind last year's volume. Business has been tough—the economy is in a downslide and the competition within the intimate apparel industry has increased dramatically. Sam is disturbed as he peruses the accounting ledgers. He determines that there are only a couple of months remaining in which to salvage this season. He decides that he must come up with a plan immediately to offset the company's current decline in sales.

Sam walks through the factory and takes a look at the large room full of returns/defective goods. These are all items that have been returned by retailers (for various reasons) and seconds that were never shipped because of the flaws noticed by the quality control personnel. Next, he enters the sample room and views hundreds of sample garments from the previous season's lines. He then checks out several racks of past season goods—left-over merchandise resulting from overproduction. Additionally, he notes the racks of goods that were not ready to deliver until after the cancellation dates on various retailers' orders. Finally, he takes a look at the extensive inventory in the fabric warehouse to evaluate the types and amounts of piece goods that have been purchased but remain uncut.

Sam then decides to create some promotional packages to generate end-of-the-season sales volume, to produce cash flow, and to clear out space in both the factory and warehouse. He will promotionally price these goods so that retailers can sell the merchandise during their end-of-the-season sales as special purchases. Sam determines that he will offer the promotional packages to both new and current retail accounts. He believes that he will add to his regular-priced clientele list later by offering the new accounts the promotionally priced merchandise now. "If the goods sell for the new retailers," Sam thinks, "they may come back next season to purchase the new line." He believes that his current retail accounts will appreciate the opportunity to purchase the promotional goods as merchandise for planned sales or as goods that can provide extra initial markup.

1   If you were in Sam's position, what promotional packages would you develop to generate sales volume now and later?

2   If you were the buyer of one of Sam's retail accounts, how would you use this promotional merchandise in your store?

52 How Low Can She Go?

After a week of viewing lines during the holiday apparel market in Manhattan, Lily Williams is getting down to the intense business of writing her orders for the misses' sportswear department of Parisian Fashions, a specialty store chain located in the Northwest. While sorting through her notes of the manufacturers' new lines, Lily is selecting the specific styles, colors, and sizes that will comprise the sportswear department's merchandise assortment for this coming spring season. Additionally, she is planning a particular flow of merchandise into the department by carefully examining the delivery dates quoted by each manufacturer. She is also considering those items that she will advertise as she plans quantities for each item within her style selection. Finally, Lily is ready to determine the retail prices for the merchandise assortment before reconciling the proposed orders with her open-to-buy budget.

The merchandising division of Parisian Fashions has an established policy in regard to requirements for the departmental merchandising statistics. The buyers are required to show a minimum 55 percent overall initial markup in their respective departments. Markdowns must also be limited to a maximum of 18 percent of the department's annual sales volume. Individual departmental statistics have been assigned in regard to stock turn goals. The individual buyers are then reviewed at the close of each season by analyzing actual departmental performance as it compares to the planned merchandising statistics. Lily is keeping the initial markup requirement in mind as she prepares to calculate retail prices for the merchandise she plans to purchase for the store.

Lily plans to place a substantial order for a basic T-shirt from a manufacturer that has been successfully carried in past seasons by competitive stores. She wants to put the shirts on the retail sales floor at a 45 percent initial markup. She believes that it would be beneficial to Parisian Fashions to undercut the competitors in retail price. It is also her belief that the consumer will notice the lower retail price offered on this in-depth basic item and will assume that the store offers better prices than its competitors. Additionally, Lily feels that the reduced price may help generate reorders on the T-shirt, creating larger sales volume. Although a lower retail price seems logical, Lily is concerned about how a lower initial markup on this order would affect the total department.

1   If you were in Lily's shoes, what would you decide in regard to the retail pricing of this order?

2   What additional alternatives can you provide that will enable Lily to reach her initial markup goal?

53 Ad-Dressing Rising Costs and Hemlines

Brooke Zunkel, the dress designer for the petite division of David Warton Dresses, Inc., has worked day and night for weeks to develop the new line. She is extremely pleased with the results of her hard work and feels that the designs are creative, exciting, and ideal for the petite career woman. Brooke now has six months of design experience under her belt with this company and believes that she understands just what her customer is looking for in a contemporary dress. Brooke presents the sketches with their corresponding fabric swatches to the company owner and the merchandise manager, then waits for their reaction. Both are extremely pleased with Brooke's creative work and compliment her for these fashion-forward, yet marketable designs. However, as the three of them begin to analyze the styles one by one, Brooke's positive visions of the new dress line begin to deteriorate.

The company owner and the merchandise manager start the critique session by questioning Brooke's choices of fabric suppliers. They suggest that she could utilize less expensive piece goods and still produce very similar garments. Next, they analyze ways of reducing the yardage required for some of the fuller skirts and longer hemlines. They recommend making alterations on these styles in an effort to decrease the amount of fabric required. The company owner also suggests using fabric-covered belts that the firm can produce, rather than the novelty belts that must be purchased from a supplier—yet another method of cutting costs. Finally, the merchandise manager examines the design details of each garment. She makes notes on construction technicalities that can be changed or eliminated to reduce the labor costs involved in producing each style. She recommends removing the welt pockets from one style, deleting the bodice lining from another, and changing French cuffs to a banded sleeve for ease of construction on yet another style. The merchandise manager develops a lengthy list of similar changes on many of the remaining styles.

Suddenly, Brooke felt as though she did not even recognize the collection she had worked so diligently to create. She asked the company owner and the merchandise manager if it was their intention to reduce the wholesale prices of the petite dress line. They replied that they were not decreasing the line's cost prices; however, increased labor rates were making it necessary for them to find ways to maintain the company's price range. The higher hourly wages paid to the garment workers could be reflected either in higher prices to the consumer or they could be absorbed through subtle changes in the production of the garments. The merchandise manager and the company owner stated that they would prefer not to pass these cost increases on to the consumer because they believe that they have reached the pinnacle of the pricing zone acceptable to their particular customer.

As this is her third season with David Warton Dresses, Inc., Brooke has the experience to recognize which of the new designs will be top-sellers at the retail level. She believes that several of the styles, which have been dramatically altered, were among the best in the entire collection.

1   **If you were in Brooke's position, what would you do about this situation?**

2   **If you were Brooke's merchandise manager, how would you work with Brooke in regard to the design changes?**

Figure 7.1 *This is an example of a garment costing sheet used by a manufacturer to determine the wholesale price of a product.*

Jessica Hamilton Blouse Company Costing Sheet

Date:_____

Style:_____

Patternmaker:_____

Designer:_____

    ☐ Miter

Label:_____

    ☐ End Fold

Stock Pattern Reference:_____

Thread Color:

_____Matching @_____

_____

_____Contrast @_____

_____

Topstitching:

_____Edge @_____

_____

_____1/4 @_____

_____

_____Double Needle/Other @_____

_____

Elastic:

_____Width-Cut Length_____

_____

_____Width-Cut Length_____

_____

Zipper Length:_____

Placement:_____

Curtain Color:_____

☐ Single ☐ Double

Shoulder Pad Mill: _____$_____

Style #_____

Button Placement:_____

_____

Center Back Finished Length:_____

Special Notes:_____

_____

_____

_____

Yardages:_____

_____

Pattern Pieces-Fuse_____

_____

_____

Comments:_____

_____

_____

_____

_____

_____

Cutting Instructions:_____

_____

_____

_____

Figure 7.2 *This Kimball ticket below illustrates how the product is identified through perforated and number coding.*

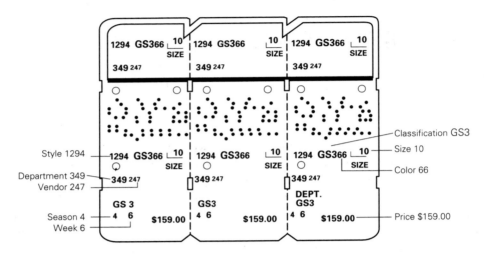

Figure 7.3 *The product identifier below features a Universal Product Code that enables electronic scanning of the merchandise.*

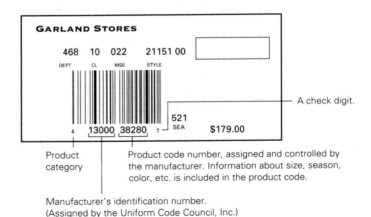

54   **Reaching Out By Mail**

The executives of the large home accessories catalog company, The Postage Stamp, are meeting with the representatives of a major market research firm with two primary objectives in mind:

1 To project ways to enlarge their customer following.

2 To determine methods to further satisfy the needs of their present mail order clientele.

Last year, the catalog company's management team hired the marketing research firm to conduct a survey using a nationwide sample of current and prospective customers. The Postage Stamp has benefited greatly from this in terms of new orders and annual sales volume as a result of the information the company gathered from the previous survey. As The Postage Stamp features specialty accessories for the home, the company believes its target market expects exclusive merchandise, exceptional service, and ease of shopping through the firm's catalogs.

The Postage Stamp's executives were informed that their specialized target consumer wanted the simplified and inexpensive return privileges that were not previously available from the catalog company. In response, free U.P.S. pick-up service for customer returns was implemented. Additionally, the catalog company's management staff learned from the market research firm's survey that the mail order customer did not want to pay a shipping and handling fee. As a result, the costs of transporting merchandise to the customer were incorporated into the retail price of the goods through an additional markup percent. The implementation of these two new policies resulted in increased revenue and a larger customer following for the catalog company.

From the most recent survey conducted by the market research company, the executives of The Postage Stamp are learning that there is one major concern in regard to mail order purchasing shared by both prospective and current customers. The issue reflects the consumer's desire to comparison shop for the best price on merchandise. The consumer would prefer a merchandise policy that would ensure the lowest possible price. In other words, when the customer sees an item in another catalog at a lower price after purchasing the identical item from The Postage Stamp, the customer wants the price difference. The representatives of the market research firm suggest that many potential consumers hesitate to shop by mail because of their perceived inability to obtain the best price possible on merchandise. The market research firm is recommending that the executives of The Postage Stamp establish a company policy to resolve this consumer concern.

The executive team of The Postage Stamp is concerned about the potential costs of meeting competitors' prices. These costs are greater than price reductions as there are related expenses of customer service and accounting activities. Additionally, the executives question the market research firm's representatives about time limitations on price reductions for customers. Next, they discuss the costs of customer services (e.g., gift wrap and no-cost returns) which are offset by the retail pricing. As competitors may offer limited services and lower prices, The Postage Stamp executives are not certain that a "price war" would allow the company to continue all consumer services.

1   **If you were a member of The Postage Stamp's executive staff, what would you suggest in regard to competitive pricing of the catalog merchandise?**

2   **If you were a representative of the market research firm, what policy recommendations would you make to the executives of The Postage Stamp?**

Chapter 8
Product Placement—Marketing Channels of Distribution

Understanding Marketing Channels

A conventional marketing (or distribution) channel performs the function of moving goods from producers (e.g., manufacturers, service providers, sales representatives) to consumers. Participants in the marketing channel may perform a variety of functions, including research, promotion, negotiation, physical distribution, financing, and risk-taking. Many producers lack the financial resources or interest in carrying out direct marketing. When the manufacturer shifts direct marketing functions to middlemen, the producer's costs and prices are often lowered. However, producers who can afford to establish their own channels can often earn a greater return by increasing their investment and expanding into retail sales. An example of the potential profit that may be generated by this decision is illustrated by the influx of manufacturer-owned and operated retail stores, often called factory outlets.

Channel Design Alternatives

A conventional marketing channel consists of an independent producer, wholesaler(s), and retailer(s). Each is a separate business entity, working to maximize its own profits. No channel member has substantial control over the other members. Examples of conventional marketing channel levels are:

1 Manufacturer to consumer; for example, direct mail from the manufacturer, factory outlets, home sales parties.

2 Manufacturer to retailer to consumer; for example, Bloomingdale's, Dillards, Nordstrom.

3 Manufacturer to wholesaler to retailer to consumer; for example M and S Jewelry Wholesalers.

4 Manufacturer to wholesaler to jobber to retailer to consumer; for example, Vern Smith Discount Resale, Inc.

The organizations composing a conventional marketing channel are connected by physical, title, payment, and information flows. The physical flow refers to the movement of the actual product from raw materials to end users. The title flow denotes passage of ownership from one marketing organization to another. Payment flow describes both the methods channel members use to pay their bills and to whom the payments are made. Finally, the information flow pertains to directed promotion efforts that are used to influence product sales from one party to other parties in the channel.

When formulating an effective channel design, decisions regarding types of business intermediaries, cost, control, and length of commitment are evaluated by channel members. The company sales force, a manufacturer's promotional agency, and industrial distributors are examples of business intermediaries, which should be considered when determining channel design. Sometimes a company attempts to develop a preferred channel, but ventures into another channel because of cost or other difficulties. For example, the U.S. Timex Company originally tried to sell its inexpensive Timex watches to fine jewelry stores. However, as most jewelry stores refused to purchase the low-end watches, Timex turned to mass-merchandise outlets. The choice was advantageous due to the future rapid growth of mass-merchandising that occurred from the 1960s to the present.

Vertical Channels

A vertical marketing channel (i.e., vertical integration) consists of producer(s), wholesaler(s), and retailer(s), cooperating as a unified group. One channel member either owns the others, franchises them, or dominates them. The new competition in retailing is no longer between independent business units, but between whole systems of vertical marketing who compete against each other to achieve the best cost economies and customer response. An example of a vertical marketing system is Benetton, a manufacturing and retail company that produces and distributes its own merchandise. Benetton sells its goods through its own sales force of company representatives to independently owned Benetton franchise stores. Additionally, the company operates its own retail stores and factory outlets. In essence, Benetton controls all facets of distribution from production of its apparel and soft goods to the sales to the ultimate customer.

Horizontal Channels

The horizontal marketing channel is the joining of two or more companies to take advantage of an emerging marketing channel opportunity by contracting on a permanent or temporary basis, or by creating a separate company. For example, a manufacturer may decide to directly sell its apparel products through the home shopping show of a cable television network. The executives of the manufacturing firm and the cable network may develop a separate company or product line to maximize to market potential of the home shopping clientele.

Multichannels

Multichannel marketing systems operate on two different customer levels (i.e., dual distribution). They usually combine several styles of retailing with an integration of some distribution and management functions. For example, Guess markets its product line directly to the consumer through its own retail outlets, retail boutiques, and direct mail pieces; however, it also sells its product line to other retail stores that market the products to the consumer.

Distribution Strategies

Distribution strategies refer to the marketing decisions related to delivering the product to the ultimate consumer. One of the distribution strategy decisions involves selecting the types and numbers of the marketing channel's intermediaries—whether intensive, exclusive, or selective. Hanes hosiery utilizes an intensive distribution strategy, selling its products to discount and moderate-priced retailers throughout the country. The company's goal is to make its product line available to as many different types of retail operations as possible, the objective of intensive distribution. Guess uses a selective distribution strategy, choosing to sell its lines to moderate and better department and specialty stores. Chanel has chosen an exclusive distribution strategy, selecting preferred better stores. Chanel's high-end price points and limited production capacity demand this marketing strategy. An exclusive distribution strategy satisfies Chanel's desire to make its high quality, limited product available to a specific high-end clientele.

Physical Distribution

Physical distribution describes how organizations store, handle, and move goods so that they will be available to the consumer at the right time and location. It involves the tasks of planning, implementing, and controlling the physical flow of materials and final goods from points of origin to points of use. The objective of physical distribution is to get the right goods to the right places at the right times for the least cost. The seven major physical distribution cost are (the first on the list costs the most; the last on the list, costs the least):

1 Transportation

2 Warehousing

3 Inventory carrying

4 Receiving and shipping

5 Packaging

6 Administration

7 Order processing

Next, you will find a series of case studies examining the types of distribution problems that may arise for retailers and manufacturers.

55   Going After Another Piece of the Pie

Lauren Ashton, Inc. is a ladies' and girls' apparel manufacturing corporation, which produces quality garments that reflect the classic English country look. Additionally, the corporation licenses its name to a wide range of manufacturers that produce such items as hair accessories, eyeglass frames, bed linens, stationery, wallpaper, lamps, millinery, and fragrances—each under the Lauren Ashton label. All of Lauren Ashton's product lines, those manufactured through licensed companies and those the firm itself produces, are currently distributed through retailer-operated stores located around the world.

Recently, Lauren Ashton, Inc. has decided to examine possible alternatives to the conventional distribution channel it is now utilizing. Initially, the corporate executives discussed the option of opening a division of retail boutiques. They discussed the two major advantages to the company-owned boutique alternative, which are: (1) the boutiques could provide a testing ground for the firm's newest styles and products; and (2) the additional profits from the higher markup margin provided by selling directly to the ultimate consumer at full retail prices, rather than at wholesale prices to other retail accounts.

The executives then examined the disadvantages of owning a division of retail boutiques. They analyzed the costs associated with building, operating, stocking, promoting, and managing retail operations. Additionally, the executives debated the notion that the corporation's area of expertise is in apparel production, not apparel retailing. Later, they discussed the impact the manufacturer-owned boutiques may have on their current and future retail store accounts. Some of the executives believe that many of their retail accounts would elect to drop the Lauren Ashton, Inc. line if faced with direct competition from the manufacturer.

This discussion of opening a chain of manufacturer-owned boutiques led to an analysis of the option of offering franchised retail operations. The corporate executives examined the option of selling franchises to prospective retailers. They recognized that this option would give them control over the way the company's products would be presented and where the stores would be located. The corporation would benefit financially from the sale of the franchise operations and from a percentage of the resulting sales volume produced by the franchised stores. Disadvantages cited for the franchise concept were similar to those related to opening a division of boutiques.

Finally, the Lauren Ashton, Inc. executive staff examined the alternative of opening a chain of manufacturer-owned outlet stores. This type of store would carry the corporation's merchandise at greatly reduced retail prices. End-of-the-season goods, seconds, returns, closeouts, and overproductions could be moved through these outlet stores. This would provide the company with a potentially profitable method of clearing out its warehouses at the end of each season. The firm could also use excess piecegoods to manufacture basic stock for the outlet stores. Profit margins would be consistent with those of their current manufacturer-to-retailer channel of distribution. A primary disadvantage of the factory outlet is that existing retail accounts may be threatened by outlet stores that carry similar merchandise at reduced prices. Additionally, the manufacturer's outlet can be a costly enterprise for the manufacturer in terms of rental fees, utilities, promotions, and personnel salaries and benefits.

1   If you were a member of the Lauren Ashton, Inc. executive staff, what would you recommend in regard to the company and channel(s) of distribution?

2   If you were the buyer of one of Lauren Ashton's large retail accounts, what would you do in regard to carrying the line if Lauren Ashton opened a boutique or factory outlet in your retail trade area?

56   The Death of a Salesman

Elizabeth Anne is major manufacturer in the U.S. misses' sportswear industry. The company has been a major player for almost a decade as a top-selling misses sportswear resource in large retail operations internationally. Its retail clientele consists of major specialty and department store chains across the U.S. and in Europe. In addition to selling to retailers globally, the company owns a chain of manufacturer's outlet stores that it uses to profitably dispose of merchandise over-runs and seconds. The parent corporation also operates several other soft goods and apparel divisions, including men's wear, children's wear, large-sized women's and petite women's dresses and sportswear, home accessories, and fashion accessories. The Elizabeth Anne label is respected and loved by the company's ultimate consumer, the middle-aged, middle-income woman who has conservative fashion taste and an eye for quality. Elizabeth Anne is a giant in both the apparel and soft goods industry and the company continues to prosper with each new season.

Recently, the vice-president of the misses' sportswear division has made an announcement to the division's personnel concerning the distribution of the apparel line. In a divisional memorandum, she stated that the corporate executives have made a major decision that will challenge the traditional method of product distribution in the apparel industry. They have decided to both eliminate one level of the sportswear line's distribution channel and to add a new one. The misses' sportswear line will no longer be sold to the retail store buyers through manufacturers' representatives. Instead, the manufacturers' reps' positions will be eliminated by the first of the year, at which time the company plans to hire a team of merchandise coordinators.

She went on to explain that the merchandise coordinator position will represent a new career option in the fashion industry. The merchandise coordinators will be hired and salaried by Elizabeth Anne and their assignment will be to work directly with the company's major retail accounts. The merchandise coordinator's job responsibilities will include:

- Working with the department's buyers and sales associates to display the merchandise attractively in the stores.

- Training the store's sales associates to sell the product line more effectively.

- Presenting trunk shows and similar special events to the retailers' clientele.

- Writing reorders for fill-ins on available top-selling styles.

- Acting as a liaison between the staff of the company's New York headquarters and the personnel of the retail accounts regarding stock availability and selling trends.

Approximately 20 merchandise coordinators will be hired and trained and each will be assigned to a specific geographical territory.

Some of the retail buyers are extremely concerned about losing their manufacturers' representatives. All store buyers will now be required to travel to the major apparel markets to view the seasonal Elizabeth Anne lines, rather than the reps bringing the lines to their store offices or their regional apparel markets. They are worried that they will not have adequate communication with the company in regard to merchandise shipments, the availability of off-price goods, and selling trends. Because the merchandise coordinators are reserved for Elizabeth Anne's large retail accounts, the small store owners/buyers will be left to work on their own and they will have to attend the New York or Dallas markets to view the Elizabeth Anne lines. Additionally, they will be limited to communicating by telephone with a customer service representative in regard to any issues relating to delivery, reorders, and returns.

The small store buyers are not the only people who are extremely distraught over the elimination of the manufacturers' representatives' jobs. The manufacturers' reps are devastated. Financially, they will be without the substantial commission earned by selling the lucrative Elizabeth Anne line. Some of the reps previously dropped all of their other apparel lines to concentrate solely on the sales potential of Elizabeth Anne. Buyers and reps have inundated the company headquarters with complaints over the corporate restructuring of Elizabeth Anne's distribution channel.

The corporate executives have responded that they are able to lower prices on the line through the elimination of the exorbitant commission fees. The merchandise coordinators will be paid on a fixed salary that is one-quarter the amount the reps now earn. The corporate executives believe that the merchandise coordinator position more directly benefits their primary target market—the major retailer. Because the retail buyer is often dealing with minimal staff and an overwhelming workload, the merchandise coordinator can help ease the burden by assisting the sales associates, the ultimate consumers, and the buyer. Because the Elizabeth Anne management team believes that the line has established a positive reputation with the retailers and the consumers over the past ten years, they feel that the small store owners/buyers who have a successful track record with the company will continue to purchase the line. They recognize that some of the small stores may not continue buying the line because they do not attend the major markets; they believe, however, that they are focusing the company's merchandising efforts on its primary target market—the major department and specialty store chains.

1 **If you were a small store owner/buyer, what would you do in this situation?**

2 **If you were a manufacturers' representative for Elizabeth Anne, what would you do about this predicament?**

57 Can You Have Too Many Customers?

When Stan Lewis heard the receptionist page him over the inter-
com and then announce the buyer's name and her store affiliation,
he immediately had the feeling that there was trouble ahead. Stan
is the manufacturers' representative for Maggie Paris, a line of better designer dresses. The dress line is upper-priced and features
fashion-forward styling, magnificent fabrics, quality detailing, and
excellent fit. Because of its higher retail prices and exclusive styles,
Maggie Paris' retail accounts are primarily better specialty stores,
the designer departments of major department and chain stores,
and distinctive boutiques. When Stan heard the receptionist
announce the name of the store and its buyer, he realized that this
retail operation did not fit into the target market Maggie Paris had
solicited.

Connie Cook is the buyer for T.M. Jaxx, a large department
store chain that has generated its incredible growth by discounting
name brand merchandise. Connie is in the Maggie Paris showroom
to view the new line and Stan is the representative assigned to her
store's territory. He has been in the T.M. Jaxx branch stores and has
personally viewed the racks and racks of designer garments priced
far below the regular retail prices. As Stan has traveled his territory
extensively, he is quite familiar with the image of T. M. Jaxx, its
store locations, and its merchandising philosophy. T.M. Jaxx has
made its niche in retailing by offering its merchandise to the consumer at a 30 percent markup, which is 20 percent lower than the
traditional retail store. By selling goods in great quantity, offering
minimal services, and reducing overhead costs, the company has
flourished despite the minimal markup.

Stan first introduced himself to Connie and asked how he can assist her. She replied that she would like to review the new line and place an order for her stores. Stan then expressed his concern that there are several existing retail accounts near her store locations and that there may be adequate penetration of the line in that region at this time. Connie seemed to ignore the point. Stan then mentioned that the nearby current retail accounts carry the line at full retail price. Again, Connie disregarded the information and prepared her order pad to review the line. Stan acquiesced and quickly presented the line to Connie. She then wrote an extremely large order and left it with Stan along with delivery instructions to ship the goods as soon as possible.

Stan is completely confused. First, he thinks of the substantial commission check he will receive for this T.M. Jaxx order. Next, he anticipates the dozens of irate telephone calls he will receive from his current retail accounts when his store buyers find out that Maggie Paris is now being sold by a discount operation. He questions how many of these accounts will drop the line. Stan then views this situation from the consumer's perspective. Will the customer's image of Maggie Paris change when she sees the line in a discount store? Stan then goes back to thoughts of future commission checks he could receive through the large quantities T.M. Jaxx could purchase in the future. Finally, Stan wonders whether or not he has any alternatives in this situation. He questions whether or not he can legally refuse to sell the line to Connie Cook.

1   If you were in Stan's position, what would you do in this case?

2   If you were the owner/buyer of a retail store that carried the Maggie Paris dress line, what would you do if you found the line was being discounted at a nearby T.M. Jaxx store?

3   If you were the owner/manufacturer of the Maggie Paris better dress line, what would you do if presented with a large order from Stan Lewis to be discounted at T.M. Jaxx?

58   A Sock for Every Foot

Shades Hosiery, Inc., headquartered in Winston-Salem, North Carolina, is a major manufacturer of hosiery products for men, women, and children. Shades Hosiery is owned by a large corporation that also operates several divisions of product manufacturing unrelated to socks and hosiery (e.g., handbags, gloves, foods, and active sportswear). As the corporation as a whole has shown high profit margins for several years, the firm's executives have decided to expand one division annually. This year they have allocated funding for the expansion of Shades Hosiery, Inc.

Primarily, the company has sought out the target market of "middle America" with its moderately-priced and traditionally styled hosiery selection that caters to the entire family from infants to adults. The corporation has recently raised the capital needed to expand its production and distribution capabilities. The company's executives are currently evaluating various marketing and retail opportunities that could potentially increase the market share and move into an intensive distribution strategy for Shades Hosiery, Inc.

One alternative is to license a designer's name to market a line of women's and/or men's high fashion socks and hosiery. The designer's firm could determine the color and style selection for each season and coordinate the hosiery products with its ready-to-wear lines. The hosiery manufacturer could then produce the goods under the designer's label. A second option is to produce a budget line of socks and hosiery to sell to mass-merchandisers and discount stores. This merchandise line could carry a private label of the retailer's choice or a new label created by Shades Hosiery, Inc. A third choice is to manufacture a better line of hosiery and/or socks that would appeal to the higher-priced retailer operations. Again, this potential line could either feature a private label selected by the retail store or an exclusive label generated by the manufacturer. The team of corporate executives have decided to brainstorm more additional alternatives with several business consultants before determining a plan of action to implement the Shades Hosiery, Inc.'s new intensive distribution strategy.

1 **If you were hired as a business consultant for this corporation, what would you recommend? What additional marketing opportunities do you believe exist for Shades Hosiery?**

2 **If you were an executive for Shades Hosiery, what would you recommend in regard to additional marketing opportunities for the company?**

59   Getting Burned with the Swimsuits

The manufacturers' representative for Skinny Dippers, a junior swimwear line, has made Karen Allen an offer she believes she cannot refuse. Karen is the buyer for the junior department of Sun & Fun, a chain of 20 specialty swimwear stores located throughout California. Matt Miller, Skinny Dippers's sales rep, has made the following merchandise proposal to Karen:

"As Skinny Dippers will debut a seasonal preview line in December, Skinny Dippers is offering a representative selection of the entire preview collection to each of the Sun & Fun branch stores to be delivered by December 1st. This merchandise will be tendered on a consignment basis. Sun & Fun can return any of the unsold goods before January 30th for no payment or credit."

It appears to be a win/win situation for both the manufacturer and the retailer. It provides Skinny Dippers with an audience to test market new styles as the merchandise will be viewed by the ultimate consumer. Additionally, it gives the manufacturer an early indication of consumer preferences in regard to silhouette, style, color trends, as well as the opportunity to make adjustments before making large fabric and production commitments. From the retailer's perspective, the store can feature a timely, extensive merchandise assortment with no inventory investment. The buyer, too, has the advantage of an early reading on consumer favorites and can reorder styles accordingly. Karen receives approval from her merchandise manager regarding the consignment deal and then signs the agreement with Matt.

On the first of December, the merchandise is shipped to Sun & Fun's 20 branch stores as planned. Throughout the next eight weeks, Karen and Matt confer by telephone regularly in regard to those styles, colors, and sizes that are selling and those that are not selling as well. By the end of the two-month period, approximately 60 percent of the consignment stock has sold, leaving the stores with the balance to return to the vendor. Karen sends a memorandum to the store managers requesting them to transfer the remaining Skinny Dippers preview line to Sun & Fun's central distribution center. It takes about a week for all of the merchandise to arrive before the receiving personnel can begin inventorying and packing up the goods. The merchandise is then shipped to the vendor, followed by payment to Skinny Dippers from Sun & Fun's accounting office for the merchandise that was sold.

Soon after, Karen receives a call from Matt who is extremely upset. It appears that there is a discrepancy between the quantity of merchandise returned and the number of goods for which Skinny Dippers received payment. Additionally, Matt states that there are about 30 swimsuits that are damaged or soiled—either while in the stores or during shipping. Karen reviews her vendor's sales records and the central distribution center's inventory of the returned consignment goods and she agrees that there is a disparity of approximately 50 units. After she contacts the branch store managers by telephone, she is only able to come up with an additional 10 units that were overlooked when the merchandise was transferred. Karen wonders what could have happened to the missing suits and assumes that they were shoplifted.

Unfortunately, Matt is suggesting that—unless the damaged and missing merchandise is paid for—Skinny Dippers will not be interested in working with Sun & Fun on a consignment basis in the future. Karen questions whether or not her store is responsible for the unaccounted for and defective goods.

1   **If you were in Karen's situation, what would you do to resolve this problem?**

2   **If you were in Matt's position, what would you recommend as a resolution to this conflict?**

Figure 8.1 *This vendor performance analysis report provides the retail buyer with information in regard to sales, returns, markup, and gross margin of a manufacturer's line in a retail operation.*

GARLAND STORES
VENDOR PERFORMANCE ANALYSIS WEEK ENDING 5/23/96

DATE 5/23/96 PAGE: 1
TIME 2:02 PM

SEASON : LATE SPRING

VENDOR: GS43 The Western Shoe and Boot Company

DEPT: 10 Ladies Shoes and Boots

CLASS DESCRIPTION	TOTAL $ SOLD TY	LY	% SOLD REG DOL TY	LY	UNITS SOLD TY	LY	% SOLD REG UNIT TY	LY	% INIT MARKON TY	LY	% GROSS MARGIN TY	LY	DOLLARS RECEIVED TY	LY	% RECD/PURC TY	LY	% RETURNS TY	LY
CLASS : 1 Boots	142,875	130,144	90.2	88.6	1,705	1,732	96.1	93.2	51.1	52.4	50.1	50.8	190,125	180,145	90.5	88.1	1.5	4.2
2 Dress Shoes	111,125	104,457	95.7	91.0	1,949	2,009	88.6	83.4	50.5	50.8	50.2	48.7	150,172	140,123	95.7	97.2	2.1	2.4
3 Casual Shoes	57,193	48,615	91.1	84.5	1,505	1,393	90.7	89.6	50.2	51.7	51.4	49.7	75,145	80,125	98.9	98.1	1.8	1.7
TOTAL DEPARTMENT	311,193	283,216	92.3	88.8	5,159	5,134	91.7	88.4	50.6	51.6	50.6	49.7	415,442	400,393	95.0	94.5	1.8	3.1
TOTAL VENDOR	410,145	390,271	88.7	85.3	6,795	7,045	86.4	83.2	50.1	50.7	50.2	49.4	547,512	510,874	94.3	94.0	2.1	2.7
TOTAL SEASON	955,024	961,701	91.4	87.2	25,792	25,673	90.4	85.9	51.3	52.1	51.9	49.9	2074185	2023134	98.7	95.3	1.9	2.6

Figure 8.2 *This is an example of an authorization form used by the retail buyer to revise delivery dates on unshipped purchase orders.*

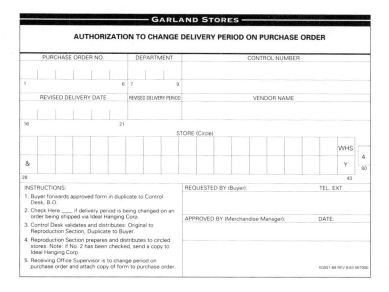

Figure 8.3 *The return-to-vendor report provides an analysis of reasons for the return of merchandise to vendors and a listing of the recipient of fees associated with returning goods.*

GARLAND STORES			
RTV REASON CODES			

REASON: Three letter code identifying the reason the merchandise is being returned to the vendor **AND who pays the freight charges outbound**.

Reason	Description	Frt. Out/HC Responsibility	Frt.-in* Respons.
DAM	Damaged Merchandise	VENDOR	VENDOR
WRG	Wrong Merchandise	VENDOR	VENDOR
NOR	Not Ordered	VENDOR	VENDOR
CAN	Order Cancelled	VENDOR	VENDOR
LAT	Received Late	VENDOR	VENDOR
AGV	Agreement—vendor pay	VENDOR	N/A
AGS	Agreement—store pay	STORE	N/A
SMV	Sample—vendor pay	VENDOR	N/A
SMS	Sample—store pay	STORE	N/A
JBV	Job Out—vendor pay	VENDOR	N/A
JBS	Job Out—store pay	STORE	N/A

*Freight In will be charged back to the vendor ONLY if the store payed the original inbound freight.

60 The Accessory Addition

Because the principals of The Total Look (a costume jewelry wholesale company) Mary Holden and Susan Coberly had been the retail
buyers of accessories departments for years, they have based their
innovative merchandising plan on a need in the accessories market
that they had personally experienced in their professional lives.
Costume jewelry goods are relatively inexpensive items that reflect
fashion trends and/or fads. The consumer purchases these items —
often on impulse—as a less costly method of updating her existing
wardrobe. It is far cheaper to buy an accessory rather than to purchase an entire new outfit in order to wear the newest fashion
trend. As fashion accessories sell quickly, the accessories departments buyers frequently find that they are out of stock on key items.

For example, if pearl choker necklaces are "hot," consumers will
purchase them immediately. The buyer is then faced with a lengthy
lead time—the time required between placing a reorder with the
manufacturers, receiving the merchandise in the store, tagging the
goods, and then displaying the jewelry on the counters and in the
display cases for the customer to purchase. Often, the lead-time
between order placement and actual sales floor placement is four to
six weeks. By then, the trend may already have faded and been
replaced by a new consumer preference. And the retail store will
have missed the opportunity to maximize the sales potential of that
particular item.

To counter this ongoing problem, Mary and Susan developed a
jewelry wholesale business that would reduce the lead time for
retail buyers of costume jewelry departments. They opened wholesale stores in major and regional market apparel centers that carry

an inventory of currently popular jewelry items. These successful wholesale outlets are located in New York City, Dallas, Chicago, Miami, and Los Angeles—with plans for even further expansion. Mary and Susan either purchase the merchandise or carry consignment lots of merchandise from a wide range of jewelry manufacturers. The retail buyer has the option of either taking the merchandise back to the store or having it shipped to the store by the next business day. The wholesale outlets are designed to resemble retail stores. The stock is warehoused in the back of the store off the sales floor; sample pieces of the inventory are featured in showcases and throughout the various merchandise displays. While visiting the wholesale showroom to purchase costume jewelry, the buyer also has the opportunity to gather ideas in regard to the presentation of the jewelry selection.

The merchandise is sold to the retail stores at 15 percent above the manufacturers' actual line prices. Although the retail buyers pay a little more for the goods than if they purchased directly from the vendor, they have the benefits of immediate delivery, reduced travel costs, and a preselected assortment. Rather than having to view full lines at all the various locations of the many different jewelry manufacturers' showrooms, the retail buyer is now able to see the merchandise from a diverse selection of vendors—all under one roof. Although Mary and Susan's wholesale prices carry the company's additional markup, there are big savings for buyers using the wholesale operation—the saving of time. Time spent traveling to the manufacturers' showrooms, time needed to view the jewelry lines, and time between ordering and receiving the goods all are reduced by this innovative jewelry wholesaler.

Although the business is widely welcomed and accepted by the retail buyers, some jewelry manufacturers are resistant to selling their merchandise to Mary and Susan. First, manufacturers are required to reduce their line prices by 10 percent so they can be carried by the wholesale operation. This helps Mary and Susan to pay their overhead costs while continuing to facilitate their below-industry initial markup. Many of these jewelry manufacturers believe that if they allow their goods to be carried by the wholesale operation, the retail accessories and jewelry buyers will not view the full lines in their showrooms. Instead, the buyers will see only a portion of their lines—those being the items that Mary and Susan have selected. The jewelry vendors are also uncertain of the profitability of having items from their lines displayed with those of their competitors'. They are also unclear about the status of merchandise returns, questioning whether defective goods will be returned to Mary and Susan or to the manufacturer.

1   If you were either Mary or Susan, how would you convince the indecisive jewelry manufacturers to allow their lines to be featured in your new wholesale outlet?

2   If you were a jewelry manufacturer, what would you do if Mary and Susan wanted to feature merchandise from your line in their wholesale operation?

3   If you were the retail buyer of an accessories department, would you choose to purchase merchandise from the accessory wholesaler? If so, why? If not, why?

Chapter 9
Promotion

Promotion Decisions

Promotion communicates the product attributes to the target consumers through the use of four major tools: (1) advertising; (2) sales promotion; (3) publicity; and (4) personal selling. Promotion decisions incorporate:

- Identifying the target market
- Choosing a message
- Choosing a communication channel
- Choosing the media
- Setting the total promotion budget and mix
- Evaluating the promotion results

Each of these decisions is explained more fully in the following sections.

Identifying the Target Market

The preliminary stage of promotion decision-making includes first identifying the target market and then determining that target market's readiness state, which is used to establish the desired audience response. The buyer readiness state refers to the type of motivation that encourages a customer to purchase a product. The three distinct buyer readiness states are:

1 Cognitive, which utilizes the consumer's awareness and knowledge of new product developments as a purchasing motivation.

2 Affective, which refers to consumer liking, preference, and conviction of product performance. It is often used to promote existing products, for example, cosmetics and health products.

3 Behavioral, which focuses on motivating the consumer to immediately purchase the product, often based on a "for a limited time only" special. Illustrations of the behavioral readiness state include K-Mart's use of the "blue light special" and the television home shopping network's use of time and quantity limitations to encourage customers to quickly place their orders.

Developing the Message

The second stage of the promotion decision-making is to develop an effective message that will generate attention, stimulate an interest, promote a desire, and induce action. The message can be segmented into three parts, which are:

1 Content, which reaches out to the target market through a rational, emotional (positive or negative), or moral appeal. The rational appeal stresses self-interest by showing that the product will produce claimed benefits. The positive or negative emotional appeal may be based on fear, love, humor, pride, romance, or joy. An example of a positive emotional appeal is the appeal made by a fragrance company that states that the use of a specific perfume will result in romance and love. Moral appeals reflect the audience's sense of what is right or wrong. An illustration of a moral appeal is the mass merchandiser's advertising approach that buying U.S.-made products is the right thing to do as it increases job opportunities for Americans. On the other hand, an advertisement by an animal-rights organization may attempt to impact the consumer's sense of what is wrong by portraying the purchase of apparel made of fur or leather as immoral.

2 Message structure, which may be open-ended or closed, one or two-sided, or present the strongest argument first or last. An open-ended message allows the consumer to complete the thought, to fill in the blank. For example, an advertisement for fine watches may imply that the purchaser must have a certain socioeconomic status and leave consumers asking themselves if they are worth the investment. This open-ended message presents an emotional appeal. A one-sided message often uses a spokesperson as an authority on the product type, while the two-sided message incorporates an opposing view for either realism or contrast.

3 Message format, which is analyzed when determining a promotional effort. Print or display media messages include an analysis of size, color, and illustration. For such verbal messages as radio and television advertisements, speech pace and background music are segments of the message format.

Choosing a Communication Channel

In the third stage of the promotion decision-making process, either personal or nonpersonal communication channels are selected. Personal communication channels are classified as advocate, expert, or social channels. The advocate channel uses salespersons to contact potential buyers in the target market. The expert channel presents an individual person with expertise who makes statements about the product to the target market. The social channel is composed of word-of-mouth from neighbors, family, friends, and associates. Further, personal communication channels are stimulated by:

- Identifying influential individuals and organizations.

- Creating opinion leaders who will sway potential purchasers.

- Working through influential community leaders.

- Developing advertising with high conversation value.

Nonpersonal communication channels utilize mass media (undifferentiated) or selective (specialized) media through print, electronic, or display methods. Print methods of nonpersonal communication include catalogs, newspaper and magazine advertisements, and billing statement enclosures. Electronic methods include television and radio promotional efforts, electronic billboards, and Internet advertisements. Display methods comprise point-of-purchase displays, merchandise fixtures, and similar visual merchandising efforts. Additionally, nonpersonal communication channels include atmospheres, which are designed environments that create or reinforce the buyer's product desire. For example,

Esprit apparel manufacturing company decorates its California showroom with antique Amish quilts, lush green plants, and natural wood furniture. This contemporary decor creates an exciting and colorful atmosphere that is reflected in Esprit's product line.

Events are also used as nonpersonal communication channels. These are designed occurrences that communicate particular messages to the target audience. For example, the Cotton Council sponsors video presentations that are designed to familiarize retail buyers and apparel manufacturers with upcoming fashion and color trends as they correspond with innovative cotton fabrications.

Choosing the Media

Choosing the media refers to selecting from a large number of alternatives to transport the message to the consumer. Among these alternatives are: television, telephone, newspaper, radio, direct mail, billboards, and computer networks, to name a few. When determining the media type to utilize, the following is analyzed:

1 Reach, which refers to the number of people in the target market that may be affected by the media type.

2 Frequency, which indicates the number of times the message is presented.

3 Impact, which designates the influence of the media type on the target market's buying habits.

4 Source credibility, which refers to the media effort's ability to establish expertise, trustworthiness, and likability in the consumer's mind. Many retailers, for example, K-Mart, Walmart, and J.C. Penney have established proprietary brands, using celebrities as spokespersons to establish source credibility for their labels.

In addition to reach, frequency, impact, and source credibility, other variables to consider when choosing the media type include target market media habits, the product itself, the message, and the cost of the media type.

Setting the Promotion Budget

Methods for establishing an organization's total promotion budget vary within different industries. Revlon cosmetic firm allocates 7%

of sales volume for promotion expenditures while K-Mart appropriates 2.2% of sales volume for promotion costs. The four techniques used to set the total promotion budget of an organization are:

1 Affordable method, which is the dollar amount the firm can afford at the moment.

2 Percentage of sales method, which is based on sales volume.

3 Competitive-parity method, which is based on a competitor's expenditures.

4 Analysis of communication objectives and tasks, which is based on costing and type/number of audience factors.

Additionally, promotion budget assistance is often provided by external funding. Fiber, fabric, and garment producers frequently offer cooperative advertising monies. In exchange for name or brand recognition, the producer will pay a specified percentage of the promotion costs. After the promotion budget is determined, it is divided between the four promotion tools: advertising, sales promotion, publicity, and personal selling. These are examined in the next sections.

Advertising

Advertising is the use of paid media to communicate persuasive information about a product in a nonpersonal presentation that is financed by the seller. Forms of advertising media include magazines and newspapers, television and radio, outdoor displays, direct mail, novelties (e.g., calendars, memo tablets, and automotive placards), catalogs, directories, and circulars. Different types of advertising can be designed to serve several purposes. Some types are:

- Institutional advertising, which builds an organization's image and creates community goodwill.

- Brand advertising, which promotes a particular brand.

- Sale advertising, which announces specific value item(s).

- Classified advertising, which spreads information about a sale, service, or event.

- Advocacy advertising, which supports a particular cause. For example, a recent advocacy newspaper advertisement not only announced that a store's entire inventory was composed of American-made products, but also expressed the reasons for supporting domestic producers.

Personal Selling

Personal selling consists of oral presentations to one or more prospective purchasers for the purpose of making a sale. A manufacturer's representative is employed by apparel and soft goods manufacturers for the purpose of selling to the retail store buyer. A sales associate is hired by the retailer to sell merchandise to the ultimate consumer. A telemarketer is paid by a marketing company to sell goods or services by telephone to a prospective customer. Currently, technological forms of personal selling are rapidly developing through the use of salespersons on television home shopping networks. Interactive television shopping is on the horizon as the consumer will soon be able to communicate directly with the television channel representatives for an innovative form of personal selling.

Sales Promotion

Sales promotion includes short-term incentives that encourage the product sale. Examples of sales promotion techniques include samples, coupons, price packs, point-of-purchase displays, trade promotions, contests, sweepstakes, games, business conventions, and trade shows. Sales promotions can be either internally or externally sponsored. An internally sponsored sales promotion is one that is initiated and financed by the retailer, while an externally sponsored sales promotion is started and funded by a supporting organization for the retailer. An external sponsor, for example, can be an apparel or soft goods manufacturer, a fiber manufacturer, or a fashion magazine. Externally sponsored sales promotions are frequently utilized to build sales volume in the cosmetic industry. For example, when the consumer makes a minimum $17.00 purchase of Clinique products during a gift-with-purchase promotion, a free cosmetic bag filled with sample products is given to the purchaser. The promotion is of no cost to the retailer, as all expenses were incurred by Clinique.

Publicity

Publicity refers to the nonpersonal creation of demand for a product by introducing commercially significant news about the product through media efforts unpaid for by the sponsor. Press relations, product publicity, corporate communication and lobbying are examples of publicity efforts. As an example, Jones Store Company (a Kansas City department store) recruited fashion designer Bill Blass to promote his apparel and fragrances within the store. The Kansas City Star newspaper featured several articles on the designer's background, current product lines, interests, and activities, while mentioning his appearance at Jones Store Company. The retailer paid nothing for this newspaper publicity.

While positive publicity is the public relations goal of most organizations in the apparel and soft goods industries, they must also be concerned about opportunities for negative publicity. Equal opportunity employment, fair pricing, and legal advertising practices are topics that can be used against an organization by the media if it is believed that there are improprieties in the company's hiring, merchandising, or promotional practices. Today, current topics for negative publicity in the apparel and soft goods industries include the use of sweatshops by apparel manufacturers, the extensive purchasing of foreign-produced merchandise by retailers, and a lack of multicultural diversity within the employee and management divisions of retailing and manufacturing organizations.

Visual Merchandising

Visual merchandising primarily refers to store windows and interior displays. These are often called "silent salespersons." The primary purpose of windows and displays is to sell product(s) while projecting the correct image. Windows and displays communicate product information to the consumer, which affects purchasing behavior. Effective use of visual merchandising can modify consumer demand, buying habits, and patronage. Additionally, creative use of window and display space creates shopping expectations and stimulates the consumer to purchase the featured merchandise. Displays can also speed up transactions, as in a self-service operation.

Evaluating the Promotion Results

Evaluating the results of promotion efforts is the final and crucial—yet often overlooked—stage of promotion decision-making. The most common form of promotion evaluation is an analysis of sales and the impact on profit before, during, and after the promotion. Sometimes, consumer surveys are used to evaluate consumer awareness, comprehension, and attitude changes that result from promotion efforts. Advertising pre-testing includes direct ratings (e.g., which ad would influence you to buy the product?) and portfolio tests, in which a group of consumers analyzes an assortment of ads and then is tested for recall and recognition.

On the following pages, you will find a group of case studies that will examine the promotional aspects of several different types of organizations.

61 Showing Off the Shoe Business

As the new manager of a contemporary footwear retail operation, Michael Gunst is finding the shoe business exciting, fast-paced, and prosperous. The footwear company's theme, "There's no business like shoe business," reflects its dramatic and enthusiastic approach to retailing. As the stores are designed to resemble theaters, the shoe selection is showcased on miniature stages while the cash desk appears to be a ticket office. The inventory is fashion-forward, yet moderately priced. The clientele primarily consists of contemporary young men and women who are interested in the latest shoe styles. Previously, Michael was one of the store's best customers and when the company advertised for a new store manager, he was among the first applicants to interview for the position. Michael was hired by the company just two weeks ago.

Michael's job description includes responsibility for appropriating the store's quarterly promotional expenditures. Although the company's main office provides the total budgeted amount that can be spent on advertising for a three-month period, it is Michael's job to determine where, when, and how the promotional dollars will be allocated for his particular branch store. Although he has prior management experience in retailing, he has never worked with the promotional facet of the business. He believes that this promotional aspect can make or break his store's business. Because he is working on a bonus payment system, he is particularly interested in surpassing his quota goals.

After researching promotional efforts by major retailers across the country, Michael had developed several innovative promotional plans that he excitedly discussed with the store's regional manager, Mr. Claire. Mr. Claire did not share Michael's enthusiasm for attempting new advertising techniques. He suggested that Michael stick with the types of advertising the retail operation had utilized in the past because they had all been relatively successful. He further dampened Michael's excitement with a description of the store's promotional budget. The funds were extremely limited and could only support one or two monthly promotional efforts.

This week, Michael is meeting with a number of sales representatives from the primary media sources in the community. The newspaper advertising salesperson recommends using the newspaper's fashion section to promote specific styles of merchandise. The radio sales representative suggests using the airwaves for an institutional approach to advertising the store's image and personality. The television rep believes that Michael should use TV for both image and specific product advertising.

In conjunction with these major media sources, Michael is considering using part of his promotional budget to print fliers announcing a sale. Additionally, he is thinking about collaborating with an apparel store to produce a fashion show. The costs involved with a fashion show would include: advertising the event, transporting the merchandise, renting a facility, leasing light and sound equipment, paying the models, and more. Michael is still looking for other ways to stretch his promotional budget to reach the store's target market.

If you were in Michael's position, what would you decide in regard to a promotional plan for the next three months?

62   The Runway Riddle

Although the new fabric store owner, Courtney Blair, is eager to gain favorable publicity and recognition for her store in the community, she is unsure today about how she should respond to the request from the local business women's organization. The organization's program chairwoman contacted Courtney this morning in regard to a fashion show scheduled for next month. She invited Courtney to be the featured retailer in a holiday fashion show at the local country club. If she accepts the invitation, Courtney will be responsible for the total production of the show. Her store will provide the merchandise shown in the fashion show; Courtney will recruit the models and commentator; and she will produce the actual show. In turn, the business women's organization will take responsibility for promoting the event, selling tickets to the fashion show, and incurring the fashion show production costs of lighting, sound, and staging. The women's organization guaranteed that a minimum of 250 people will attend the show, assuring Courtney of excellent exposure to her new business.

At first, Courtney nearly jumped at the opportunity; however, she calmed herself and asked to consider it overnight. She discussed the pros and cons of sponsoring the fashion show with her assistant manager, Jessica Martin. On the positive side, they both agreed that the positive publicity and extensive community exposure will project an excellent store image. Jessica and Courtney note that many of the costs associated with the show will be assumed by the business women's club. Additionally, Jessica suggested that they use volunteers from the business women's organization as models in the show. This would allow them to spend time on responsibilities other than recruiting models and would add excitement to the show from the audience's perspective—an audience of at least 250 people! Additionally, Courtney and Jessica discussed that the models would be excellent potential customers when they came to the store for merchandise selection and fittings. On a final positive note, both women admitted that it would be a fun and inspiring event in which to participate.

On the down side, they both recognize that the store will incur some expenses. They will need to construct garments from the store's fabric inventory—garments that may or may not sell after the show. In addition to the cost of the materials, they will have to hire assistance with the sewing. Courtney and Jessica estimate that a 30-minute fashion show would require the construction of at least 25 outfits over the next four weeks! They discuss the time that will be needed to make the show garments, to fit the models, to write the commentary and to rehearse the show—time that will be taken from the sales floor. Most important, neither Courtney nor Jessica have ever directed a fashion show. They are concerned that, if the show appeared disorganized and amateur, the new store's image will be negatively affected.

As the two women weigh the pros and cons of accepting the invitation to sponsor the fashion show, they realize that they are at a standstill. The opportunity for positive public relations and free publicity seem to be exceptional, yet, at the same time, the responsibilities and time constraints seem to be overwhelming.

1   **If you were Courtney, what would you decide to do?**

2   **If you were the program chair of the local business women's organization, how would you collaborate on this fashion show event to encourage Courtney to participate?**

63 Pay Now and Play Later?

Shannon Channce is the men's casualwear buyer for a major
department store chain that is located throughout Florida. Shannon
is preparing his orders for the upcoming fall season with special
consideration given to the advertised items that he will feature in
August and September. He is frustrated that the advertising budget
for his department has been decreased significantly from last year
because of management's emphasis on lowering overhead costs.
"How can I effectively promote my department through radio and
newspaper promotions and manage to increase this year's sales volume over last fall's with only half the advertising funds I had last
year?" he asks himself. He shuffles through the notes he wrote
while previewing the manufacturers' new lines, then peruses the
advertising material the manufacturers provided. His limited
advertising budget has made him more interested than ever before
in the cooperative advertising funds offered by most of his vendors.

The majority of funds available through cooperative advertising
contracts are dependent on the dollar amount of orders placed by
the retail store with the manufacturer. For example, some vendors
will pay up to 50 percent of the cost of an advertisement; however,
the available cooperative advertising funds are based on 3 percent
of the total cost of orders placed with any particular vendor for the
year-to-date. "In other words," Shannon reflects, "the more I spend
with a manufacturer, the more they will assist me with the costs of
promoting their products." Many of the cooperative advertising
agreements have detailed, complicated requirements, for example,
featuring the manufacturer's name in the headline of a printed
advertisement and including the fabrication in the advertisement's

copy. "It takes a law degree simply to understand these contracts!" Shannon fumes.

As he juggles writing his orders for regular inventory and for advertised items, Shannon comes across his notes for a new manufacturer with whom he was extremely impressed. The merchandise is fresh and forward-looking, the prices are excellent, and the line is not carried by any of the store's competitors. Shannon believes that several of the styles are ideal for promoting the current fall trends. He excitedly telephones the manufacturers' representative of the new line to discuss the availability of cooperative advertising funds.

Unfortunately, the manufacturers' representative has bad news for Shannon. There are no available advertising funds. The rep explains that because the line is brand new, the company is putting all of its monies into the production and distribution of its quality merchandise. "Cooperative advertising funds would mean higher cost prices on the garments," the rep continued. "Let's work together now and, as the company grows, you will be the first to receive coop funds. We can guarantee you exclusivity at this point, Shannon. We won't sell the styles you select to advertise to any of your competitors," the rep concluded.

Shannon is confused. He must decide whether or not he selects advertisement styles from a vendor with whom there is the greatest availability of cooperative advertising funds or from the vendor he believes has the top-selling merchandise with an offer of exclusivity. If he chooses a vendor offering little or no cooperative advertising dollars, he must pay the price from his limited advertising budget to promote the merchandise. If he selects a vendor with whom there is cooperative advertising funds, the advertisement may generate more traffic because of a larger promotional effort than Shannon could support with his advertising budget. On the other hand, the new line without cooperative advertising may generate big profits through exclusive and forward-looking styles.

If you were in Shannon's position, which line would you advertise and how would you promote it?

Figure 9.1 *This is an example of an intimate apparel manufacturer's cooperative advertising plan for retail accounts.*

◆ RICARDO BORGIA LINGERIE, INC. ◆

Ricardo Borgia Cooperative Advertising Plan

Because we recognize the importance of newspaper advertising as a valuable means of promoting increased sales of all Ricardo Borgia Lingerie (RBL) products, we offer to our esteemed customers the following cooperative advertising plan. We have set this forth because we believe that it will assist both our retail customers, the ultimate consumer, and RBL in maintaining the very highest standards with regard to the public's perception and awareness of the quality found in the RBL lines, their image, and their status.

This plan is in effect until further notice for all ads run on or after June 1, 1996.

1 RBL and Customer Share. RBL will share 50% of the space-cost in accredited newspapers, based on the store's lowest earned rate, up to an amount not to exceed 4% of first quality, branded net purchases at wholesale for each season. This plan only covers first quality, branded net purchases (applied to all RBL lines).

2 Charges. Net cost is limited to your actual space-cost only. This agreement shall not include the cost of special preparation, art work, cuts or any other advertising or production costs. We do not share in the cost of agency fees or special service charges. We will share in 50% of the cost of newspaper color change. We do not share in mechanical or production costs for color reproduction.

3 Enclosure Advertising. Each season RBL will make attractive statement enclosures available. Enclosures are to be ordered on the special forms provided by our advertising department. Minimum quantity orders are necessary to qualify to receive these enclosures. Check with your sales representative for the minimum quantity necessary. A fraction of the actual cost of enclosures, $6.00 per thousand has been established and this amount will be applied against the 4% RBL cooperative advertising limit as set forth in this agreement.

4 Media. This plan covers newspaper advertising in all daily, weekly, and Sunday newspapers (no special editions), with recognized audited circulation and published rates. At our discretion, we will participate in the cost of magazine, television, and radio advertisements, as well as theatre programs, souvenir programs, circulars, or billboards under terms similar to those outlined in this plan for newspaper advertising. Final approval of the content of such ads and our share of the broadcast costs are contingent on our approval. To receive approval, see your sales representative. After receiving approval, a notarized affidavit from the station, which itemizes specific times and the commercial, must accompany your invoice.

5 Copy Requirements.
    a The RBL product-logotype must appear prominently in the advertisement. The Ricardo Borgia name must also appear in the heading or subheading as the use of the RBL product-logotype in graphics only will not meet our requirements. The Ricardo Borgia name must be as large as the largest type in the advertisement exclusive of the store's own logotype. We will supply the scan of the Ricardo Borgia logotype on a Macintosh diskette.
    b Competitive merchandise cannot appear in the same advertisement with the RBL name or product-logotype. If the advertisement shows other merchandise, this other merchandise must be goods other than lingerie, innerwear, robes, loungewear, or sleepwear. In addition to this requirement, the RBL portion of the advertisement must be separate and clearly defined, either outlined with a rule, or a surrounding white space of not less than 1/8 of an inch (.31 cm). If any other merchandise is shown in the advertisement, we reserve the right to final approval on such advertisement.
    c No advertisement in any media shall show a sale price or a markdown price on any RBL product. If a price is listed, it must be the full list price, given in an even dollar amount (e.g., $100, $148, $65). In addition to this requirement, any advertised sale that shows or presents any RBL product or that uses the RBL or the Ricardo Borgia name must obtain approval from our advertising department.

6 Payment. Invoices must be submitted within 45 days of publication. An advertising credit will be issued for the Ricardo Borgia share. No deductions are to be made for advertising prior to receiving the credit memo authorizing the amount to be deducted.

Please submit invoices accompanied by tearsheets for each advertisement to:

RBL Advertising Department
Ricardo Borgia Lingerie Products, Inc.
P.O. Box 456734
New York, NY 10109

We reserve the right to change or terminate this agreement at any time upon 30 days notice.

Figure 9.2 *This is an illustration of a manufacturer's cooperative advertising contract with a retail account.*

◄ **RBL PRODUCTS** ►

Ricardo Borgia Cooperative Advertising Plan

Ricardo Borgia Lingerie, Inc.
P.O. Box 456734
New York, NY 10109

Store_____Dept._____

Address_____

City_____State_____Zip Code_____

Buyer_____

Salesman_____Date_____

The above account has agreed to run the advertisements listed below, in accordance with our current cooperative advertising contract on the approximate date(s) that are indicated. The invoices will be sent to the RBL Products, Ricardo Borgia Lingerie, Inc., Cooperative Advertising Department, P.O. Box 456734, New York, NY 10109. RBL Products will be charged with no more than the amount that is indicated below as "RBL Share."

Important—The only logo or brand name identification to use for any advertising or promotional material is ◄ **RBL PRODUCTS** ►

Approximate Date of Ad	Styles to be Advertised	Name of Media	Ad Size	Lineage Rate	Cost of Ad	RBL Share

Prior Calendar Year   **Orders to Cover Ad(s)**

Volume $_____   Innerwear $_____

Coop $_____   Sleepwear $_____

Current Year to Date   Robes/Loungewear $_____

Shipped $_____   Advertising Department Approval_____

Unshipped $_____   _____

Coop Spent $_____   Date_____

◄ **RBL PRODUCTS** ► copy

---

64 **An Advertising Assessment**

Roseann Block is overwhelmed with one decision after another as she makes plans to finally open her own store—Mother Goosebumps. To own a successful retail business has been her professional objective for the past ten years. Her personal goals have come to fruition as she is the wife of a young farmer and the mother of four beautiful children. At this point in her life, she is combining her two goals by opening a children's wear boutique.

Roseann has leased the downtown retail building in which Mother Goosebumps has been located for the past five years under the previous store owners. After consulting with a bank, she purchased the existing inventory, the customer and vendor listing, the financial records, and all the fixtures from the retiring owners. She also made arrangements to assume the store name and logo. Roseann began her store ownership by marking down the remaining inventory and selling it out at greatly reduced prices. She is now ready to start fresh with the back-to-school season—which starts in a month.

Remodeling the store, purchasing fall merchandise, and installing a computer system required a tremendous amount of decision-making and expenditures by Roseann over the past few weeks. Although she dealt effectively with each of these steps, she is particularly perplexed with the choices to be made in regard to promoting her new business. Newspaper, radio, television, and novelty company sales representatives from the city have contacted her to present promotional packages that are designed to introduce the new Mother Goosebumps to the community. Although she recognizes the importance of informing potential consumers about the store's new ownership and her exciting plans for the store, Roseann is surprised at the expenses involved with all types of media promotions. She can envision spending several thousand dollars to announce the opening of her store; however, she needs to be extremely cost-conscious because of her family expenses and the unpredictable income generated by their farm.

Roseann has asked the media sales representatives about the cost-benefits of institutional advertising. They could not provide her with an actual return on investment calculation. They discussed the negative consequences of not promoting the store, yet were ambiguous about the potential sales volume that may be generated with each advertising dollar spent. When dealing with institutional advertising, it appears that it is extremely difficult to determine how much promotional expenses directly impacted consumer traffic and the subsequent sales volume.

Telling herself to "bite the bullet," Roseann decides to sample three types of media—television, newspaper, and radio. She purchases small promotional packages from the community's highest-rated television channel, the top radio station, and the newspaper with the largest circulation. She then decides to formulate a plan to evaluate the effects of these promotional endeavors.

1 **If you were the owner of Mother Goosebumps, how would you assess the impact of these promotional efforts?**

2 **If you were a media advertising executive, what would you offer Roseann to secure her business with your media company?**

3 **If you were the owner of a promotional firm, how would you advise Roseann in terms of formulating a promotional plan?**

Figure 9.3 *This is an illustration of a print advertisement produced by a retail operation to feature specific fashion merchandise.*

GARLAND STORES PRESENTS

A casual career look at a great price!

The look for versatility, comfort, simplicity and, of course, style. Our sandwashed silk blazer in both indigo and slate easily complements skirts, jeans and tights. Perfect for the Office or Weekends. Sizes 4-14. $179.00.
At all Garland Stores locations.

Figure 9.4 *This advertising checklist provides evaluation criteria for a newspaper advertisement.*

GARLAND STORES

CHECKLIST FOR ADVERTISING

Audience Appeal

		Yes	No
1	Does the advertisement contain information on advantages and benefits to our target shopper?	☐	☐
2	Does the advertisement appeal to the target shopper's needs and interests?	☐	☐
3	Does the advertisement make the target shopper aware of their needs and interests?	☐	☐
4	Does the advertisement present a positive image of both the product and the store?	☐	☐

Copy Guidelines

5	Does the copy use sentences of 10-11 words in length?	☐	☐
6	Is the copy in the present tense?	☐	☐
7	Is the copy brief and simple?	☐	☐
8	Is the store name in a prominent location in the advertisement?	☐	☐
9	Is the store name used in more than one place in the advertisement?	☐	☐

Content

10	Is the copy content appropriate to the store and to the product?	☐	☐
11	Does the copy state all the facts needed for understanding?	☐	☐
12	Is the illustration appropriate for the product and the store image?	☐	☐
13	Is the copy free of errors?	☐	☐

Layout

14	Does the advertisement use more than one color?	☐	☐
	How many colors? Specify_____		
15	Does the advertisement use a photograph(s)?	☐	☐
	How many photographs? Specify_____		
16	Does the advertisement use a line drawing(s)?	☐	☐
	How many line drawings? Specify_____		
17	Is store logo in a prominent location?	☐	☐
18	Is the letter/word spacing effective?	☐	☐

65   The Silent Salesperson

"You tell him," the store manager pleaded. "Not me," the visual merchandising assistant replied, "You don't understand—I have to work with him every day." Arlene Millstein, the store manager, is concerned about the window display decisions made by the company's visual merchandising director, Travis van Gundy. The department store chain, which has 15 locations in New York state, carries a full-range of budget to better apparel, soft goods, and home furnishings. The visual merchandising director and his team of assistants travel from branch store to branch store to install the primary window and interior displays. Travis is responsible for selecting the featured merchandise and for designing the actual displays. Once again, Arlene dissatisfied with his choices of window merchandise.

Arlene believes that the featured merchandise in the windows and displays should reflect the items that have been purchased in large quantities by the store's buyers. She thinks the window and interior displays are the most effective tools for promoting the quantity merchandise that she and her sales associates must sell. Items carried in depth for newspaper and catalog advertising and those of large, private label purchases are the goods Arlene thinks should be promoted through these primary displays.

Travis, on the other hand, believes that the window and interior displays should be designed to catch the consumer's eye. He thinks that unique items from the inventory should be showcased through the windows and displays. It is his theory that the windows should attract the customers and draw them into the store. He believes that such alternative promotional efforts as newspaper and catalog advertising will support the sales of the merchandise that has been purchased in great depth. Travis does not want the store to look like all of its competitors by featuring basic merchandise in its primary displays. He believes that the store's displays should be dramatic and innovative, envisioning his role as the visual merchandising director as that of a stage designer. Travis is not pleased that Arlene does not appreciate his creative work.

Arlene finally brings up her concerns about the selected display merchandise to Travis. Arlene is determined to convince Travis that the merchandise featured in the store's advertising should also be displayed in the windows and interior displays. Travis, on the other hand, is adamant that his philosophy of display design is correct. After all, he thinks, he is the one who has studied and trained in the field of visual merchandising. The discussion evolves to a heated debate that ends in an impasse. At Travis's suggestion, they decide to meet with Tom Green, the general merchandise manager, to discuss their conflicting views about the windows and interior displays. Both parties agree that they will conform to Mr. Green's decision.

1   **If you were in Arlene's position, what information would you present to convince the merchandise manager that your view of visual merchandising is the correct choice?**

2   **If you were in Travis' position, what would you say to the merchandise manager to persuade him that your perception of visual merchandising is the right one?**

3   **If you were in the general merchandise manager's position, what would you recommend?**

66 The Communication Connection

"The price is what really matters," shrugs the young man leaning back in his chair with his feet on the table. "No, I disagree," a tall woman in black quietly interjects, "It is the product image—its status. I believe we should go for snob appeal." "You are both wrong," the older man remarks, "It is the fit of the product that the customer appreciates." A young woman in contemporary designer apparel interrupts, "I cannot believe that none of you recognize that is the line's forward styling that makes it so appealing to the customer!"

The promotional division of Black Dog, a jeans manufacturer with an international retail distribution, is meeting to determine the corporation's seasonal campaign for back-to-school. The members of the promotional team are brainstorming the company's advertising approach to introduce the new fall line. The multitude of concepts are diverse—some are creative, while others are practical. Price, styling, fit, and prestige are among the central promotional messages the promotional staff has recommended so far. Additional ideas surface as the Black Dog team members discuss the option of using a current issue as a promotional theme. Some of their suggestions include: protecting the environment, supporting AIDS research, promoting safe sex, condemning domestic violence, and denouncing drug use.

One member of the promotional team mentions that the promotional campaign is an international effort because the primary advertisements will be featured worldwide. He believes that the corporation must express an international cultural awareness. He continues by stating that some of the popular topics in the U.S. are not necessarily issues of concern or agreement in countries abroad. The constituents of the promotional division acquiesce to this observation. They decide to take an alternative approach to using a current issue as the promotional theme for the advertising campaign.

After some discussion, the Black Dog promotional team debates using a celebrity model, a film or music industry star, and even an animated character as an advertising vehicle for the back-to-school promotion. They examine the costs, exclusivity, and international appeal associated with each of these suggestions. Following several hours of brainstorming, the group decides that they are at a stopping point and agree to return the next morning for a final meeting. At this time, each member of the promotional staff will individually present his/her preferred promotional message and a suggestion as to the vehicle by which the message will be distributed.

If you were a member of the Black Dog promotional team, what message would you recommend that the corporation disseminate through the back-to-school campaign and how would you accomplish this?

67   An Advertising Statement

Helen Haggerty, the advertising director of a department store chain, is planning the advertising mix for the retail operation's promotional campaign next month. As December traditionally provides the company's largest monthly sales volume and this year the company is planning an increase in sales, Helen is attempting to carefully balance the media types utilized for the store's promotional endeavors. Newspaper and television advertisements, special events, direct mail pieces, radio spots, and billboards are among the promotional vehicles that Helen is considering for her December promotional plan. As she evaluates all the media types, she is also determining the proportions of nonpersonal as opposed to personal messages transmitted by the various promotional efforts.

Helen decides that she will use a series of radio and television commercials as well as several billboards for the department store chain's institutional advertising campaign. She selects a number of the departmental items designated for advertising by the merchandising staff to feature in newspaper advertisements. Helen consults with the company's fashion coordinator in regard to a major fashion show production that will be presented at several of the chain store's mall locations. Finally, she concludes that items from the accessories, bed linen, and intimate apparel departments will be promoted through direct mail pieces. The merchandise promoted through direct mail will be featured as postcards, fliers, or statement enclosures. A statement enclosure—usually provided for a minimal fee by the manufacturer—is an envelope-sized page that features a photograph of the garment or item on one side and a written description of the product with a corresponding order form on the other side.

All these direct mail advertisements will be sent to the company's computerized mailing list, a compilation of the store's charge account customers and the personal customers of the firm's sales associates. Additionally, customers who have registered at the store locations to receive the company's mailings will receive the direct mail advertisements. The department store chain has an extensive mailing list that can be designated by location or customer type.

Helen meets with the intimate apparel buyer, Pat Salk, to inform her about the promotional plan for the hooded wrap robe selected as an advertised item from the intimate apparel department. Helen advises Pat that this particular item will be promoted through a statement enclosure. Pat is immediately defensive. She does not want the robe—the single item that she believes is the key to her department's holiday sales—to be advertised through a statement enclosure. She believes it will not receive adequate consumer exposure through direct mail. Instead, she insists that the hooded robe be featured as a full-page newspaper advertisement. Pat continues that she has negotiated 50 percent cooperative advertising funds from the manufacturer toward the cost of a full-page newspaper ad. Although Pat acknowledges that the robe manufacturer will provide the statement enclosures at a small fee, she denies that the cost of the postage and handling for the mailing is comparable to the price of the newspaper advertisement.

Helen leaves the meeting feeling frustrated with Pat's response to the advertising plan. Helen believes that she has spent a tremendous amount of time and effort constructing the total promotional strategy. She feels that Pat is being stubborn and that she has no basis for her perception that the robe will not sell as effectively when advertised in a statement enclosure as it would through a newspaper advertisement.

1   **If you were in Helen's position, what would you do about the advertising plan as it pertains to Pat's opposition to the statement enclosure featuring the robe?**

2   **If you were in Pat's situation, what would you do in regard to the statement enclosure as the choice of advertising media for the robe?**

Chapter 10
Human Relations in the Workplace

Careers in Retail Management

There is good news and bad news. Let us begin with the bad news and end with the good. A successful career in retail management or merchandising initially requires many long hours and hard work. Exceptions to this rule are extremely rare. Prerequisites for entering an executive career path in apparel and soft goods marketing are an appropriate education and work experience. A bachelor's degree is required by most major firms before they will consider hiring you as a management or merchandising trainee. Additionally, the vast majority of industry employers expect entry-level executives to have obtained work experience, such as summer employment and/or an internship enrollment. While the employment expectations are high (long hours, hard work, prior work experience, and a college degree), the opportunities are diverse, profitable, and exciting.

What qualifications and attributes do employers look for in prospective employees? Effective communication skills are essential. These communication abilities should be verbal and written. Quantitative or mathematical skills are equally important, as is computer literacy. Managerial skills are necessary, particularly the ability to delegate authority and responsibility. Managerial attributes should also include effective time management, a fair and impartial attitude, and a tactful approach. From a personal standpoint, employers seek candidates who exhibit flexibility, energy, creativity, enthusiasm, and curiosity. Entry-level executives are expected to be healthy, both emotionally and physically. Finally, employers prefer management and merchandising employees who have a keen ability to get along with others—superiors, subordinates, peers, vendors, and customers.

In the following case studies, you will investigate career obstacles and opportunities for the merchandising and management employee. From recognizing career obstacles to adapting to company ownership changes, the young executive is frequently faced with decision-making and problem-solving that may determine a future career path.

68 **Musical Chairs in Fashion Retailing**

Megan Meyer had been an assistant buyer in the misses' dress department of a family-owned specialty store chain for two years. She loved her job, admired her buyer, and was working toward a promotion to the accessories buyer position within the next year. Then it happened—suddenly and unexpectedly. The specialty store chain operation verified in a corporate memo that it had been purchased by a major department store ownership group. The new corporate management staff would arrive within a few weeks to meet with all current employees in regard to future employment concerns. Rumors flew within the buying office. Some buyers believed that the entire buying office would be eliminated as the ownership group had its own centralized buying staff and resident buying office in New York. In anticipation of this prediction, a few of the buyers mentioned that they would begin a job search immediately. Others speculated that everything would remain the same; it was simply a financial ownership change. Some on the buying staff were extremely positive that the new ownership group would have the funds to put additional monies into the stores for larger inventories, additional advertising, and higher salaries. The only thing that the buying personnel agreed upon was that no one agreed on what would happen next.

Megan was completely confused and somewhat frightened. She worried about maintaining her present lifestyle through a continued income, starting over on her career path, and possibly relocating to find a new equitable position. Megan asked for advice from her buyer, Annie Wilson. Annie began, "It's probably premature to panic at this point, but I'm going to update my resumé and get my personnel file in order. I want to make sure that my curriculum vitae reflects my successes, which are a 20 percent increase in sales volume last year, my involvement in the community, and the promotions I negotiated with our vendors over the past few seasons. Those are the types of accomplishments I want the new owners to know about. I'd suggest you do the same. Also, it's a good idea to do some research on this new ownership group to find out the other companies that it owns and how those transitions went. I'll telephone some of our major vendors to see if they have additional information." Annie concluded, "Megan, don't worry about it now. Before you make a decision, wait until the new corporate representatives have spoken with us and until you've gathered more information. You'll know what to do and I'll keep you updated." Megan was relieved to have a plan of action and to have a colleague of such compassion and calmness.

A couple of weeks later, the new ownership group sent representatives from its management staff to the specialty store buying office. After meeting with the representatives, the future of the buying staff was still unclear. The representatives were not specific about the ownership group's plans for centralized or decentralized buying. They simply assured the buyers and assistant buyers that their job descriptions, salaries, and employment benefits would remain the same for the next six months. During that time period, the ownership group would evaluate and determine the future of the specialty store buying office in collaboration with the specialty store chain's buying staff. Monthly meetings were scheduled as the buyers' and assistant buyers' recommendations would be incorporated into the decision-making process. Additionally, the representatives would meet individually with each of the buyers and assistant buyers to review their credentials, to solicit suggestions for the buying function, and to answer questions.

Megan was concerned with the prospect of waiting for six months before learning about her future potential with the company. "The stress and uncertainty may be overwhelming," she thought. Megan decides that her first priority is to effectively prepare for her individual meeting with the ownership group representatives. She plans to develop a portfolio representing her personal accomplishments. She will also construct a list of recommendations in regard to the buying division for the ownership group meeting. Megan determines that she will meet with the corporate representatives before developing a further plan of action to deal with the ambiguity of her current job situation.

1   What materials, information, and questions would you prepare for your individual meeting with the ownership group representatives if you were in Megan's position?

2   What recommendations would you make to the ownership group representatives in regard to the buying function of the store?

3   If you were in Megan's position, what would you determine as a plan of action following your meeting with the ownership group representatives?

69　The Too Good to be True Assistant Buyer

Thomas Scott was concluding his first twelve months as an assistant buyer in the men's wear division of a major resident buying office located in New York. He was scheduled to receive a first year evaluation through a personnel review with Michael Johnson, the men's wear division buyer, as a requirement for a potential salary increase and possible promotion. Mr. Johnson is a respected executive in the men's wear market with nearly forty years of buying experience under his belt. He has worked successfully as a retail store buyer, then as a resident buyer in both ladies' and men's apparel.

Thomas was confident that his first year evaluation would be a positive experience. He was anxious to receive the recommendation that would support his promotion to the position of buyer. Almost daily, Mr. Johnson commented on Thomas' superior work performance. Over the past twelve months, Thomas had learned quickly and worked diligently. Johnson had come to count on Thomas in nearly every aspect of the buying function. Mr. Johnson had expended much time and effort to train Thomas to handle responsibilities greater than those of most of the other departmental assistant buyers.

After his initial months of exposure to the assistant buyer position, Thomas eventually became responsible for communicating with the client stores monthly, following up on shipments due from the manufacturers, placing reorders on hot-sellers, maintaining the on-order records, visiting the vendors to preview new items or lines, and summarizing the sales reports. Michael Johnson frequently referred to Thomas as his "right arm." The client store buyers regularly relied on Thomas for assistance with returns to vendors, cooperative advertising requests, and promotional suggestions. He felt appreciated by his supervisor and valued by the buying office's retail accounts. Thomas believed that he would soon receive the promotion he had been working toward. His evaluation meeting next week would determine whether or not Thomas had reached this goal.

As they sat down for their evaluation meeting, Mr. Johnson brought out a list of summarizing Thomas' strengths and his areas for improvement. The number of strengths substantially outweighed the areas for improvement. Johnson cited Thomas' strengths as his exceptional oral and written communication skills, his quantitative analysis abilities, his "people skills," and his ability to learn quickly and to retain information. Mr. Johnson indicated that Thomas needed to work on his delegation skills when given a major project and his enthusiasm when presenting merchandise to the client store buyers. Thomas agreed with the evaluation points and was pleased to receive a fair and helpful review.

Mr. Johnson concluded, "Thomas, I don't believe that you're ready yet for the buyer position that will be available next month in ladies' accessories. First, you need more time in the field, time to learn more about the business and to work on the areas in which you need improvement. You're young and have just started in this business. You will have plenty of opportunities to move into a buying position. Secondly, you don't have any resident buying office experience in the ladies' apparel division. Finally, I can't imagine how I'd get along without your help. Normally it takes years to train an assistant to do what you do." He continued, "I am going to recommend you for the optimum salary increase for an assistant buyer. However, I can't recommend you for the buying position at this time, Thomas. Don't let it get you down—your time will come soon enough. I will be retiring in a couple of years and, by then, you will be the ideal candidate for this buying job." Thomas thanked Mr. Johnson for his candid evaluation and quietly left the office.

By the time Thomas arrived home, his head was whirling. He had really wanted that promotion to ladies' accessories buyer. He questioned whether or not he had made himself too valuable in his present assistant buying position. Thomas began to feel resentment toward Mr. Johnson as he wondered if Johnson was intentionally holding him back for his own personal benefit.

Thomas replayed the evaluation session in his mind and attempted to formulate the questions he should have asked. He decided that he would develop a plan tonight and deal with his questions and concerns at work the next day.

1   **If you were in Thomas Scott's position, what would you do?**

2   **If you were in Michael Johnson's place, what would you do?**

3   **Additionally, develop a brief response that Thomas Scott could have provided for Michael Johnson during the evaluation session.**

Figure 10.1 *The employee evaluation form below is used to assess the performance levels of the assistant buyer.*

GARLAND STORES
EXECUTIVE PERFORMANCE EVALUATION MX 10535 (1/77)
ASSISTANT BUYER

NAME

Spring ....
Fall ....

1 = Unacceptable	2 = Marginal	3 = Good	4 = Very Good	5 = Outstanding
☒ ☐ ☐ ☐ ☐ 1 2 3 4 5	☐ ☒ ☐ ☐ ☐ 1 2 3 4 5	☐ ☐ ☒ ☐ ☐ 1 2 3 4 5	☐ ☐ ☐ ☒ ☐ 1 2 3 4 5	☐ ☐ ☐ ☐ ☒ 1 2 3 4 5

1	2	3	4	5	**MERCHANDISE RESPONSIBILITY**
☐	☐	☐	☐	☐	1. Initiates plans/actions to optimize sales.
☐	☐	☐	☐	☐	2. Understands the importance of floor presentation by proper classification, color, or trend.
☐	☐	☐	☐	☐	3. Understands the components of coordinated merchandise presentation by proper arrangement/assortment.
☐	☐	☐	☐	☐	4. Understands the importance of proper stock levels relative to the business.
☐	☐	☐	☐	☐	5. Sees that stock is filled in, labelled accurately as to price and size, counted per schedule, and is neat and accessible.
☐	☐	☐	☐	☐	6. Department records are kept up to date correctly (RTVs, markdowns, recaps, turnover, etc.)
☐	☐	☐	☐	☐	7. Plans actions and recommendations for assigned classification, which reflect an understanding of the department's current potential, trends, seasonal needs, and past experience.

1	2	3	4	5	**MERCHANDISE KNOWLEDGE**
☐	☐	☐	☐	☐	1. Understands the Open-to-Buy concept.
☐	☐	☐	☐	☐	2. Understands merchandising reports/information and effectively utilizes them.
☐	☐	☐	☐	☐	3. Understands the flow of paperwork and related systems.
☐	☐	☐	☐	☐	4. Able to project and forecast in a concise and precise manner (rates of sale, reorders, etc.)

1	2	3	4	5	**LEADERSHIP RESPONSIBILITY**
☐	☐	☐	☐	☐	1. Constantly apprises and informs sales staff is of merchandise selection and trends.
☐	☐	☐	☐	☐	2. Is flexible and can adapt to the changing needs of the business within the context of the department's goal and objectives.
☐	☐	☐	☐	☐	3. Is well informed of the merchandise situations (on hand, on order, best seller by store, stock conditions); the action of the competition; department problems and recommended solutions.
☐	☐	☐	☐	☐	4. Informs suburban department managers (through communication, store visits, etc.)
☐	☐	☐	☐	☐	5. Interacts well and deals effectively with other divisions in the store.
☐	☐	☐	☐	☐	6. Takes constructive criticism well and tries to correct shortcomings.
☐	☐	☐	☐	☐	7. Is well motivated and a self-starter.
☐	☐	☐	☐	☐	8. Maintains high standards for self and department.

1	2	3	4	5	**PLANNING AND ORGANIZATION**
☐	☐	☐	☐	☐	1. Is well organized and apportions time constructively and wisely.
☐	☐	☐	☐	☐	2. Meets deadlines and schedules.
☐	☐	☐	☐	☐	3. Reacts to the changing needs of the business by taking actions which reflect a basic understanding of priorities.
☐	☐	☐	☐	☐	4. Learns quickly and effectively.

Figure 10.1 (Continued)

ACCOMPLISHMENTS

What specific measurable results has this individual accomplished in the appraisal period (sales growth, profit):

....

....

....

....

OBJECTIVES

What specific business objectives are to be achieved by the next evaluation period:

....

....

....

....

....

....

....

....

....

FUTURE GROWTH AND DEVELOPMENT

What ideas and thoughts do you have for this individual's professional development:

....

....

....

....

....

....

....

....

....

....

....

1	2	3	4	5	**OVERALL EVALUATION**
☐	☐	☐	☐	☐	Performance as a merchant
☐	☐	☐	☐	☐	Performance as a leader
☐	☐	☐	☐	☐	Potential for advancement

Discussed With Assistant Buyer:

Signature .... Date ....

Rater's Signature .... Salary Action ....

70 Lost Lace, Misplaced Money, and Burgled Buttons

Rachel Roberts is the sole proprietor of a fabric shop, Fabrics Facile, located in a Kansas City suburb. Rachel has six employees in her store—an assistant manager and five sales associates. Rachel loves her work; her employees are a unified team and her customers are loyal and pleasant to serve. She earns a substantial income as a business owner and is able to arrange a somewhat flexible schedule. Usually, Rachel manages Fabrics Facile from nine o'clock in the morning to five o'clock in the afternoon while her assistant manager Corrine manages the store nights and weekends.

Corrine Smith is a middle-aged woman who knows the "ins and outs" of the fabric business because she has worked in fabric stores since high school. Rachel values Corrine's knowledge of fabric resources and appreciates her assistance in buying and pricing merchandise. Corrine also assists Rachel with accounting, inventory, and payroll duties. Rachel hired Betty Larkin as a sales associate because of her knowledge of sewing and smocking clothing for her children and grandchildren. Another sales associate, Debra Jones, is a young mother with tailoring experience who enjoys working at Fabrics Facile, which allows her a flexible schedule. Brooke Gold is a high school student who works at the store part-time during evenings and weekends—she is planning a career in the fashion industry. Lea Jeffers has extensive experience as a quilter and provides quilting lessons for the store's interested clientele. Finally, Christine Dean is a part-time sales associate who specializes in bridal sewing needs. She also works as a wedding consultant outside of her hours at Fabrics Facile.

For the past two months, the records have indicated that the register has been short 20 dollars on five separate occasions. At first, Rachel assumed that the shortages were caused by clerical errors, resulting from giving the customer incorrect change. Later, she began to suspect that one of her sales associates may be stealing from the cash register. When reordering items in the locked bridal case, Rachel noticed that several expensive buttons and two bolts of beaded lace were missing from the shelves. Because employees alternate monitoring the cash register and all have access to the bridal case key, Rachel feels certain that internal theft is being committed by one or more of her employees. She reflects that none of her employees have exhibited suspicious behavior. She does not want to damage the morale of her staff by pointing a finger at an innocent worker. However, if she allows the theft to continue any longer, her profits will suffer because of this employee dishonesty.

Rachel determines that she must directly deal with the problems of missing funds and inventory. She has grown to think of her employees as friends, perhaps even as family. She feels disappointed and betrayed by the situation of internal theft, but she is determined to learn who is stealing from her.

If you were Rachel Roberts, what would you do?

71   On The Take?

Specialty Stores Limited is one of the well-known New York resident buying offices that services small specialty store chains. Its clientele is located throughout the U.S. with the vast majority of its accounts in the midwest. One of the office's most successful accounts—Eureka!—is located in St. Louis, Missouri and specializes in contemporary junior apparel.

The owners of Eureka! have recently hired a new dress buyer, Emmi Green. Emmi is an energetic and intelligent young woman who has worked several years as a buyer for the junior dress department of a smaller specialty store. She is delighted to have the exceptional opportunity to work for a chain store of this caliber and is eager to prove herself to her new employer. She has met with the resident junior dress buyer of Specialty Stores Limited, Kathryn King, and has followed her advice to view the new resource that Kathryn has been touting. Pizazz is a fairly new dress manufacturer that Kathryn highly recommended.

Emmi previewed the new line at Pizazz and was not overly impressed. She placed a small order, however, based on the high ratings that Kathryn had given the vendor. While Emmi was working the line, Kathryn came into the showroom and was treated like a queen by the showroom manager and salespeople. Later, when the merchandise arrived at the store, Emmi felt that the quality was poor and the fit was less than satifactory. As the retail selling performance of Pizazz was mediocre, Emmi was glad that she had not purchased the line in any depth.

A few weeks ago, Emmi received a resident office bulletin featuring two of the Pizazz styles she had ordered as "reorder styles."

She could not believe her eyes and double-checked their sales figures on her inventory records. She found that these styles were among her slowest-sellers! On a hunch, she then visited a competitive store and found these two Pizazz styles on a markdown rack. Emmi could not understand why Kathryn would continue to recommend this resource—particularly these styles. She began to believe that Kathryn must be receiving a "payoff" from Pizazz for pushing the line to the resident buying office's client stores.

Although Emmi feels confident that Kathryn is "on the take," she is worried if she tells the Eureka! store owners about her concerns, word will get back to the resident buying office. There is the possibility that Kathryn will hear of this speculation and perceive it as a breach of trust. It would then be extremely difficult for Emmi and Kathryn to work together effectively. If Emmi is correct and the acceptance of graft can be proven, Kathryn may be fired. But this would be nearly impossible to prove as the resident buyer and the manufacturer will naturally deny collusion. More important—who would the retail store and the resident buying office believe—a new, young retail buyer or an experienced, older resident buyer?

1 If you were in Emmi's position, what would you do?

2 If you were in Kathryn's position, how would you justify your recommendation of Pizazz?

72   A Mixed Message

The Zipper is an apparel chain of over 100 store units that caters to a target market of males and females between the ages of 12 and 30 years old. The merchandise is fun and fashionable and the sales staff is young and energetic. 19-year-old Nanci Hubbard has been with the company for over two years as a part-time sales associate. She is presently working in one of the branch stores located in a Los Angeles suburb; however, she is leaving this area in a few months to attend college in San Diego. Nanci hopes to secure a position with The Zipper's San Diego branch store in order to continue her part-time employment while attending classes at the university.

Nanci is informed by her present store manager, Melody Place, that there will be a position for her with The Zipper team in San Diego. Melody indicates that all Nanci will need to do is to contact Mary Jean Zachary, the San Diego store manager, upon her arrival at the university. She stated that Nanci should schedule an appointment to go into the store for a brief, informal meeting with Mary Jean. "You will have no problem getting a job there," she concluded, "It will be a simple transfer that will not even require another interview." Nanci is relieved that she will be able to maintain employment with The Zipper because she enjoys working at the store and knows the merchandise and store policies and procedures well. "It will be great to have a job that I am familiar with," she thinks, "because I will need to really concentrate on my classes."

When Nanci arrives in San Diego, she contacts Mary Jean and arrives at the store to meet her a few days later on Saturday. When she finally arrives, Mary Jean asks her to come back at the beginning of the week when the store is not so busy. As Nanci's schedule is hectic, several days pass before she is able to return to the store. Mary Jean hands Nanci an employment application to complete before they begin their discussion. Although Nanci is a little surprised that she is required to fill out the form, she assumes that it was necessary for her employment file at this branch store. Mary Jean then briefly interviews Nanci, concluding with the question, "What do you believe that you can do for our team here?" Nanci replies, "I think that I have a good deal of knowledge that I can share with your employees and that I could become a leader on the sales floor."

Mary Jean wraps up the interview by thanking Nanci for her time and interest in employment with The Zipper. "It was a pleasure to meet you, Nanci," she says, "If you do not receive a telephone call from me by the end of the week, then good luck with your job search."

"Good luck with my job search?" Nanci thinks as she leaves the store. "I am not supposed to be job hunting. This is my job—it was to be a simple transfer between stores!" Nanci hopes she is wrong, but does not receive a phone call from Mary Jean by the end of the week.

1   If you were in Nanci's position, what would you do?

2   If you were Melody Place, what would you do to help Nanci secure a job at the other Zipper store?

Figure 10.2 *The following employment application is used as part of the interview process for prospective employees of a retail operation.*

GARLAND STORES, INC.

EMPLOYMENT APPLICATION

Our employment policy is equal opportunity for all without discrimination because of race, color, creed, sex, age, religion, or national origin.

Name : First Middle Last Today's date:

Social Security No.: Present Address: Street City State Zip Code

How long at address? Phone Number:

Prior Address: Street City State Zip Code How long at address?

Former Name: Date of Change:

Position Applied for: Other positions for which you are qualified:

Schedule desired: ◯ Full-time days ◯ Full-time evenings ◯ Part-time days ◯ Part-time evenings Will you work weekends? ◯ Yes ◯ No

When can you start? Are you a U.S. citizen? ◯ Yes ◯ No Visa No.:

Do you have any impairments, physical, mental, or medical which would place restrictions on your ability to work in any capacity? If yes, please describe

Have you been convicted of a crime within the last ten years? ◯ Yes ◯ No If yes, please give details:

What means of transportation will you use to get to work? Are you currently employed? ◯ Full Time ◯ Part Time ◯ Not Employed

How were you referred to us? Have you ever applied to a Garland Store before (including any GS Superstore)? ◯ Yes ◯ No

If yes, please specify store, job, and duties:

List all friends and relatives currently working for Garland Stores.

Please specify store(s).

Work History (Include Military duty, if applicable)

Current or Most Recent Employment	Name of Company		Address		
Job Title/Duties	From:	To:	Start Salary	End Salary	
	MO YR	MO YR			
Reason for Leaving			Supervisor's Name, Title, Phone #		

Previous Employment	Name of Company		Address		
Job Title/Duties	From:	To:	Start Salary	End Salary	
	MO YR	MO YR			
Reason for Leaving			Supervisor's Name, Title, Phone #		

Previous Employment	Name of Company		Address		
Job Title/Duties	From:	To:	Start Salary	End Salary	
	MO YR	MO YR			
Reason for Leaving			Supervisor's Name, Title, Phone #		

Please complete reverse side.

Figure 10.2 (Continued)

Education

School:	Name and Address of School	Course of Study	Date From:	DateTo:	Circle last Year Completed	Did you Graduate?	List Diploma or Degree
College			MO YR	MO YR	13 14 15 16		
High School (or G.E.D.)			MO YR	MO YR	9 10 11 12		
Other (Specify)			MO YR	MO YR	17 18 19 20		

Hours Available for Work   Comments

Mon.	From	To	
Tues.	From	To	
Wed.	From	To	
Thurs.	From	To	
Fri.	From	To	
Sat.	From	To	
Sun.	From	To	

Important: Read Carefully

I certify that the information in this application is correct to the best of my knowledge and I understand that falsification of this information is grounds for dismissal in accordance with Garland Stores policy. Garland Stores, in considering my application for employment, may verify the information set forth on this application and obtain additional information relating to my background. I authorize all persons, schools, companies, corporation, credit bureaus, and law enforcement agencies to supply any information concerning my background, and release all parties from all liability for any damage the may result from furnishing same to you. In accepting employment, I acknowledge that the policies, benefits, and other programs listed in the benefits booklet and policy manuals do no infer or imply a contract of employment between Garland Stores and myself. I realize that the aforementioned benefits, policies, and programs ar provided at Garland Stores discretion and may be changed or eliminated at any time. In consideration of employment, I agree to conform to the rules and regulations of Garland Stores. I also realize that my first 90 days of employment is considered to a probationary period and that during that time my employment and compensation can be terminated, with or without notice, at any time, at the option of Garland Stores or myself.

I acknowledge that I read and understand this statement.

Signature of Applicant (Do Not Print)   Date:

Please Do Not Write Below This Line

Post Employment Information

Marital Status: ○ Divorced ○ Married ○ Single ○ Widowed   Birthdate:

Spouse's Name (If Applicable)

In Case of Emergency, Notify: Name   Address   Relationship   Phone

Non-Hire Information   Reason for Non-Hire:

○ Candidate not interested because   ○ Candidate not qualified because

○ No suitable openings at this time   ○ Better candidate available

○ Other   Manager's Signature   Date

73 The New Boss

Baxter's is a specialty women's clothing store located in San Antonio, Texas. The store employs ten sales associates and a store manager. Because the store owner operates several other businesses, he only briefly visits Baxter's weekly to oversee the general operation of the company. After the store manager of ten years left because of her husband's job relocation, the company owner recently hired a new manager, Bob Davis.

Upon his arrival, Mr. Davis immediately began making changes in the employee policies. He altered the dress code that previously permitted jeans and shorts to more professional apparel of skirts and pants. As most of the employees were students, they had limited funds to purchase new work wardrobes. There were other more uncomfortable changes. When the store closed at the end of the day, Mr. Davis often offered to buy the employees drinks. Additionally, the employees saw him leaving the store a few times during the course of each day to visit the local bar. When he returned, he smelled of cologne and breath mints.

Within two weeks, Mr. Davis threatened all the employees with termination. He said that if they could not produce the sales volume quotas, he would find sales associates who could. The employees became more and more nervous and angry and as the tension grew to an uncomfortable level, several individual employees spoke with the owner about the decline in employee morale.

Mr. Davis seemed as though he was simply waiting for the employees to resign or to find a reason to fire them. And the store owner was doing nothing about the situation.

If you were one of the employees at Baxter's, what would you do?

74 I'd Rather Do It Myself

Brandi Gann is an executive trainee in the management training program of Dryer's, a large department store chain. She is a conscientious and ambitious employee who has aspirations of eventually becoming a store manager for Dryer's. Brandi is enjoying the management training program and has learned much about the company and the retailing business in general through its class sessions. As the training program is coming to a close, the management trainees are now receiving the key assignment that will determine their placement in the company's management staff at the close of the program.

The trainees are divided into groups of five persons and given a project that they will complete as committees. Brandi's team is charged with development of a plan to reverse the declining sales in the children's wear department of the flagship store. It is an exciting and familiar challenge for Brandi because she was employed as a sales associate in the children's wear area during her internship. The class of trainees has dispersed to begin work on their committee projects.

From the initial meeting, Brandi's committee members simply do not get along together. One of the members attempts to take charge and totally dominate the discussion. Two other trainees sit back and appear to be totally disinterested in the proceedings. The fourth member of the team plays devil's advocate and disagrees with every suggestion the participating committee members offer. Brandi is both frustrated and worried. If the committee does not receive a high score on this project, the team members will receive low placement for the available management positions. Rather than receiving the preferred position of assistant store manager, the trainees with the lowest evaluations will be assigned to the department manager positions. These trainees will have to work their way up to the assistant manager slots through several positive six-month reviews.

In addition to the group score assigned to the project by the directors of the executive training program, the trainees will receive separate scores for their personal contributions to their respective committees. The team members will individually submit confidential evaluation forms for each of the peers on their team. Brandi is concerned that if she was overly aggressive and controlling, her peer evaluations will portray her as an ineffective team player. As the ability to work successfully with others is an important attribute in employees to the company's management staff, the peer assessments are a critical factor in the placement of the executive training program graduates.

Brandi decides to prepare for the second meeting of the committee with a new positive attitude and an organized approach to the project. She constructs a list of suggestions to turn around the children's wear department's sales volume and develops the pros and cons to each suggestion. She plans a strategy that will enable the committee members to work effectively as a team. Brandi decides that she will politely attempt to draw all of the committee members into the discussion. She intends to solicit recommendations from each team member and alternate between taking the roles of leader and listener. Brandi is looking forward to the committee's next meeting because she believes it will be a productive session.

She is so wrong! It is a disastrous rerun of the first meeting—the team members argued, sulked, withdrew, and eventually came to a stalemate. Nothing productive has been accomplished in two meetings and the committee has just one week to submit their final project. Brandi is so upset that she is considering requesting permission from the executive training program directors to complete the project on her own. She feels that she simply cannot work with this group.

1   **What would you do if you were in Brandi's position?**

2   **If you were one of the program directors and you found out about Brandi's problem with this particular group, what would you do to remedy the situation?**

Glossary

Administered vertical marketing system A type of *marketing channel* that coordinates successive stages of production and distribution through the size and power of one of the parties, not through common ownership. See case number 18, page 95.

Advertising A group of activities that involves the presentation of a mass message about a product or an organization; the message is paid for by an identified sponsor. See case number 61, page 235.

Advocacy advertising A type of promotional *advertising* designed to support a particular cause, such as the "Made In America" campaign. See case number 12, page 75.

Advocate communication channel A promotional method that uses salespersons to contact potential buyers in the *target market*. See case number 13, page 81.

Affective The *buyer readiness state* of a *target market* in which consumer liking, preference, and conviction is often used to promote existing products. See case number 34, page 144.

Affordable method A technique used to determine *promotion budgets;* based on the dollar amount a company can afford at the moment. See case number 61, page 235.

Analysis and costing of communication objectives and tasks A method used to determine *promotion budgets*, which examines the expenses involved in supporting individual communication efforts; this is weighed against the anticipated impact (i.e., the benefit) each effort will provide. It is a type of cost effectiveness method for communication budgets. See case number 64, page 243.

Assortment The total number of items in the *product mix*.

Basic stock An assortment of items that have consistent customer demand.

Behavioral The *buyer readiness state* of awareness and knowledge that focuses on motivating the consumer to immediately purchase the product.

Biogenic buying motive Consumer purchasing incentive that relates to physical needs (e.g., food, shelter, sex).

Branch division Functional division of an organization that is responsible for the operation of the multiple units (i.e., branches) of an organization. See case number 8, page 66.

Brand A name, term, sign, symbol, design, or any combination of these; intended to identify the goods or services of one seller or group of sellers; also used to differentiate these products or services from those of competitors. See case number 37, page 155.

Brand advertising A type of advertising effort designed to promote a particular *brand*. See case number 37, page 155.

Brand mark The part of a *brand* that can be recognized, but not be spoken. Usually a type of symbol.

Brand name The part of a *brand* that can be vocalized. See case number 37, page 155.

Breadth That characteristic of an *inventory* assortment, which offers a large number of different types of products, but not necessarily a large stock of any one style. See case number 44, page 177.

Break even analysis A method used to determine the price (this can be wholesale or retail) at which any product will have to be sold in order to cover all the costs.

Buyer readiness state Term used to identify the potential purchasing behavior of a *target market*. See case number 14, page 84.

Buying process Steps (i.e., process) the consumer goes through when deciding what, when, where, and how to buy; these steps include need recognition, information search, evaluation, purchase decision, and post-purchase behavior. See case number 14, page 84.

Chain store A type of business ownership, which comprises multiple retail outlets under common ownership. In this type of ownership, major functions (e.g., buying, advertising, employment) are usually controlled by a central headquarters. See case number 70, page 263.

Chain operation Multiple operations under common ownership whose major functions (e.g., buying, advertising, human resource management) are often controlled by a central headquarters; the operations handle or carry similar lines of merchandise. See case number 71, page 265.

Classified advertising Notices and advertising by classification under headings; sold by the line or by the number of words. See case number 64, page 243.

Cognitive A *buyer readiness state* of awareness and knowledge; commonly used for new product introduction. See case number 42, page 166.

Competitive-parity method A technique for setting a promotion budget as based on competitors' expenditures.

Consistency The relationship of the various *product lines* to each other in end use, production requirements, or distribution channels.

Consumer cooperative association A type of business ownership in which consumers own shares in the operation. Owners decide business policy and actual operations are determined and maintained by a manager.

Content The informational part of a promotional message. See case number 59, page 220.

Contractor A manufacturing company that produces finished merchandise for a company; may be domestic (i.e., made in the U.S.) or foreign (i.e., made overseas). See case number 36, page 148.

Contractual vertical system A *marketing channel*, which consists of independent firms at different levels of production and distribution. These different levels integrate their programs on retailer cooperatives and franchise organizations. See case number 7, page 62.

Control Division of an organization charged with safeguarding the company's financial status; responsibilities include accounting and record keeping, credit and collections, budgeting, and inventory control. A functional division in the *Mazur Plan*. See case number 11, page 73.

Convenience goods Those goods the consumer usually purchases frequently, immediately, and with minimum effort in comparison and buying. This is merchandise the consumer expects to have readily available at a convenient location.

Conventional marketing channel Traditional distribution arrangement of separate business entities (i.e., independent producer, wholesaler, and retailer), which moves the product from the manufacturer to the consumer. See case number 58, page 218.

Cooperative advertising A type of advertising arrangement in which a manufacturer provides advertising funds to a retailer in exchange for the purchase of goods and name recognition in promotional efforts. See case number 37, page 155.

Copyright The legal right granted to an author, a designer, a composer, a playwright, or distributor to exclusive publication, production, sale, or distribution of a literary, musical, dramatic, or artistic work; also applies also to *brand names*, slogans, and other marketing verbage. See case number 42, page 166.

Corporate vertical system A *marketing channel* that combines successive stages of production and distribution under a single ownership. See case number 55, page 211.

Corporation Legal form of business organization in which stockholders invest in the company, but do not necessarily share in management decisions. Usually, major decisions are made by a board of directors, while daily operations are conducted by executives and employees of the operation. Stockholders have limited personal responsibility for the firm's debts, as determined by the amount of their investments. See case number 55, page 211.

Cost factors The variables that are combined to determine the selling price of an item of merchandise. See case number 53, page 201.

Cost-plus pricing A method for determining a price of an item or service, which is based on the cost of an item with the addition of a dollar amount, usually based on a predetermined markup percent. See case number 41, page 164.

Culture A type of market segmentation, which is inseparable from lifestyle; term refers to the behavior typical of a group or class. See case number 17, page 93.

Customary pricing A pricing strategy that assumes the customer expects a certain product to be available at a certain price; this strategy also assumes that any significant deviation in either direction from that customary price will result in decreased demand. See case number 57, page 216.

Demand pricing A pricing strategy that assumes there is a relationship between the selling price of an item and the amount that can be sold. See case number 50, page 194.

Demographics Term that refers to the breakdown of the consumer population into statistical categories. Category examples include age, gender, education, occupation, income, households, and marital status. See case number 19, page 99.

Depth Refers to the number of variants within each product of a full line; also used to describe an inventory assortment offering limited versions of popular styles (e.g., large number of colors or sizes in a limited number of styles). See case number 44, page 177.

Direct purchasing Buying merchandise directly from a source, rather than through a middleman. See case number 55, page 211.

Direct ratings A method of collecting feedback on types of promotions in which consumers determine the type of advertisement that would influence them to buy the product. See case number 64, page 243.

Discount terms A manufacturer's reduction in the price of goods offered to the retailer for early order placement, early payment, quantity purchases, and so forth. See case number 6, page 57.

Domestic manufacturers Producers that are based in and which produce goods in the U.S. See case number 36, page 148.

Downward vertical communication channel Communication that extends from manager to employee. See case number 56, page 213.

Dual distribution Multichannel marketing systems that operate on two different consumer levels; for example, a manufacturer that sells to retail stores and also operates its own factory outlets. See case number 55, page 211.

Durable goods Tangible products that normally survive many uses. See case number 39, page 159.

Economic environment An external influence on business that includes consumer and governmental spending, consumption, and saving. A component of the *external environment*. See case number 30, page 134.

Emotional appeal Promotional effort to induce consumer purchasing; based on positive or negative feelings (e.g., fear, love, humor, pride, romance, joy.) See case number 16, page 90.

Emotional buying motive A consumer's intent to purchase a product based on feelings developed without logical thinking (e.g., love, vanity, fear). See case number 66, page 249.

Employee pilferage Losses of merchandise or dollars because of theft by the company's personnel. See case number 9, page 68.

Exclusive distribution strategy A distribution channel alternative that uses a minimal number of retail outlets; used because of a manufacturer's limited production capacity, also the product's high-end price point. See case number 57, page 216.

Exclusivity Merchandise that is made available without competition to a specific retailer in a particular trade area. See case number 63, page 239.

Expert communication channel A form of promotion that presents an individual person who has expertise or knowledge and also who is recognizable to the general public or to the target market. This expert makes positive statements about the product to the *target market*. See case number 66, page 249.

External environment Those influences and events that are outside an organization, but which affect the business. Subsets include economic, social/demographic, political/legal, natural, technological, and competitive environments. Also referred to as the macroenvironment. See case number 33, page 142.

Fashion goods Usually refers to tangible items that are only popular for a specific, limited time. See case number 56, page 213.

Foreign manufacturers Companies who are headquartered overseas (i.e., outside the U.S.) and also produce their goods abroad. See case number 29, page 131.

Formal communication Communication within an organization that involves the use of employee handbooks, suggestion systems, newsletters, bulletins, meetings, and education departments. See case number 43, page 174.

Formal internship program A type of employment program that is usually offered by a large company, which takes a group of students (i.e., interns) through preplanned classes and activities to gain exposure to the organization. See case number 25, page 116.

Format The structure of a promotional message.

Franchise A type of business ownership in which a manufacturer, wholesaler, or service company sells the right to conduct a business in a specified manner within a certain period of time; this right is usually sold to a smaller firm or individual for a fee. See case number 7, page 62.

Frequency The number of times the message is presented in a promotional effort.

General line The wide variety of goods within a *product assortment*.

Hard goods Merchandise that includes appliances, small electronics, and home furnishings.

High-end The higher-priced goods within a given *inventory*.

Horizontal marketing channel The joining of two or more companies to develop an emerging *marketing channel* opportunity by establishing a contract on a permanent or temporary basis, or by creating a separate company.

Horizontal communication channel Communication that flows from manager to manager. See case number 23, page 111.

Human resource management The personnel division within a company; concerned with hiring, training, motivating, and understanding the needs of employees in order to develop a productive and satisfied work force. See case number 8, page 66.

Impact The effect or impression that results from the use of a specific media type in a promotional effort.

Independently owned A type of business ownership in which there is usually only one outlet, which is often owner-managed. See case number 70, page 263.

Industrial goods Those products used to manufacture other products; these are classified as *materials and parts*, capital items, or *supplies and services*.

Informal communication The use of vertical and horizontal communication channels for verbal exchange; often referred to as "the grapevine," it reflects unofficial communication within an organization. See case number 62, page 237.

Informal internship program The internship employer and student develop an internship program to meet the employer's needs and the student's academic internship requirements. See case number 22, page 109.

Institutional advertising Advertising that is designed to build the organization's image and create community goodwill. See case number 67, page 251.

Intensive distribution strategy A channel design alternative in which the manufacturer's objective is to make the product available to as many different types of retail operations as is possible. See case number 58, page 218.

Information flow A directed promotion effort, which is used to influence product sales from one party to other parties in a *marketing channel*.

Inventory Merchandise kept on hand for sale by a manufacturer or retailer. See case number 10, page 71.

Keystone markup Term used to describe a retail price that is established by doubling the cost price of an item.

Key vendors The primary manufacturers that are responsible for the majority of merchandise within the inventory of a retail department. See case number 30, page 134.

Label/Labeling A part of *packaging*, which consists of printed information that describes or identifies the product and which appears on the merchandise or the package. See case number 40, page 162.

Layout A floor plan of the internal arrangement of a department store with allocated space for each department; the plan also includes nonselling space. See case number 48, page 186.

Lead time The amount of time required between different receiving stages of the distribution channel. From a manufacturer's perspective, this would be the number of days or weeks that exist between the receipt of an order for certain goods and the production of these goods. From a retailer's viewpoint, this would be the number of weeks or months between the placement of an order for specific goods with a manufacturer and the receipt of those goods at the retail operation. See case number 60, page 224.

Leased department A type of business ownership in which a retailer arranges to rent actual space within the retail store to another retailer for selling space.

Letter of application Cover letter to a prospective employer. Usually includes brief explanations of the job for which the candidate is applying, the source of the job information, and a summary of the applicant's attributes as they relate to the position being sought or offered.

Lifestyle A type of *market segmentation*, which uses the unique attributes of a particular consumer group that sets it apart from other groups as part of a marketing strategy.

Limited line A particular type of merchandise assortment (e.g., ladies' career apparel, home accessories, better shoes). See case number 61, page 235.

Loss leader A product offered at an extremely low price, which thereby generates no profit and possibly produces a loss; this strategy is used with the intent of attracting customers and building consumer traffic. See case number 50, page 194.

Loss prevention Activities used by an organization to discourage or eliminate shortages and losses because of theft, employee pilferage, and clerical errors. See case number 28, page 127.

Low-end Lower-priced merchandise within a product mix.

Macroenvironment Also referred to as the *external environment*.

Management A functional department organization within the *Mazur Plan* whose activities include personnel (human resources), store maintenance, purchasing of supplies and equipment to operate the store, operations, customer services, and business security. See case number 4, page 53.

Manufacturers' representative (manufacturers'rep) A salesperson that represents more than one manufacturer; usually works on commission by selling merchandise from various manufacturers to retail store buyers. See case number 13, page 81.

Manufacturer/retailer A type of business ownership in which the manufacturer operates its own retail outlets, thereby eliminating wholesalers and gaining absolute control of the distribution process. See case number 55, page 211.

Manufacturer's brand Also referred to as a *national brand*.

Marketing channel The arrangement of business entities that moves a product from the manufacturer to the ultimate consumer. Types include *administered vertical marketing system*, *contractual vertical system*, *conventional marketing channel*, *corporate vertical system*, *horizontal marketing channel*, *multichannel marketing system*, *vertical marketing channel*.

Market positioning A term used to describe the occupation of a product in a clear, distinctive, and desirable place in the market and in the minds of consumers. See case number 28, page 127.

Market segmentation The process of dividing a large consumer population into smaller homogenous sections, which include *culture*, *lifestyle*, *reference groups*, and *social classes*. See case number 15, page 86.

Market week See *regional marts*.

Mass media The use of undifferentiated media communication channels for promotional efforts.

Materials and parts Types of *industrial goods* that enter the manufacturer's product completely, for example, raw materials and/or manufactured materials and parts.

Mazur Plan A concept that was developed to organize store departmentalization by functions (i.e., *merchandising, publicity, management, operations, control*).

Merchandising An operational division within the *Mazur Plan* that includes the responsibility for all activities involved in buying and selling merchandise. See case number 69, page 258.

Mission statement A document that provides guidance to create a shared sense of direction, opportunity, significance, and achievement for an organization's executives and employees. See case number 22, page 109.

Moral appeal A promotional effort that reflects a *target market's* sense of what is right and wrong. See case number 17, page 93.

Multichannel marketing system A *marketing channel* that usually combines several styles of retailing with an integration of some distribution and management functions. See case number 55, page 211.

National brand A brand, which is familiar to consumers and which is owned by a manufacturer or distributor. This type of brand is available throughout the U.S. and is distributed competitively by wholesalers and retailers. See case number 50, page 194.

Natural environment An external influence on business that encompasses the natural elements. Examples of natural influences include flood, fire, and severe weather changes. A component of the *external environment*. See case number 31, page 136.

Nondurable goods Tangible goods that are normally consumed in one or few uses.

Nonpersonal communication channel A type of promotional effort that utilizes mass and specialized media to reach a wide range of consumers. See case number 12, page 75.

Nonstore selling An alternative *marketing channel* that does not require a physical plant. Examples include direct selling, party plans, mail order retailing, catalog retailing, telephone and television selling, and electronic retailing (including computer selling). See case number 54, page 205.

Operations management A functional division that includes receiving, marking, checking of merchandise receipts; also warehouse distribution and shipping of merchandise. A part of the *Mazur Plan*. See case number 38, page 157.

Opinion leader A term used to identify a member of a *reference group* who exerts influence over consumer decision-making by colleagues in that reference group. See case number 13, page 81.

Order processing A part of *physical distribution*; it is how orders are handled. See case number 54, page 205.

Ownership group A type of business ownership in which a parent corporation owns divisions of retail institutions. See case number 68, page 255.

Packaging The activities of designing and producing the container or wrapper for a product; also used in reference to the actual wrapper of a product. See case number 38, page 157.

Partnership A legal form of business organization in which two or more persons invest their time and money while maintaining liability for business debts. See case number 1, page 44.

Patronage buying motive Term used to describe the reasons why consumers choose one place to shop rather than another. See case number 49, page 188.

Payment flow Method(s) used by *marketing channel* members to pay their bills; also includes the parties to whom the payments are made. See case number 59, page 220.

Penetration pricing A pricing strategy that is designed to capture a large mass market by offering the product at a low price. See case number 52, page 199.

Percentage of sales method A technique for setting the *promotion budget* that is based on the organization's sales volume.

Personal communication channel A type of promotion that involves direct people-to-people communication; types include *advocate communication channel*, *expert communication channel*, and *social communication channel*.

Personal selling A type of selling that involves actual human contact between a representative of the seller and the prospective consumer. Includes wholesale selling or contact selling, in which the seller usually contacts the customer; also includes retail selling in which the customer usually approaches the retail operation. See case number 45, page 180.

Personnel The employees of an organization.

Physical distribution This describes the tasks of planning, implementing, and controlling the *physical flow* of raw materials and final goods from points of origin to points of use; usually devised as a strategy to meet the needs of customers at a profit. See case number 55, page 211.

Physical flow The movement of the actual product from raw materials to end users.

Political/legal environment An external influence on organizations that includes political and governmental issues such as import quotas, trade restrictions, and business regulations. A component of the *external environment*. See case number 29, page 131.

Portfolio tests A method of collecting feedback on types of promotions in which groups of consumers analyze assortments of advertisements and then are tested for recall and recognition.

Prestige pricing A pricing strategy that assumes the customer infers a relationship between price and quality and will not buy a product if the price is too low. See case number 57, page 216.

Private brand A brand name owned by a middleman, distributor, or dealer.

Private label A brand name that is exclusive to the distributor. See case number 40, page 162.

Private label source Manufacturer that makes products under a label other than its own name. See case number 40, page 162.

Product Any "thing" offered to a market for attention, acquisition, use, or consumption; capable of satisfying a consumer's wants or needs, it may be an object, a service, an activity, a person, a place, an organization, or an idea.

Product life cycle The time period during which a particular item, classification, color, or style will sell well enough to generate a profit.

Product assortment Also referred to as the *product mix*.

Product line A group of products that are closely related because they: 1) function in a similar manner; 2) are sold to the same customer groups; 3) are marketed through the same types of outlets; or 4) fall within given price ranges. See case number 70, page 263.

Product mix The set of all products that a particular seller offers for sale to buyers; also referred to as the *product assortment*. See case number 48, page 186.

Promotional pricing A method of pricing merchandise so that the retail price infers a value or bargain to the consumer. See case number 51, page 197.

Promotional sources Manufacturers that offer merchandise that can be sold as special purchase or that provide value items at promotional prices. See case number 51, page 197.

Promotion budget The total amount of funds to be spent on promotional efforts and the allocation of these funds to individual public relations activities. See case number 61, page 235.

Psychogenic buying motive A consumer buying incentive that stems from psychological needs (e.g., to enhance the ego, to protect, to provide security). See case number 16, page 90.

Psychological pricing A pricing strategy, which assumes that consumers relate certain types of prices with sale or special value merchandise, for example $7.99 or 2 for $10.00. See case number 50, page 194.

Public relations Organizational activity that is concerned with all nonpersonal selling activities including sales promotions, advertising, and special events; utilized to project the character and image of the organization. See case number 26, page 119.

Rate method A method of pricing products that includes a standard initial markup, for example, doubling the cost price of a product to determine the retail price (this rate method is also referred to as a *keystone markup*).

Rational appeal Promotional effort that stresses self-interest by showing that the product will produce claimed benefits; it is a promotional appeal that is based on logic and knowledge. See case number 16, page 90.

Rational buying motive A term used to describe the purchasing incentive of consumers that involves judgment and logical thinking (e.g., security, durability). See case number 16, page 90.

Reach The number of persons communicated with by a certain media type in a specific target market.

Reference groups
Type of *market segmentation* that analyzes those consumers who are influential in shaping the attitudes and opinions of others. See case number 24, page 114.

Regional marts Buildings that house showrooms for manufacturers, wholesalers, and importers in which store buyers and merchandise managers can inspect lines presented by resources under one roof. The 5- to 7-day period during which seasonal lines are shown is referred to as market week. See case number 13, page 81.

Regular-priced sources Vendors who provide merchandise that retail buyers sell at nonsale prices. See case number 50, page 194.

Resident buying office A company to which a retail organization pays a fee in exchange for consultation about merchandise selection and a variety of services; examples of these services include direct mail, private label, and quantity purchases. It is an outside agency whose primary responsibility and specialization is coverage of the various merchandise classifications it represents. See case number 71, page 265.

Resumé A brief account of a person's professional or work experience and education, which is often submitted by a prospective employee with a *letter of application*.

Sale advertising Advertising designed to announce specific value items.

Sales promotion Any promotional activity other than advertising, publicity, and personal selling that attracts the public to an organization, stimulates purchasing, and makes a profit for that organization. See case number 50, page 194.

Sample line A representation of styles within a manufacturer's seasonal line that is presented by the *manufacturer's representative* to the retail store buyer. See case number 51, page 197.

Selective distribution strategy Distribution channel design alternative in which the manufacturer sells the product line to a limited number or type of outlets. See case number 47, page 184.

Selective media Specialized print, electronic, or display methods used for promotional efforts. See case number 34, page 144.

Secondary vendors Manufacturers whose goods are carried in lesser amounts or numbers than those products of the key vendors within a retailer's inventory.

Service An intangible product offered for sale; general examples include activities, ideas, benefits, or satisfactions. See case number 46, page 182.

Shopping goods Merchandise that the consumer usually compares on basis of quality, price, style. See case number 23, page 111.

Shortage The financial difference between an organization's book *inventory* and physical inventory; also referred to as shrinkage. See case number 28, page 127.

Shrinkage Also referred to as *shortage*.

Soft goods Term used to describe textiles and apparel products.

Social classes A type of *market segmentation* in which homogeneous divisions of families and individuals within a society are determined by occupation, source of income, education, family background, dwelling type and other variables. See case number 19, page 99.

Social communication channel Word-of-mouth communication among neighbors, family, friends, and associates. See case number 72, page 267.

Social environment An external influence on businesses that includes such social attitudes and changes as population shifts, attitudes about behaviors, and geographical residence patterns. A component of the *external environment*. See case number 32, page 140.

Sole proprietorship A legal form of business organization in which one person owns the business and assumes personal responsibility for its debts. See case number 5, page 55.

Source credibility Media effort that attempts to establish expertise, trustworthiness, and likability for a company and its products or services.

Specialty goods Products with unique characteristics and/or brand identification for which a significant group of consumers is habitually willing to make a special buying effort. See case number 48, page 186.

Staple goods Type of merchandise that the average customer expects to be in stock at all times; also refers to merchandise that is not readily influenced by fashion trends.

Structure The format of a promotional message.

Supplies and services Types of *industrial goods* that do not enter the finished product in any form, but which help to form the ultimate product. Examples include operating supplies and maintenance and repair items, maintenance and repair services, and business advisory services.

Target market The group of consumers to whom a particular organization is aiming their product. See case number 15, page 86.

Technological environment An external influence that affects business; technological influences include computers, manufacturing equipment, newly developed textiles and related products. A component of the *external environment*. See case number 27, page 125.

Title flow The passage of ownership of a product from one marketing organization to another. See case number 59, page 220.

Trade shows Market exhibitions presented by a substantial number of manufacturers' representatives who show and sell seasonal product lines to retail buyers. See case number 30, page 134.

Trademark A device (as a word or a name) that points distinctly to the origin or ownership of merchandise to which it is applied and is legally reserved to the exclusive use of the owner as the maker or the seller. See case number 42, page 166.

Transportation The physical distribution of merchandise; also how products are shipped. See case number 29, page 131.

Uncontrollable variables External influences of social, technological, natural, and economic environments (i.e., the *external environment*) that affect organizations, but which organizations cannot readily impact or manipulate. See case number 30, page 134.

Unsought goods Products that a customer may or may not know about. Usually the customer does not think of buying these products first, but rather the customer is first made aware of the product through advertising. See case number 42, page 166.

Upward vertical communication channel An employee to manager form of communication. See case number 3, page 50.

Vertical marketing channel Producer(s), wholesaler(s), and retailer(s) who are cooperating as a unified group to move a product from manufacturer to consumer. See case number 60, page 224.

Warehousing That aspect of physical distribution where the *inventory* is located. See case number 38, page 157.

Reference Readings

Bohlinger, Maryanne, *Merchandise Buying: A Practical Guide, 4th Edition*. Newton, MA: Allyn & Bacon, 1993.

Donnellan, John, *Merchandise Buying and Management*. New York, NY: Fairchild Publications, 1996.

Granger, Michele, *A Guide to Analyzing Your Fashion Industry Internship*. Albany, NY: Delmar Publishers, 1996.

Guerreiro, Miriam, LaDonna Garrett, *The Buyer's Workbook, 2nd Edition*. New York, NY: Fairchild Publications, 1994.

Jarnow, Jennette, Miriam Guerreiro, *Inside the Fashion Business, 5th Edition*. Macmillan Publishing Company/Prentice Hall, 1992.

Jernigan, Marian, Cynthia Easterling, *Fashion Merchandising and Marketing*. Englewood Cliffs, NJ: Macmillan Publishing Company/Prentice Hall, 1990.

Rath, Patricia, Jacqueline Peterson, Phyllis Greensley, Penny Gill, *Introduction to Fashion Merchandising*. Albany, NY: Delmar Publishers, 1994.

Index of Cases